13-99

BRIEF RATIONAL EMOTIVE BEHAVIOUR THERAPY

WILEY SERIES
in
BRIEF THERAPY AND COUNSELLING

Editor
Windy Dryden

Brief Rational Emotive Behaviour Therapy
Windy Dryden

Further titles in preparation

BRIEF RATIONAL EMOTIVE BEHAVIOUR THERAPY

Windy Dryden

Goldsmiths College, University of London, UK

JOHN WILEY & SONS

Chichester · New York · Brisbane · Toronto · Singapore

Other Wiley Editorial Offices

John Wiley & Sons, Inc., 605 Third Avenue,
New York, NY 10158-0012, USA

Jacaranda Wiley Ltd, 33 Park Road, Milton,
Queensland 4064, Australia

John Wiley & Sons (Canada) Ltd, 22 Worcester Road,
Rexdale, Ontario M9W 1L1, Canada

John Wiley & Sons (SEA) Pte Ltd, 37 Jalan Pemimpin #05-04,
Block B, Union Industrial Building, Singapore 2057

British Library Cataloguing in Publication Data:

A catalogue record for this book is available from the British Library

ISBN 0-471-95786-0 (paper)

Typeset in 10/12pt Palatino by Dorwyn Ltd, Rowlands Castle, Hants
Printed and bound in Great Britain by Biddles Ltd, Guildford, Surrey
This book is printed on acid-free paper responsibly manufactured from sustainable
forestation, for which at least two trees are planted for each one used for paper production.

CONTENTS

ABOUT THE AUTHOR

Windy Dryden   *Department of Psychology, Goldsmiths College, University of London, New Cross, LONDON SE14 6NW, UK*

Windy Dryden is Professor of Counselling at the Psychology Department, Goldsmiths College, University of London. He is also a practitioner with his own psychotherapy practice. He has written and edited numerous books in psychotherapy and counselling, and is general editor for several distinguished book series, including the Wiley Series in Brief Therapy and Counselling, in which this book appears.

SERIES PREFACE

In recent years, the field of counselling and psychotherapy has become preoccupied with brief forms of intervention. While some of this interest has been motivated by expediency – reducing the amount of help that is offered to clients to make the best use of diminishing resources – there has also developed the view that brief therapy may be the treatment of choice for many people seeking therapeutic help. It is with the latter view in mind that the Wiley Series in Brief Therapy and Counselling was developed.

This series of practical texts considers different forms of brief therapy and counselling as they are practised in different settings and with different client groups. While no book can substitute for vigorous training and supervision, the purpose of the books in the present series is to provide clear guides for the practice of brief therapy and counselling, which is here defined as lasting 25 sessions or less.

Windy Dryden
Series Editor

PREFACE

I have written this book for two main reasons. First, there is a need for it. Brief therapy is attracting increasing interest from a field that is becoming preoccupied with cost effectiveness and cost efficiency. By its nature, rational emotive behaviour therapy (REBT), which is best placed within the cognitive-behavioural tradition in psychotherapy, has all the hallmarks of an effective approach to brief therapy. It advocates that the therapist assumes an active-directive stance in therapy; it encourages clients to be specific about their problems; it is goal-directed; and it urges clients to help themselves between therapy sessions. While there are many clinically oriented texts on REBT, this is one of the few that considers it as a brief, session-limited treatment modality.

The second reason why I have written this book is because I wanted to write a book for John Wiley & Sons, in general, and for Michael Coombs and Wendy Hudlass, my editors, in particular. I have long admired their work from afar and it is a pleasure to have worked with them on this book.

I wish to thank 'Carol', the client whose therapy illustrates the principles that I have discussed in this book, for giving me permission to use our work in modified form. Without her, this book would have been harder to write. I also wish to thank Amstrad for making such a reliable machine in the shape of the NC 200, Stephen Godwin for writing the program which enabled my disks to be used in WordPerfect format, Maurice Douglas for effecting the transfer from one format to another and Marion Jackman and Lisa Faulds for typing the revisions of the manuscript.

WD
1995

DEDICATION

I dedicate this book to
Dr Paul Hauck
who first introduced me to
REBT

BRIEF RATIONAL EMOTIVE BEHAVIOUR THERAPY: CONTEXT AND RATIONALE

Currently, there is a great deal of interest in brief therapy and most of the predominant therapeutic orientations have spawned brief forms of treatment. The number of books that have been published on this subject is growing and there is now a *Handbook on the Brief Psychotherapies* (Wells & Gianetti, 1990). In this opening chapter, I will do the following. First, I will consider the reasons for the growth of brief therapy; second, I will consider the issue of who is suitable for brief rational emotive behaviour therapy; and finally, I will provide a brief outline for the rest of the book.

THREE REASONS FOR THE GROWTH OF BRIEF THERAPY

It seems to me that the stimulus for the growth of brief therapy is three-fold. First, there is the question of finance. In North America, insurance companies which are responsible for funding, at least in part, the psycho-therapeutic services received by many people are increasingly un-prepared to pay for long-term therapy. The tremendous growth of 'managed' mental health care schemes that has occurred recently in the States is designed to keep treatment brief and therefore cost-effective for the insurance companies. Whether they like it or not, many American therapists are turning to the brief therapy literature to discover how they can practise therapy briefly in order to maintain their livelihood.

Second, there is the related question of resources. In Britain, the field of counselling and psychotherapy has recently come under close crit-ical scrutiny (e.g. Dryden & Feltham, 1992; Persaud, 1993). This is a sure sign that these activities are being increasingly accepted by the general public. Agony aunts and uncles are constantly recommending their correspondents to seek counselling or therapy for their problems and it is not unusual for soap opera characters to be seen going off for a counselling session or even talking in the session itself. What this has meant is that currently in Britain it is far less 'shameful' to seek therapeutic help than in the past. This has led to an increase in the demand for counselling and psychotherapy in both the public and private spheres.

In the private sphere, this is not a problem when counselling and therapy are inexpensive, since clients are usually prepared to pay for it out of their own pockets. However, when such private help is more expensive, and this usually means that private psychiatric services are involved, there is greater reliance on insurance companies which, in Britain, are even more reluctant to pay for long-term 'outpatient' therapy than their American counterparts. This again has led private hospitals and clinics to think in terms of short-term psychotherapeutic intervention.

In the public sphere, the increased demand for services has not been met by increased resources. In short, a growing number of people in distress are seeking counselling and psychotherapy services from a static or even shrinking population of public-sector professionals. This again has led these professionals to offer brief (and sometimes very brief) intervention. Again these workers are looking for information on how to practise briefly and are turning to the literature and brief (naturally!) training workshops.

The impetus for offering brief intervention can also be seen in the voluntary helping sector in Britain. Counselling agencies run by MIND, for example, offer a set, small number of sessions to clients (e.g. six sessions) which in some cases can be renewed for a further set number of sessions. However, long-term therapy is not generally on offer. An exception to this norm of brief interventions is found in centres run under the auspices of Relate: National Marriage Guidance who according to its Head of Counselling discourage the blanket application of the practice of brief therapy (Hill, personal communication).

The third impetus for the development of brief therapy is the realization that a number of clients do not require long-term therapy and actually benefit from a brief intervention. The idea that more therapy is better for everyone is now considered a very outmoded one. In the past, therapy was brief by default which meant that clients dropped out early from therapy, while increasingly now therapy is brief by design in that this intervention is regarded as a treatment of choice for some clients. The development of brief therapy by design rather than by default has itself led to an interest in (i) assessment for brief therapy (i.e. who will benefit from a brief intervention and how we can identify them), and (ii) the ingredients of an effective brief intervention. In this book, I will address these questions from the perspective of Rational Emotive Behaviour Therapy (REBT), a system of therapy which I will introduce in Chapter 2. However, readers interested in how practitioners from other perspectives address these questions should consult Budman (1981).

Readers may be wondering what exactly constitutes brief therapy. As might be expected there is no consensus on this point. Brief therapy can range from one session to 50 or 60 sessions depending on which authority one consults. Most people, however, would probably agree with Budman and Gurman (1988) who say that brief therapy is 25 sessions or less. To complicate matters, the approach to brief therapy that I discuss in this book is based on 11 sessions. It would be nice if such diversity did not exist, but the reality is different and as we shall see, REBT urges us to accept reality even if we dislike it!

WHO IS SUITABLE FOR BRIEF REBT?

There is much debate in the brief therapy literature concerning who is suitable for brief intervention. Some theorists (e.g. see Davanloo, 1978) argue in favour of stringent inclusion criteria while others (e.g. Budman & Gurman, 1988) are more liberal in their views on who is suitable for brief therapeutic intervention. In this section, I will outline my views on the question: who is suitable for brief REBT?

Suitability Criteria

In my view, there are seven indications that a person seeking help will benefit from brief REBT.

1. The person is able and willing to present her problems in a specific form and set goals that are concrete and achievable.

It often occurs that at the outset people seeking therapeutic help talk about their problems in vague, abstract terms. Your task as a brief REBT therapist is to help them as quickly as possible to translate these abstractions into specific problem statements. You will be able to do so with most people, but a minority are either unable or unwilling to discuss their problems or goals in a concrete form. If the person is able to specify her problems and goals, but is not willing to do so, perhaps because she doesn't think it would be helpful to do so, then this person is not a good candidate for brief REBT or even for longer term REBT. In such instances it is useful to discover what she thinks will be therapeutic for her and then make a relevant referral. When a person appears unable to discuss her problems and goals in concrete terms, she is also not a good candidate for brief REBT, but may do better in longer term REBT, where you may be able to train her to be specific. You need to be cautious here, however, as some individuals have cognitive deficits which prevent them from being concrete. If you suspect that this is the case you may wish to refer the person for a neuropsychological assessment in the first instance.

2. The person's problems are of the type that can be dealt with in 11 sessions.

In my opinion, brief REBT is indicated when the person's problems are not severe. They may 'feel' severe to the person, but this is not what I am referring to. Rather, by the term 'severe' I am talking about problems that are chronic (i.e. not of recent onset) AND that significantly disrupt the person's life. It is the presence of both of these problem characteristics that, for me, contraindicates brief REBT. It could well be that a person may have a chronic problem that does not significantly disrupt his life or he may have a significantly disruptive problem that is acute (i.e. of recent origin). By themselves, these problems are not contraindications for brief REBT. However, like all forms of brief therapy, brief REBT works best when the person's problems are not in the severe range.

It is important to recognize that the person seeking help may come to therapy with a number of problems, some severe and some not. The person may be a good candidate for brief REBT if he is prepared to target his less severe problems for intervention AND the existence of his severe problems does not prevent him from doing so. However, unsurprisingly, it is more often the case that he will wish immediate help for his severe problems. In which case, longer term REBT should be offered instead of brief treatment.

3. The person is able and willing to target two problems that she particularly wants to work on during therapy.

It is as important to realize the limitations of brief REBT as it is to appreciate its strengths. One of its limitations is that, in all probability, you will not have the time to deal with all of your client's problems in depth. My view is that in 11 sessions you only have time to deal with two of your client's problems in depth, while perhaps having the time to see the linking themes across her problems and doing SOME work on what I call the CORE irrational beliefs that underpin these problems (see Chapter 8). Given this, if the person seeking help cannot, for whatever reason, limit herself to working on two target problems, then brief REBT is not the modality of choice for this person and longer term REBT should be considered. I should add that if the person targets only one problem for change, then brief REBT is indicated. She doesn't have to target exactly two target problems. One will do!

4. The person has understood the ABCDEs of REBT and has indicated that this way of conceptualizing and dealing with his problems makes sense and is potentially helpful to him.

As will be shown in Chapters 2 and 3, REBT is based on a specific model of psychological disturbance and its remediation. In my view, it is important that the person seeking help understands the nature of this model so that he can make an informed decision whether or not to commit himself to brief REBT. This is why I believe that in this approach to brief treatment it is important for you to explain the REBT model of psychological problems and their treatment in the first session. This is done by teaching your client the ABCDEs of REBT (see Chapter 3). If your client has understood this model and thinks that this way of conceptualizing and dealing with his problems makes sense and is potentially helpful to him, then this is a good sign that he could benefit from REBT. If he thinks that it is not relevant to his problems and/or not useful then this is a contraindication for brief REBT. If the person is undecided about the potential relevance and utility to his problems, then you need to address this issue more fully before asking him to commit himself to brief REBT.

5. The person has understood the therapist's tasks and her own tasks in brief REBT, has indicated that these seem potentially useful to her and is willing to carry out her tasks.

Various codes of professional ethics stipulate that a person seeking help has to give informed consent before the therapist uses a therapeutic intervention. In brief REBT, we take this seriously by explaining in the first session what our tasks are as brief REBT therapists and what we consider our clients' tasks to be. This, of course, has to be explained in terms that clients can understand and I deal with this issue in Chapter 3. Your client is a good candidate for brief REBT in this respect if she has understood your respective therapeutic tasks, has given some indication that she believes that these tasks may be useful to her and she has said that she is willing to carry out her tasks.

You need to take care in forming your opinion of your client's suitability for brief REBT on this criterion. For example, your client may say that she understands what you both need to do to make brief REBT effective, but she may think that these tasks will not be helpful to her. Or she may understand the tasks, see their potential utility, but not be prepared to carry them out, hoping that you will do the work for her. You need to explore and respond constructively to any doubts and reservations that she may have about the task domain of REBT. This may involve correcting any misconceptions that she might have about this approach to therapy. Finally, you need to form an opinion concerning whether or not the person seeking help has the ability to put her therapeutic tasks into practice. If you judge that she does not, you need to effect a suitable referral.

6. The person's level of functioning in his everyday life is sufficiently high to enable him to carry out his tasks both inside and outside therapy sessions.

Most proponents of brief therapy recognize that this approach works better with clients who are functioning relatively well in life (e.g. see Davanloo, 1978). Consequently, my view is that it is best to offer brief work to this clinical population. I do not go along with the view that is sometimes expressed that brief therapy can be offered to everybody because all will gain SOMETHING from this approach. I believe in tailoring the therapy modality to the person rather than offering everyone a single modality (Dryden, 1993). Consequently, you need to make a judgment concerning whether or not your client is functioning sufficiently well in life to respond productively to brief REBT. This can be done in a number of ways.

First, as various authorities advocate (e.g. Malan, 1980) you can carry out a thorough formal assessment of the person's level of psychological functioning or arrange for someone to do this for you. Some therapy agencies have an intake interview policy where everyone seeking help receives an assessment-oriented intake interview with someone who will not become that person's therapist, but will refer the person to a therapist if he or she judges that this is someone suitable for brief therapy.

Second, you can rely on the judgment of an external referral agent. Thus, many of my referrals come from psychiatrists who carry out a full mental status examination and take a full history from the people whom they refer to me. A full report invariably accompanies the referral. In the vast majority of cases where they have referred to my brief therapy practice, I have found that their judgment has been accurate. This is also true of a smaller number of General Practitioners who refer to my brief therapy practice (including the GP who referred Carol to me).

Third, in the absence of a full report on the person's level of psychological functioning from someone whose judgment you trust, and when you do not yourself carry out such a full assessment, you may decide to assume that the person is healthy enough to be suitable for brief REBT unless and until you have evidence to the contrary. If and when you gain such evidence, you will decide to refer the person to a more suitable treatment modality. For reasons discussed earlier, I do not agree with this approach. I prefer to make a judgment myself whether the person is suitable for brief REBT or to rely on the judgment of someone whose opinion I trust that this is the case rather than make the assumption, on limited information, that the person is suitable for brief REBT until proven otherwise.

7. There is early evidence that a good working bond can be developed between you and the person seeking help.

The approach to brief REBT described in this book lasts 11 sessions. Given this, it is important that you are able to develop a good working bond very early in therapy. On this criterion, a person is a good candidate for brief REBT when she is able to discuss her problems openly with you and a good rapport develops between the two of you. However, if in the first session the person is very reticent with you and there seems to be an antipathy between the two of you that cannot be easily remedied, then the person is not a good candidate for brief REBT, at least with you as her therapist. If this occurs, it is sensible for you to make a suitable referral.

Having described the seven indications that suggest that a person is suitable for brief REBT, let me consider the contraindications for brief therapy. While there is no definitive answer to this question in the brief REBT field, my view is that if any of the following conditions exist, I will not offer the person a contract for brief therapy:

1. the person is antagonistic to the REBT view of psychological disturbance and its remediation;
2. the person disagrees with the therapeutic tasks that REBT outlines for both therapist and client;
3. the person is unable to carry out the tasks of a client in brief REBT;
4. the person is presently seriously disturbed and has a long history of such disturbance;
5. the person seeking help and the therapist are clearly a poor therapeutic match;

6. the person's problems are vague and amorphous and cannot be specified even with the therapist's help.

Between the definite indications and contraindications for brief REBT lies the
grey area where a person may meet some of the indications for brief REBT,
but not others. As long as the person does not meet any of the contraindications listed above, the only guidance I can give is that the greater the number
of indications present, the more likely it is that the person is suitable for brief
REBT. It is useful to discuss cases that fall into the grey area with your
supervisor.

The other factor to take into account is the client's actual response to brief
REBT. This cannot be known until you have begun therapy, but it is
worthwhile to point out that a person may meet all the suitability criteria
that I have outlined, but still respond poorly to REBT. The reverse is also
true. I have occasionally taken the risk and offered a person who has met
few of the indications for brief REBT (but none of the contraindications) a
brief therapy contract and have been pleasantly surprised at his positive
response. My view concerning the client's response to brief REBT has
been put succinctly by Budman and Gurman (1988: 25):

> 'Our recommendations in patient selection are to monitor the patient's re-
> sponse to treatment on a trial basis; to be prepared to make creative modi-
> fications as necessary (two such modifications may involve the patient's
> seeing another therapist or including the patient's family) and to be pre-
> pared to use various alternatives, including longer and more open-ended
> treatment.'

I would only add one thing to this statement. Be aware of and do not
exceed your own limitations. Thus, if you consider that involving a client's family would be a helpful, creative modification, but you do not
have the skills to do this, either refer the case to an REBT therapist with
expertise in family work or involve such a therapist in the family sessions
as a co-therapist.

THE BOOK'S STRUCTURE

Having considered the context of and rationale for brief REBT, let me
bring this chapter to a close by outlining the structure of the rest of the
book. First, in Chapter 2, I will provide a brief introduction to the basic
principles and practice of REBT. Then, in Chapter 3, I will discuss how to
form a working alliance quickly with brief therapy clients and show how
to prepare them to get the most out of REBT. In Chapter 4, I will deal with

the important issue of assessing clients' problems from an REBT perspective which is a core task before change-directed interventions are employed. In Chapter 5, I will show you how to help your client to understand the rational solution to her problems whereby she gains intellectual insight into the determinants of her problems and what she needs to do to effect change. Chapter 6 is devoted to teaching your client what she needs to do to move from intellectual to emotional insight or, to put it differently, to understand what is involved in integrating the rational solution into her belief system so that she can overcome her problems. Chapters 7 and 8 are devoted to helping your client to initiate and maintain the integration process both inside (Chapter 7) and outside therapy (Chapter 8). In Chapter 9, I will discuss the process of brief REBT and finally in Chapter 10, I will illustrate this process by describing my work with a single case (Carol) from beginning to end.

Throughout this book, I will use my work with Carol to illustrate the ideas that I discuss. This case is a real one and I have obtained written permission from the client concerned to use it for educational purposes. However, I have changed all identifying material to preserve client confidentiality. I have chosen this case because it demonstrates what can be achieved from brief REBT with a well-motivated client in a therapy that went relatively smoothly. While I fully recognize that not all cases are as smooth as the one selected, this case does allow me to present brief REBT as clearly as possible. However, I shall discuss the many obstacles that can occur in brief REBT and how to address these in Chapter 9.

2

SOME BASIC PRINCIPLES AND PRACTICE OF RATIONAL EMOTIVE BEHAVIOUR THERAPY

In this chapter, I will outline the basic principles and practice of REBT. In particular, I will tailor my discussion to the concepts that you, the reader, will need to understand in order to get the most out of this book. This chapter will therefore be selective rather than comprehensive. For an up-to-date and full presentation of the theory and practice of REBT, you are advised to consult Ellis (1994). The topics I will cover in this chapter concern: (i) the two principles of emotional responsibility; (ii) the two types of psychological disturbance; (iii) the REBT model of healthy and unhealthy negative emotions; (iv) the principle of psychological interactionism; and (v) the process of therapeutic change. I will also introduce the now famous ABCDEs of REBT.

THE TWO PRINCIPLES OF EMOTIONAL RESPONSIBILITY

If I have learned anything about clients from my 20 years experience as a counsellor and therapist, it is that at the beginning of therapy they adhere to what might be called the principle of emotional irresponsibility. In a nutshell, they tend to believe that the way they feel is caused by factors outside themselves. This is by no means a characteristic of clients alone. If you listen to how people talk about emotional issues, you will hear that talk peppered with phrases such as: 'He made me so angry', 'It really made me anxious', 'If they do that, they will make me very depressed', and so on.

As these statements show, we tend to believe that our emotions such as anger, anxiety and depression are caused directly by the actions of others and by life events or what I call the 'its' of this world. This 'naïve' view of the determinants of human emotion can be contrasted with the cognitive view of human emotion.

The GENERAL Principle of Emotional Responsibility

As any introductory book on psychology will tell you, there has been a cognitive revolution in mainstream psychology, which used to be dominated by behavioural principles. This cognitive revolution stresses the importance of the way we transform the information that we detect with our senses. It claims that such transformations have a critical influence on the way we feel and act. This idea has permeated all areas of psychology including psychotherapy and counselling. Actually, this is far from being a novel idea, since the Stoic philosopher Epictetus said many years ago that we are disturbed not by things themselves, but by the views we take of them. This later statement nicely describes what I have called the GENERAL principle of emotional responsibility (Dryden, 1995) which can be stated more formally thus: *We are largely, but not exclusively, responsible for the way we feel and act by the views we take of the events in our lives.* To say that we are exclusively responsible for the way we feel and act is a dogmatic position which negates the influence of these events and, as we shall see presently, REBT takes a stand against dogmatic positions. The REBT general principle of emotional responsibility states that events contribute to the way we feel and act, but do not cause these reactions which, as I have said, are largely determined by our views of events.

The SPECIFIC Principle of Emotional Responsibility

At the heart of the general principle of emotional responsibility is the concept of 'view'. While this points to the importance of understanding the cognitions or thoughts that your clients have about themselves, other people and the world, it is by itself too vague to provide you with the detailed information that you need as a therapist to understand precisely how clients disturb themselves and what you need to focus on to help them overcome their emotional problems. For such detailed information you need to understand the second principle of emotional responsibility – what I have called the SPECIFIC principle of emotional responsibility (Dryden, 1995).

The specific principle of emotional responsibility is so termed because it specifies precisely the kinds of 'views' that are at the core of psychological disturbance and, as importantly, the kinds of 'views' that are at the core of psychological well-being. In outlining the rational-emotive position on this issue, I will present below four belief pairs. The first belief in the pair will be that associated with psychological health and the second that associated with psychological disturbance. In the language of Rational Emotive Behaviour Therapy, the first are known as rational beliefs and the second as irrational beliefs. Before I present the four belief pairs that describe precisely how people disturb themselves about self, others and life conditions and what we would have to think to be healthy instead, let me briefly discuss the terms 'rational' and 'irrational' as they are used in REBT theory.

The Meaning of the Terms 'Rational' and 'Irrational' in REBT

The term 'rational' in REBT theory refers to beliefs which are: (i) flexible; (ii) consistent with reality; (iii) logical; and which (iv) promote the person's psychological well-being and aid her pursuit of her personally meaningful goals. In contrast, the term 'irrational' in REBT theory refers to beliefs which are: (i) rigid; (ii) inconsistent with reality; (iii) illogical; and which (iv) interfere with the person's psychological well-being and get in the way of her pursuing her personally meaningful goals. Having outlined the meaning of the terms 'rational' and 'irrational' as they refer to beliefs, I will distinguish among four types of cognition before discussing the four belief pairs which embody the specific principle of emotional responsibility and which delineate precisely the 'views' that people hold about self, others and the world that lead either to psychological well-being or psychological disturbance.

The Four Types of Cognition

REBT therapists distinguish among four types of cognition: descriptions, interpretations, inferences and evaluations (Wessler & Wessler, 1980; Dryden, 1994a). I will briefly discuss these different types of cognition since an understanding of the differences among them will help you to understand fully the specific REBT principle of emotional responsibility.

The first type of cognition, DESCRIPTION, seeks to describe the nature of a stimulus without adding any non-observable meaning. As such, descriptions can be accurate (e.g. 'The man is walking along the street' when this is so) or inaccurate (e.g. 'The man is running along the street' when, in fact, he is walking).

The second type of cognition, INTERPRETATION, goes beyond the data at hand, but is non-evaluative. Thus, we make interpretations in non-emotional episodes, i.e. when our emotions are not involved (e.g. 'The man is going to the post box to post a letter'. This statement is an interpretation because (i) it goes beyond the data at hand – I do not know whether or not the person is going to post a letter – and (ii) my emotions are not involved).

The third type of cognition, INFERENCE, also goes beyond the data at hand and is partly evaluative. Thus, we make inferences in emotional episodes, i.e. when our emotions are involved. Even though our inferences influence the type of emotion we experience (e.g. annoyance or anger as opposed to remorse or guilt), they do not fully account for our precise emotion (i.e. they do not explain why we feel anger as opposed to annoyance or guilt as opposed to remorse). That is why I say that inferences are partly evaluative. An example of an inference might be 'The man is going to the post office to post a letter to my boss that may lead me to lose my job'. This statement is an inference because (i) it goes beyond the data at hand – I do not know whether or not the person is going to post a letter to my boss that may lead me to lose my job – and (ii) my emotions are involved. Thus, I may feel anxiety or concern.

It is important to note that interpretations and inferences are similar in that they are both hunches about reality rather than factual. As such, they need to be tested against the available evidence. The fourth type of cognition, EVALUATION, as its name implies is fully evaluative and is centrally involved in our emotional experiences. Most often, an evaluation involves a person making a positive or a negative appraisal. In addition an appraisal can be neutral as in the statement: 'I don't care whether or not I pass my driving test'. The following four belief pairs can be viewed as evaluative beliefs since they are evaluative in nature and they point to what people believe.

The Four Belief Pairs

Preferences vs musts: Evaluative beliefs which are flexible in nature are often couched in the form of preferences (or their synonyms, e.g. wishes, wants, desires, etc.). Preferences can point to what we want to happen (e.g. 'I want to pass my driving test') or to what we do not want to occur (e.g. 'I don't want to get into trouble with my boss'). However, to understand the full meaning of a preference, its non-dogmatic nature needs to be made explicit in the person's statement. To take the two examples that I have just mentioned, we can tell that they are really preferences thus:

'I want to pass my driving test, BUT I don't have to do so.'

'I don't want to get into trouble with my boss, BUT there's no reason why I must not do so.'

The reason why it is so important for preferences to be put in their full form is that if they are expressed in their partial form (e.g. 'I want to pass my driving test'), then it is easy for us to change it *implicitly* to a dogmatic must (e.g. 'I want to pass my driving test [and therefore I have to do so]'). As I have shown elsewhere, the stronger our preferences, the more likely we are, if left to our own devices, to change these preferences into musts (Dryden, 1994a).

Preferences are rational because they are: (i) flexible (i.e. they allow for what is not preferred to occur); (ii) consistent with reality (i.e. they are consistent with the inner reality of the person's preferences); (iii) logical; and they (iv) promote the person's psychological well-being and aid her pursuit of her personally meaningful goals (i.e. they lead to healthy negative emotions when the person's preferences aren't met which in turn facilitate effective problem-solving or constructive adjustment if changes cannot be made).

Evaluative beliefs which are rigid in nature are often couched in the form of musts (or their synonyms, e.g. absolute shoulds, have tos, got tos, etc.). Musts indicate that we believe that what we want absolutely has to occur (e.g. 'I absolutely have to pass my driving test') or that what we don't want absolutely should not happen (e.g. 'I must not get into trouble with my boss').

Musts are irrational because they are: (i) inflexible (i.e. they do not allow for what must happen not to occur); (ii) inconsistent with reality (if there was a law of the universe that says I must pass my driving test, I could not possibly fail. This law, of course, does not exist); (iii) illogical (i.e. they do not logically follow from the person's preferences); and they (iv) interfere with the person's psychological well-being and get in the way of her pursuing her personally meaningful goals (i.e. they lead to unhealthy negative emotions when the person's demands aren't met which in turn impede effective problem-solving or constructive adjustment if changes cannot be made).

Albert Ellis (1994), the founder of REBT, holds that non-dogmatic preferences are at the very core of psychological health and that three other major rational beliefs are derived from these preferences. Similarly, Ellis believes that dogmatic musts are at the very core of emotional disturbance and that three other irrational beliefs are derived from these musts.

While other REBT theorists hold different views on this issue, I will take Ellis's position in this book. As such, the following three belief pairs should be regarded as derivatives from preferences and musts respectively.

Anti-awfulizing vs awfulizing: Anti-awfulizing evaluative beliefs are rational in the sense that they are first and foremost non-dogmatic. These beliefs, which in their full form are expressed thus: 'It would be very bad if I failed my driving test, but it wouldn't be awful', are flexibly located on a continuum ranging from 0 to 99.9 per cent badness. The stronger a person's unmet preference, the higher her evaluation will be placed on this continuum. However, an anti-awfulizing belief cannot reach 100 per cent, since as Smokey Robinson's mother used to tell her young son: 'From the time you are born 'till you ride in the hearse, there's nothing so bad that it couldn't be worse.' In this sense, an anti-awfulizing belief is consistent with reality. This belief is also logical since it makes sense in the context of the person's preference. Finally, it is constructive since it will help the person take effective action if the negative event that the person is facing can be changed and it will aid the person to make a healthy adjustment if the situation cannot be changed.

Awfulizing beliefs, on the other hand, are irrational in the sense that they are first and foremost dogmatic. They are rigidly located on a magical 'horror' continuum ranging from 101 per cent badness to infinity. They are couched in such statements as 'It's horrible that . . .', 'It's terrible that . . .', 'It's awful that . . .' and 'It's the end of the world that . . .' When a person is awfulizing, he literally believes at that moment that nothing could be worse. In this sense, an awfulizing belief is inconsistent with reality. This belief is also illogical since it is a nonsensical conclusion from the person's implicit rational belief (e.g. 'Because it would be very bad if I failed my driving test it would therefore be awful if this happened'). Finally, an awfulizing belief is unconstructive since it will interfere with the person taking effective action if the negative event that is being faced can be changed, and it will stop the person from making a healthy adjustment if the situation cannot be changed.

High frustration tolerance (HFT) vs low frustration tolerance (LFT): High frustration tolerance beliefs are rational in the sense that they are again primarily flexible and not grossly exaggerated. These beliefs are expressed in their full form, thus: 'Failing my driving test would be difficult to tolerate, but I could stand it'. The stronger a person's unmet preference, the more difficult it would be for her to tolerate this situation, but if she holds an HFT belief it would still be tolerable. In this sense, an HFT belief is consistent with reality. It is also logical since it again makes sense in the context of the person's preference. Finally, like a preference and an anti-awfulizing belief, it is constructive since it will help the person take effective action if the negative event that is being faced can be changed and it will encourage the person to make a healthy adjustment if the situation cannot be changed.

Low frustration tolerance beliefs, on the other hand, are irrational in the sense that they are first and foremost grossly exaggerated. They are couched in such statements as 'I can't stand it . . .', 'I can't bear it . . .', 'It's intolerable . . .'. When a person has a low frustration tolerance belief, she means one of two things: (i) she will disintegrate or (ii) she will never experience any happiness again. Since these two statements are obviously untrue, an LFT belief is inconsistent with reality. It is also illogical since it is a nonsensical conclusion from the person's implicit rational belief (e.g. 'Because it would be very bad if I failed my driving test, I couldn't stand it if I did fail'). Finally, like musts and awfulizing beliefs, it is unconstructive since it will interfere with the person taking effective action if the negative event that the person is facing can be changed and it will stop the person from making a healthy adjustment if the situation cannot be changed.

Self/other-acceptance vs self/other-downing: Acceptance beliefs are rational in the sense that they are again primarily flexible. In discussing acceptance beliefs, I will focus on self-acceptance, although exactly the same arguments apply to other-acceptance. When a person accepts herself, she acknowledges that she is a unique, ongoing, ever-changing fallible human being with good, bad and neutral aspects. In short, she is far too complex to merit a single, global rating. Self-esteem, on the other hand, is based on the idea that it is possible to assign a single rating to the 'self'. An example of a self-acceptance belief expressed in its full form follows: 'If I fail my driving test due to my own errors, I could still accept myself as a fallible human being who has failed on this occasion. I would not be a failure.' As this example shows, a self-acceptance belief is consistent with the reality of a person being too complex to merit a single global rating. A self-acceptance belief is also logical since it is logical for a person to conclude that he is fallible if he makes errors. Finally, as with the other three rational beliefs I have discussed, a self-acceptance belief is constructive since it will once again help the person take effective action if the negative event being faced can be changed and it will also aid the person to make a healthy adjustment if the situation cannot be changed.

Self-downing beliefs, on the other hand, are irrational in the sense that they take a rigid, grossly exaggerated, view of the 'self'. They are couched in such statements as 'I am bad', 'I am a failure', 'I am less worthy', 'I am undeserving'. When a person holds a self-downing belief, he is working on the assumption that it is legitimate to assign a global (in this case, negative) rating to his 'self'. Since this, in fact, cannot be legitimately done, a self-downing belief is inconsistent with reality. It is also illogical since in making a self-downing statement, the person is making the 'part-whole error', i.e. he is correctly rating an aspect of himself, but then he rates his entire self based on the evaluation of the part. Finally, like the other three irrational beliefs I have discussed, a self-downing belief is unconstructive since it will interfere with the person taking effective action if the negative event being faced can be changed and it will stop the person from making a healthy adjustment if the situation cannot be changed.

Having now introduced the four rational beliefs and four irrational beliefs deemed by REBT theory to lie at the core of psychological well-being and psychological disturbance respectively, let me formally state the specific principle of emotional responsibility:

'The REBT specific principle of emotional responsibility states that events contribute to the way we feel and act, but do not cause these reactions which are largely determined by our rational or irrational beliefs about these events.'

THE TWO TYPES OF PSYCHOLOGICAL DISTURBANCE

Having outlined the four irrational beliefs that underpin psychological disturbance, I will now proceed to discuss the two different types of such disturbance: ego disturbance and discomfort disturbance.

Ego Disturbance

As the name implies, ego disturbance concerns psychological problems that ultimately relate to the person's view of herself. Sometimes such problems are obviously related to the self as when a person is depressed and says, almost without prompting: 'Because I failed my driving test, I am a failure'. At other times, ego disturbance is not so transparent. For example, a person might claim to be anxious about travelling by underground. Put like that, it is not at all obvious that the person's problem may be an example of ego disturbance. However, on much closer examination, this turns out to be the case when the person reveals that he is anxious about travelling by Tube because he might get panicky and as stated in his own words, '. . . make a fool of myself by passing out'. As will be discussed later in this book, effective therapy is based on an accurate assessment of a client's problems and this assessment will reveal whether or not a particular problem is related to ego disturbance.

Ego disturbance occurs when a person makes a global, negative rating of him or herself. Such ratings can be made in different areas and are related to different disorders. Let me provide a few examples to illustrate my point:

1. When a person believes that she is a failure or a loser then it is likely that she will be depressed when she has failed or anxious when there exists a threat of failure which hasn't yet occurred.
2. When a person believes that she is bad then it is likely that she will experience guilt.
3. When a person believes that she is defective or weak then it is likely that she will experience shame.

The self-ratings that are involved in ego disturbance are usually expressed quite starkly as in the statements: 'I am bad' or 'I am a bad person'. However, they can also be expressed more subtly as in the statements: 'I am less worthy' or 'I am undeserving'. Generally speaking, the more starkly they are expressed in the person's belief structure, the greater that person's ego disturbance will be.

Finally, as noted above (see p. 14), ego disturbance is derived from dogmatic, musturbatory beliefs as in the following example: 'I am a failure because I did not pass my driving test as I absolutely should have done'. According to this view, if the person in this example had a preferential belief about failing such as: 'I would have preferred not to have failed my driving test, but there's no reason why I absolutely should not have done', then she would be far less likely to condemn herself than she would if she held a demanding belief about failure as shown at the beginning of this paragraph.

Discomfort Disturbance

As the name implies, discomfort disturbance concerns psychological problems that ultimately relate to the person's sense of comfort and discomfort. In REBT, the concepts of comfort and discomfort cover a wide range of issues. For example, they may relate to justice/injustice, fulfilment/frustration, positive/negative feelings. What they have in common, however, is they do not refer to the person's view of himself. Rather, as the name implies, discomfort disturbance relates to the person's perceived inability to tolerate discomfort, whether this is in the area of feelings (e.g. anxiety) or life situations (e.g. unfairness).

Like ego disturbance, discomfort disturbance can be obvious or more subtle. An example of discomfort disturbance that is obvious is when a person says (and truly believes) that she can't stand waiting for the traffic lights to change. A more subtle example of discomfort disturbance is when a person says that she is afraid of failing her driving test. It might appear, at first sight, that the person's anxiety is an example of ego disturbance. However, on much closer examination, this turns out not to be the case when the person reveals that she is anxious about not getting the £1000 that her father promised her if she passed the test. As she said, 'I couldn't bear to lose out on all the goodies I had planned to buy with the money'. This is clearly an example of discomfort disturbance. As I mentioned earlier (p. 18), careful assessment is needed to tease out discomfort disturbance-related irrational beliefs.

Discomfort disturbance occurs when a person's LFT beliefs come to the fore (see p. 16). Such beliefs can be held in different areas and related to different disorders. Let me provide a few examples to illustrate my point:

1. When a person believes that she cannot stand being blocked or frustrated then it is likely that she will be angry.
2. When a person believes that she cannot tolerate losing a prized possession then it is likely that she will experience depression if she loses it.
3. When a person believes that she can't bear feeling anxious then it is likely that she will experience increased anxiety.

The evaluations that are involved in discomfort disturbance can be explicit, as when the person says that she cannot bear the discomfort of speaking in public. However, they can also be implicit when people avoid facing uncomfortable situations. It is as if the person is implicitly saying: 'I'll avoid that situation because I couldn't stand the discomfort of facing it'. The more widespread the person's avoidance, the greater that person's discomfort disturbance is likely to be.

Finally, as noted above (see p. 14), discomfort disturbance is derived from dogmatic musturbatory beliefs as in the following example: 'I can't stand being deprived because I absolutely must get what I want'. As discussed in the section on ego disturbance, if the person in this example had a preferential belief about being deprived such as: 'I would like to get what I want, but I don't have to get it', then she would be far less likely to disturb herself about the deprivation than she would if she held a demanding belief about her failure to get what she wants.

While Albert Ellis (1994) has argued that in psychological disturbance musts are primary, and awfulizing, low frustration tolerance and self-downing beliefs are derived from these musts, it is not possible to tell from a person's must whether he is experiencing ego or discomfort disturbance. For example, a young man holds the following musturbatory, irrational belief: 'I must get promoted at work'. Does this belief lead to ego or discomfort disturbance? The only way to answer this question is to inspect the derivatives of his must. Once you have specified the person's must and its derivatives you have identified what I call the person's full irrational belief.

Thus, if his full irrational belief is as follows: 'I must get promoted at work and if I don't it would prove I am an inadequate person', then he is experiencing ego disturbance, when this self-downing belief is stronger than any LFT belief that he might have. On the other hand, if his full irrational belief is: 'I must get promoted at work and if I don't my life will be more uncomfortable if I'm not and I couldn't stand this discomfort', then he is experiencing discomfort disturbance, if his LFT belief is stronger than any self-downing belief that he might have. Thus, while musts may be primary in a person's disturbance, it is only by identifying the secondary irrational belief derivatives that we can understand the true nature of his disturbance.

Incidentally, the presence of awfulizing beliefs also does not help us to determine whether the person is experiencing ego or discomfort disturbance. Thus, if the person says: 'I must get promoted at work and it is awful if I don't', he could mean it is awful because it would mainly prove him to be an inadequate person or because the discomfort of not being promoted would be unbearable. So if a client provides a demanding belief and an awfulizing belief, you still need to identify the presence or absence of an LFT belief and/or a self-downing belief in order to determine whether his problem reflects mainly ego or discomfort disturbance.

Table 2.1 provides a summary of the points I have made in this section. However, a good rule of thumb is this: when a person has a demanding belief, but no associated self-downing belief (or when this belief is quite weak), he is probably experiencing discomfort disturbance. However, if a self-downing belief is present and is stronger than any associated LFT belief, the person is probably experiencing ego disturbance.

Table 2.1: Guidelines for Determining Ego and Discomfort Disturbance

EGO DISTURBANCE
Must + Self-downing (awfulizing and LFT beliefs may also be present) [self-downing belief is stronger than the LFT belief]

DISCOMFORT DISTURBANCE
Must + LFT belief (awfulizing belief may also be present) [self-downing belief is absent or is weaker than the LFT belief]

NATURE OF DISTURBANCE UNKNOWN
1. Must + awfulizing belief [LFT and self-downing beliefs not assessed]
2. Must + awfulizing belief + LFT belief [self-downing belief not assessed]
3. Must + awfulizing + LFT belief + self-downing belief [strength of LFT and self-downing beliefs not assessed]

Ego Disturbance and Discomfort Disturbance can Interact

To complicate matters even further, ego disturbance and discomfort disturbance can interact, often in complex ways. For example, let's suppose that a person believes that she must do well at a job interview and if she doesn't that means that she is less worthy than she would be if she did well. This ego disturbance belief leads the person to feel anxiety as the date of the interview draws near. At this point the person becomes aware that she is feeling anxious and tells herself implicitly that she must get rid of her anxiety straightaway and that she can't stand feeling anxious. As the result of this discomfort disturbance belief, her anxiety increases. Realizing that she is getting very anxious for what to her is no good reason and that she absolutely shouldn't do this, she concludes that she is a weak pathetic person for getting matters out of proportion. This second ego disturbance adds to her emotional distress which activates a further discomfort-related irrational belief about losing control.

It is important to note that this interaction between ego disturbance and discomfort disturbance can occur very quickly and outside the person's awareness. Dealing therapeutically with complex interactions between the two types of disturbance as exemplified above is quite difficult and involves the therapist dealing with one link of the chain at a time.

THE REBT VIEW OF HEALTHY AND UNHEALTHY NEGATIVE EMOTIONS

One of the unique contributions of REBT theory to therapeutic practice is the distinction it makes between healthy and unhealthy negative emotions. I have outlined this viewpoint in Table 2.2 and suggest that you familiarize yourself thoroughly with the information I provide therein before you attempt to practise brief REBT. The following is a brief guide to the form and its different components. I will start from the left-hand column (column 1) and move to the right-hand column (column 6).

Column 1: Emotion

In this column, I provide pairs of emotions and in doing so, I use the REBT emotional lexicon. As you will see from the next column, the first emotion of the pair is unhealthy, while the second is the alternative healthy negative emotion. I should stress that while it is not essential to use the emotional lexicon in the precise way that it is used in REBT, it is important to develop a shared language with each of your clients so that you both have an agreed way of differentiating between healthy and unhealthy negative emotions.

Column 2: Healthy or Unhealthy

In this column, I indicate which of the two negative emotions is unhealthy and which is healthy. As noted above, the first of the pair is unhealthy and the second, healthy.

By a negative emotion, I mean an emotion which is unpleasant to experience. Thus, I want to stress that I am not making a moral judgment when I refer to an emotion as negative. Having emphasized this point, let me differentiate between a healthy negative emotion and its unhealthy counterpart.

A healthy negative emotion is an emotion which can be seen as a rational response to an actual or inferred negative event in that it helps the person to change what can be changed and to adjust constructively to what can't be changed. It encourages the person to pursue her personally meaning-ful goals by encouraging her to think (see column 5) and act (see column 6) in helpful ways.

In contrast, an unhealthy negative emotion is an emotion which can be seen as an irrational response to an actual or inferred negative event in that it gets in the way of the person changing what can be changed and impedes her from adjusting constructively to what can't be changed. It interferes with the person's attempts to pursue her personally meaningful goals and does so by influencing her to think (see column 5) and act (see column 6) in unhelpful ways.

Table 2.2: A Diagrammatic Summary of Healthy and Unhealthy Negative Emotions

Emotion	Healthy or Unhealthy	Inference[a] in Relation to Personal Domain[b]	Type of Belief	Cognitive Consequences	Action Tendencies
Anxiety (ego or discomfort)	Unhealthy	• Threat or danger	Irrational	• Overestimates negative features of the threat • Underestimates ability to cope with the threat • Creates an even more negative threat in one's mind • Has more task-irrelevant thoughts than in concern	• To withdraw physically from the threat • To withdraw mentally from the threat • To ward off the threat (e.g. by superstitious behaviour) • To tranquillize feelings • To seek reassurance
Concern	Healthy	• Threat or danger	Rational	• Views the threat realistically • Realistic appraisal of ability to cope with the threat • Does not create an even more negative threat in one's mind • Has more task-relevant thoughts than in anxiety	• To face up to the threat • To deal with the threat constructively

continued over

[a] Inference – Personally significant hunch that goes beyond observable reality and which gives meaning to it; may be accurate or inaccurate.
[b] Personal Domain –The objects – tangible and intangible – in which a person has an involvement (Beck, 1976). REBT theory distinguishes between ego and comfort aspects of the personal domain although those aspects frequently interact.

Table 2.2: (cont.)

Emotion	Healthy or Unhealthy	Inference[a] in Relation to Personal Domain[b]	Type of Belief	Cognitive Consequences	Action Tendencies
Depression (ego or discomfort)	Unhealthy	• Loss (with implications for future) • Failure	Irrational	• Only sees negative aspects of the loss or failure • Thinks of other losses and failures that one has experienced • Thinks one is unable to help self (helplessness) • Only sees pain and blackness in the future (hopelessness)	• To withdraw from reinforcements • To withdraw into oneself • To create an environment consistent with feelings • To attempt to terminate feelings of depression in self-destructive ways
Sadness	Healthy	• Loss (with implications for future) • Failure	Rational	• Able to see both negative and positive aspects of the loss or failure • Less likely to think of other losses and failures than when depressed • Able to help self • Able to look into the future with hope	• To express feelings about the loss or failure and talk about these to significant ones • To seek out reinforcements after a period of mourning

Anger	Unhealthy	• Frustration • Self or other transgresses personal rule • Threat to self-esteem	Irrational	• Overestimates the extent to which the other person acted deliberately • Sees malicious intent in the motives of others • Self seen as definitely right; other(s) seen as definitely wrong • Unable to see the other person's point of view • Plots to exact revenge	• To attack the other physically • To attack the other verbally • To attack the other passive-aggressively • To displace the attack onto another person, animal or object • To withdraw aggressively • To recruit allies against the other
Annoyance	Healthy	• Frustration • Self or other transgresses personal rule • Threat to self-esteem	Rational	• Does not overestimate the extent to which the other person acted deliberately • Does not see malicious intent in the motives of the other • Does not see self as definitely right and the other as definitely wrong • Able to see the other's point of view • Does not plot to exact revenge	• To assert self with the other • To request, but not demand behavioural change from the other

continued over

Table 2.2: (*cont.*)

Emotion	Healthy or Unhealthy	Inference[a] in Relation to Personal Domain[b]	Type of Belief	Cognitive Consequences	Action Tendencies
Guilt	Unhealthy	• Violation of moral code (sin of commission) • Failure to live up to moral code (sin of omission) • Hurts the feelings of a significant other	Irrational	• Assumes that one has definitely committed the sin • Assumes more personal responsibility than the situation warrants • Assigns far less responsibility to others than is warranted • Does not think of mitigating factors • Thinks that one will receive retribution	• To escape from the unhealthy pain of guilt in self-defeating ways • To beg forgiveness from the person wronged • To promise unrealistically that she will not 'sin' again • To punish self physically or by deprivation • To disclaim responsibility for wrong doing
Remorse	Healthy	• Violation of moral code (sin of commission) • Failure to live up to moral code (sin of omission) • Hurts the feelings of a significant other	Rational	• Considers behaviour in context and with understanding in making a final judgement concerning whether one has 'sinned' • Assumes appropriate level of personal responsibility • Assigns appropriate level of responsibility to others • Takes into account mitigating factors • Does not think one will receive retribution	• To face up to the healthy pain that accompanies the realization that one has sinned • To ask, but not beg for forgiveness • To understand reasons for wrongdoing and act on one's understanding • To atone for the sin by taking a penalty • Makes appropriate amends • No tendency to make excuses for one's behaviour or enact other defensive behaviour

Emotion		Inferences		Cognitions	Action tendencies
Shame	Unhealthy	• Something shameful has been revealed about self (or group in whom one identifies) by self or others • Others will look down or shun self (or group with whom one identifies)	Irrational	• Overestimates the 'shamefulness' of the information revealed • Overestimates the likelihood that the judging group will notice or be interested in the information • Overestimates the degree of disapproval self (or reference group) will receive • Overestimates the length of time any disapproval will last	• To remove self from the 'gaze' of others • To isolate self from others • To save face by attacking other(s) who have 'shamed' self • To defend threatened self-esteem in self-defeating ways • To ignore attempts by others to restore social equilibrium
Regret	Healthy	• Something shameful has been revealed about self (or group with whom one identifies) by self or others • Others will look down or shun self (or group with whom one identifies)	Rational	• Sees information revealed in a compassionate self-accepting context • Is realistic about the likelihood that the judging group will notice or be interested in the information • Is realistic about the degree of disapproval self (or reference group) will receive • Is realistic about the length of time any disapproval will last	• To continue to participate actively in social interaction • To respond to attempts of others to restore social equilibrium

continued over

Table 2.2: (cont.)

Emotion	Healthy or Unhealthy	Inference[a] in Relation to Personal Domain[b]	Type of Belief	Cognitive Consequences	Action Tendencies
Hurt	Unhealthy	• Other treats self badly (self undeserving)	Irrational	• Overestimates the unfairness of the other person's behaviour • Other perceived as showing lack of care or indifference • Self seen as alone, uncared for or misunderstood • Tends to think of past 'hurts' • Thinks that the other has to put things right of own accord first	• To shut down communication channel with the other • To criticize the other without disclosing what one feels hurt about
Disap-pointment	Healthy	• Other treats self badly (self undeserving)	Rational	• Is realistic about the degree of unfairness of the other person's behaviour • Other perceived as acting badly rather than as uncaring or indifferent • Self not seen as alone uncared for and misunderstood • Less likely to think of past hurts than when hurt • Doesn't think that the other has to make the first move	• To communicate one's feelings to the other directly • To influence the other person to act in a fairer manner

				Thinking	Action tendencies
Jealousy	Unhealthy	Threat to relationship with partner from another person	Irrational	• Tends to see threats to one's relationship when none really exists • Thinks the loss of one's relationship is imminent • Misconstrues one's partner's ordinary conversations as having romantic or sexual connotations • Constructs visual images of partner's infidelity • If partner admits to finding another attractive, believes that the other is seen as more attractive than self and that one's partner will leave self for this other person	• To seek constant reassurance that one is loved • To monitor the actions and feelings of one's partner • To search for evidence that one's partner is involved with someone else • To attempt to restrict the movements or activities of one's partner • To set tests which partner has to pass • To retaliate for partner's presumed infidelity • To sulk
Concern for one's relationship	Healthy	Threat to relationship with partner from another person	Rational	• Tends not to see threats to one's relationship when none exists • Does not think that the loss of one's relationship is imminent • Does not misconstrue ordinary conversations between partner and other men/women • Does not construct visual images of partner's infidelity • Accepts that partner will find others attractive but does not see this as a threat	• To allow partner to express love without seeking reassurance • To allow partner freedom without monitoring his/her feelings, actions and whereabouts • To allow him/her to show natural interest in members of the opposite sex without setting tests

continued over

Table 2.2: (cont.)

Emotion	Healthy or Unhealthy	Inference[a] in Relation to Personal Domain[b]	Type of Belief	Cognitive Consequences	Action Tendencies
Unhealthy Envy	Unhealthy	• Another person possesses and enjoys something desirable that the person does not have	Irrational	• Tends to denigrate the value of the desired possession • Tries to convince self that one is happy with one's possessions (although one is not) • Thinks about how to acquire the desired possession regardless of its usefulness • Thinks about how to deprive the other person of the desired possession	• To disparage verbally the person who has the desired possession • To disparage verbally the desired possession • To take away the desired possession from the other (either so that one will have it or the other is deprived of it) • To spoil or destroy the desired possession so that the other person does not have it
Healthy Envy	Healthy	• Another person possesses and enjoys something desirable that the person does not have	Rational	• To honestly admit to oneself how one desires the desired possession • Does not try to convince self that one is happy with one's possession when one is not • Thinks about how to obtain the desired possession because one desires it for healthy reasons • Can allow the person to have and enjoy the desired possession without denigrating the person or the possession	• To obtain the desired possession if it is truly what one wants

Column 3: Inference in Relation to Personal Domain

Earlier in this chapter (see p. 13) I defined an inference as a cognition which goes beyond the data at hand and occurs in an emotional episode. It differs from an interpretation in one important respect. An inference is present when a person experiences an emotion, while an interpretation occurs in a non-emotional episode. Moreover, an inference gives meaning to the observable data, but in a way that may be accurate or inaccurate. Given its involvement in a person's emotional episode, an inference is partly evaluative in that it plays an important part in determining which emotional pair a person experiences (see column 1), but it is not fully evaluative in that it cannot determine which of the two emotions within the pair a person will experience.

In order to understand inferences fully, it is important to grasp the meaning of the term 'personal domain' since inferences are with respect to an individual's personal domain. Beck (1976) said that a personal domain contains those tangible and intangible objects in which the person has an involvement. As shown in the previous section, REBT theory distinguishes between ego and comfort aspects of the personal domain although, as I have stressed, these two aspects frequently interact.

Column 3 therefore lists the most prominent inferences that are made by people when they experience anxiety or concern, depression or sadness, anger or annoyance and so on. It should be clear from this column that since the same inference is involved, for example, in anxiety and concern, changing this inference will mean that the person will experience neither unhealthy anxiety nor healthy concern. The first effect is certainly acceptable, but the second isn't since it is often important that the person reacts to threat with concern even if it can be shown on a given occasion that no threat exists. Given this, we need to find a more profound and longer lasting way of helping a person to overcome his unhealthy anxiety while encouraging him to experience healthy concern. It is for this reason that REBT therapists encourage their clients to accept temporarily that their distorted inferences are true. Doing so helps both therapist and client to identify the irrational beliefs which, according to REBT theory, are the most important determinants of clients' unhealthy negative emotions.

Column 4: Type of Belief

In the first section of this chapter, I distinguished between rational beliefs and irrational beliefs. If you recall, rational beliefs are flexible, consistent

Table 2.3

Inference × Rational Beliefs = Healthy Negative Emotion

Inference × Irrational Beliefs = Unhealthy Negative Emotion

Healthy negative emotions stem from an interaction between an inference and rational beliefs. Unhealthy negative emotions stem from an interaction between the same inference and irrational beliefs.

with reality, logical and help the person to pursue his personally meaningful goals. They take the form of preferences, anti-awfulizing evaluations, high frustration tolerance and self/other-acceptance. Irrational beliefs, on the other hand, are dogmatic, inconsistent with reality, illogical and interfere with the person's personally meaningful goals. They take the form of musts, awfulizing evaluations, low frustration tolerance and self/other-downing.

According to REBT theory and as shown in Table 2.2, irrational beliefs are at the core of unhealthy negative emotions, while rational beliefs are at the core of healthy negative emotions. Thus, the type of belief has a crucial effect on which of the two emotions within a pair a person will experience. Given the central role that irrational beliefs play in determining emotional disturbance, it is beliefs (rather than inferences), and more precisely irrational beliefs, that are the initial target of change in REBT. As we shall see later in the book, once you have helped your client to change his irrational beliefs to rational beliefs, then you can help him to challenge other kinds of faulty cognitions such as distorted inferences.

Table 2.3 shows how healthy negative emotions stem from the interaction of inferences and rational beliefs and how unhealthy negative emotions stem from the interaction of these same inferences and irrational beliefs.

Column 5: Cognitive Consequences

Once a person experiences an unhealthy negative emotion because she is holding an irrational belief about a negative activating event, then she will have a tendency to think in certain overly negative, unhelpful ways. On the other hand, when that person has a healthy negative emotion because she is holding a rational belief about that same negative event, then she will tend to think in more constructive ways. These cognitive consequences of rational or irrational beliefs are important to understand because they have an effect on the person's subsequent problem-solving.

Column 6: Action Tendencies

In addition to beliefs affecting a person's thinking processes, they also have a decided influence on the ways in which that person will tend to act. Thus, when a person is thinking irrationally and experiencing unhealthy negative emotions, she will tend to act in self-defeating and goal-impeding ways. However, when she is thinking rationally and is experiencing healthy negative emotions then she will tend to act in more self-enhancing and goal-directed ways.

Just because a person has a tendency to act in a certain way does not mean that he will always act in accordance with this action tendency. It is almost always possible for a person to go against his action tendency and doing so is very important if he is to overcome his psychological problem. Thus, he can choose from a selection of more healthy response options and act against his unhealthy behavioural tendencies. Table 2.2 outlines both self-defeating action tendencies and those associated with more healthy functioning. The ability to act against our action tendencies is, as we shall see, central to our understanding of the REBT theory of therapeutic change.

THE ABCDEs OF REBT

You are now in a position to understand what have been called the ABCDEs of REBT. You will find this formulation in virtually every book that has been published on REBT and as such you need to become very familiar with it.

(A) stands for activating event. As you will see when I discuss the assessment of A in Chapter 4, when considering one of your client's emotional episodes, you are looking for the aspect of the activating event that triggered the client's irrational belief at B. Following the lead of Don Beal (personal communication) I call this the critical A. Critical As can be actual events, but are more likely to be inferences.

(B) stands for your client's rational and irrational beliefs which, as discussed on p. 13, are evaluative in nature. I have also presented the four major types of rational and irrational beliefs as they are featured in REBT (see pp. 13–18). While some REBT therapists prefer to place all cognitive activity under B, it is my practice to put only rational and irrational beliefs under B and to place other cognitions (e.g. inferences) at A.

(C) stands for the person's emotional and/or behavioural response to the beliefs that he holds about the event (or inference) in question. Table

2.2 is relevant here in that it outlines the REBT view of the difference between healthy negative emotions and their unhealthy counterparts. It is easy to forget that C also stands for a behavioural response. Sometimes your client will exhibit self-defeating behaviour based on a set of irrational beliefs she holds about a critical A. When this occurs, either the behaviour occurs without corresponding emotion or it is designed to 'ward off' your client's disturbed feelings.

(D) stands for disputing. In particular, it stands for disputing your client's irrational beliefs by asking questions that encourage the person to question the empirical, logical and pragmatic status of her irrational beliefs. I will discuss disputing irrational beliefs in Chapter 5.

(E) stands for the effects of disputing. When disputing is successful it helps the client to change her feelings and actions at C because she has changed her thinking at B. In addition, when disputing is successful, it helps the person to make more functional inferences at A.

Having spelled out the ABCDEs of REBT, I will show how some of these interact in complex ways.

THE PRINCIPLE OF PSYCHOLOGICAL INTERACTIONISM

So far, you could be forgiven if you thought that REBT considers that thinking, feeling and behaviour are separate psychological systems. However, this is far from being the case. When Albert Ellis originated REBT in the mid 1950s, he put forward the view that thinking (including imagery), feeling and behaviour are interdependent, interacting psychological processes.

Thus, when a person experiences an emotion at C, he has the tendency to think (A and B) and act in a certain way (as shown in Table 2.2). Also when someone holds a rational or irrational belief (at B) about a negative event at (A), this will influence his feelings and behaviours (at C). Finally, if a person acts in a certain way, this will be related to his feelings and thoughts.

What follows from this is that (i) REBT therapists need to pay close attention to thoughts, feelings and behaviour in the assessment process and that (ii) they need to use a variety of cognitive, emotive and behavioural techniques in the intervention phase of therapy. I will describe some of these techniques later in the book.

THE PROCESS OF THERAPEUTIC CHANGE

In order to practise brief REBT effectively, it is important to have an understanding of the process of therapeutic change. This knowledge will help you to use REBT interventions in the most relevant sequence. I will briefly mention the steps that clients need to take in REBT to experience therapeutic change, before discussing each step in greater detail. While I will put these steps in a certain order, please note that this order is flexible and should certainly not be applied rigidly in therapy. Also, although I will not mention them here, there will be problems along the way since therapeutic change is rarely, if ever, a smooth process. Having mentioned these two caveats here are the steps:

1. understanding the principles of emotional responsibility;
2. understanding the determinants of one's psychological problems;
3. setting goals and committing oneself to achieving them;
4. understanding and committing oneself to the REBT means of achieving one's goals;
5. putting this learning into practice;
6. maintaining these gains.

Understanding the Principles of Emotional Responsibility

I discussed these principles at length at the beginning of this chapter, so I will not repeat myself here. However, I do wish to point out the following. First, of the two principles of emotional responsibility that I discussed above, it is the SPECIFIC principle of emotional responsibility that clients need to learn, since this principle outlines the REBT view of psychological disturbance and health. Second, if clients do not grasp or do not accept this principle, then they will derive little benefit from REBT.

Understanding the Determinants of One's Psychological Problems

This step concerns therapist and client pooling resources to apply the specific principle of emotional responsibility to illuminate the determinants of the client's emotional problems. This involves the therapist helping the client to specify and give examples of these problems so that they can be assessed. Assessment is directed towards identifying unhealthy emotions, the actual or inferred events that provide the context for these emotions, the behaviours that the client enacts when she is experiencing her unhealthy emotions and, most importantly, the irrational beliefs that lie at the core of the client's problems. I will discuss assessment in greater detail in Chapter 4. Unless the client understands the determinants of her problems and agrees with this assessment, REBT will falter at this point.

Setting Goals and Committing Oneself to Achieving Them

An important part of therapeutic change is setting goals and committing time, energy and effort to taking the necessary steps to achieving them. Let us consider each of these points in turn.

Goal-setting

There is an old adage that says: 'If you don't know where you're going, you won't know when you've got there'. This points to the importance of setting goals in the therapeutic change process. This is particularly important in brief therapy. If you have a short period of time with a client then if you both know where the client is going, you can tailor the therapeutic work to helping the client achieve his goals. Bordin (1979) noted that agreement on therapeutic goals is an important therapeutic ingredient and one part of a tripartite view of the working alliance that has gained much prominence in psychotherapy research (Horvath & Greenberg, 1994). Many people have outlined the nature of client goals that it is important to negotiate with clients and I will discuss this issue further in Chapter 3. Briefly, in brief REBT you should help your clients to set goals which are specific, realistic, achievable, measurable and which aid their overall psychological well-being. Your clients should 'own' their goals, which means that they should set them primarily for their own well-being and not to please anybody else (e.g. significant others or you as therapist).

However, as an REBT therapist, you have an important goal for your clients and it is essential that you are open about this and discuss it frankly with them. This goal involves your clients learning and practising the skills of what might be called REBT self-help therapy so that they can use them after brief therapy has finished. Indeed, this book is based on the idea that in brief REBT your role is to give away to your clients as much of REBT as they are able to learn. You will, of course, have to help your clients understand that learning these skills will help them to achieve their therapeutic goals, otherwise they will have little interest in learning them. As Bordin (1979) noted, helping your clients to see the relevance of your and their therapeutic tasks to achieving their goals is a central part of the process of brief REBT. Not all clients will want to learn these self-help skills and you can help them (albeit less effectively) without teaching them these skills. However, if you don't offer your clients this opportunity, they will certainly not be able to take advantage of it!

Making a Commitment to Achieve Goals

Goal-setting will be an academic exercise unless your clients are prepared to commit themselves to achieving them. A major reason why people do not keep to their new year resolutions for very long is that they are not prepared to do what is necessary to achieve what they have resolved to achieve. They want the gain without the pain. So as part of the goal-setting process, discuss with your clients how much time, effort and energy they will have to expend in order to achieve their goals. Then ask them if they are willing to make such an investment. If they are, then you may wish to make a formal agreement with them to this effect. If they are not prepared to make the necessary investment, then you will have to set new goals in line with the kind of investment they are prepared to make. Of course, this may all change once your work with your client has advanced. Nevertheless, it is important to get brief REBT off on the right foot in this respect. So, in short, set goals with your clients that they are prepared to commit themselves to before you do any further therapy work with them.

Understanding and Committing to the REBT Means of Achieving One's Goals

After you have agreed with your client goals to which she is prepared to commit herself, you then have to ensure that she understands your suggestions concerning how these goals can best be reached. This is the aspect of brief REBT where the technical nature of the therapy comes to the fore. REBT does have definite suggestions concerning what clients need to do in order to achieve their goals. These suggestions take the form of specific techniques and I will be describing some of the more important of these techniques later in the book. In order for clients to understand the nature of REBT in this respect, you need to be able to explain what you are going to do in therapy and what is expected of your client in ways that are clear and detailed. You want clients to proceed with brief therapy having made an informed decision about REBT. In your description you need to stress two things. First, you need to show your client how putting into practice the technical aspects of the therapy will help her to achieve her goals. Second, you need to explain what investments with respect to time, energy and effort your client needs to make in putting REBT techniques into practice.

I have found it very useful at this juncture to point out to clients that there are other approaches to therapy and that if what I have to offer doesn't make sense to the person, if she doesn't think that REBT will helpful to her, or if she thinks it involves too much of an investment for her, then I suggest other treatment possibilities, discuss these with the client and make a judicious referral.

Putting this Learning into Practice

It is not sufficient for clients to understand that they have to put REBT techniques into practice, nor even to commit themselves to so doing. They actually have to do it. Otherwise they will have 'intellectual insight', which in this context may be seen as a light and occasionally held conviction that their irrational beliefs are irrational and their rational beliefs are rational. While gaining this 'intellectual insight' is important, it is insufficient to help clients to achieve their goals. For this to occur, clients need a fair measure of what might be called 'emotional insight' which in this context is the same realization about rational and irrational beliefs as in 'intellectual insight', but one which is strongly and frequently held. It is this 'emotional insight' which affects a person's feelings and influences his behaviour and this is the true goal of clients' putting their learning into practice in their everyday lives.

There are several dimensions of between session practice that are important.

1. *Repetition:* It is important for clients to go over new rational beliefs many times before they begin to believe them. This repetition applies to the use of cognitive, emotive and behavioural techniques.
2. *Force and energy:* One useful way that clients can move from intellectual insight to emotional insight is to employ techniques with force and energy. However, it is important that they can understand and see the relevance of particular beliefs being rational before forcefully and energetically working to internalize them.
3. *Vividness:* The use of what I have called vivid techniques in REBT (Dryden, 1986) can help clients to bring to mind their rational beliefs

better than standard, non-vivid techniques. Vividness tends to increase the impact of rational concepts and thus makes it easier for clients to retrieve them from memory at times when it is necessary for them to do so. Consequently, they will get more practice at thinking rationally than they would ordinarily do.

It is important for REBT therapists to take great care when they negotiate homework assignments with their clients and this is particularly true in brief therapy where it is crucial to help clients make effective use of therapeutic time. However, no matter how much care you take when negotiating such assignments, your clients may still have difficulty in putting them into practice. Therefore an important part of encouraging clients to put their therapy-derived insights into practice is helping them to identify and overcome such obstacles. I will discuss this issue in greater detail in Chapter 9.

Maintaining Therapeutic Gains

Once your clients have achieved their goals, this is not the end of the thera-peutic story, although many of your clients will think or hope that it is. If they have such thoughts and hopes then they will stop using the principles that you have taught them and thus increase the chances that they will experience a lapse or, more seriously, a relapse. I define a lapse as a minor return to the problem state, while a relapse is a major return to this state. If your clients are to maintain their therapeutic gains they have to be helped to do so and to take responsibility for this maintenance work themselves. This involves (i) relapse prevention and (ii) spreading the effect of change.

Relapse Prevention

It is important to deal with relapse prevention before the end of brief REBT, otherwise the client may not be prepared for the re-emergence of his problems. As mentioned above, it is rare for clients not to experience lapses and when they do they need prior help to deal with a lapse when it occurs. If a lapse, or a series of lapses, is not dealt with it may lead to a relapse since relapses tend to occur when lapses are not identified and dealt with by the person concerned.

Relapse prevention involves the following steps:

1. recognizing that lapses are likely to occur and thinking rationally about this point;

2. identifying the likely contexts in which lapses are likely to occur and problem-solving each salient element;
3. exposing oneself to the problematic contexts and using the problem-solving skills previously learned to prevent the development of the lapse;
4. committing oneself to continue this process for as long as necessary.

If the worst comes to the worst and a relapse does occur then you should help your client to think rationally about this grim reality, and understanding of how this developed should be sought before further treatment decisions are made.

If it looks unlikely that your client will achieve her therapeutic goals by the end of therapy, it is still worthwhile raising the issue of relapse prevention, although necessarily this will have to be done rather cursorily; a written handout on relapse prevention supplementing your verbal explanation is useful here. You will need to do this after you have helped your client to formulate a plan which she can follow to achieve her goals after therapy has formally ended.

Spreading the Effect of Change

Another important way of helping to ensure that your client maintains his gains is to encourage him to generalize what he has learned about overcoming his problems in certain contexts to other contexts. Thus, if a client has overcome his fear of refusing unreasonable requests at work and is now asserting himself when relevant, he can take what he has learned to enable him to do this and use it to help him to say no when his parents and parents-in-law make unreasonable demands on him in his personal life. The more clients can spread the effect of change in this way the more they will maintain and even enhance their therapy gains.

FINAL WORD

As befits a book on brief REBT, this introduction to some of the important theoretical and practical principles of REBT has necessarily been brief. For an extended review of the theory that underpins REBT, I suggest that you consult my book, *Invitation to Rational-Emotive Psychology* (Dryden, 1994a). For a comprehensive overview of how to practise REBT in a variety of treatment modalities, I recommend a book that I wrote with Albert Ellis, *The Practice of Rational-Emotive Therapy* (Ellis & Dryden, 1987).

Now that I have presented the foundations of REBT theory and practice, we are ready to move on to the practical part of the book. One of the most important aspects of brief work is getting therapy off on the right foot. Consequently, in the next chapter, I will consider the issue of building an effective working alliance with clients.

3

BUILDING A WORKING ALLIANCE

In this chapter, I will discuss several important issues concerned with building a working alliance with your client. In doing so, I will illustrate the points that I make by providing transcript material from my work with Carol, a client who was referred to me for brief therapy.

Bordin (1979) has argued that there are three components of the working alliance. First, there are the bonds that develop between therapist and client; second, there are the goals of the therapeutic enterprise; and finally there are the tasks that both therapist and client have to carry out to help the client to achieve her therapeutic goals. Later in this chapter, I will discuss goals and tasks as they pertain to the beginning phase of brief REBT and I will elaborate on these two components of the working alliance as the book unfolds. I will concentrate on the bond component of the alliance at this point of the chapter since clients are frequently preoccupied with 'bond'-type questions at the outset of therapy. As Howe (1993) has shown, people who seek therapeutic help often ask themselves the following questions:

- 'Will the therapist accept me?'
- 'Will the therapist understand me?'
- 'Will the therapist and I get on?'

Although brief REBT is quite a technical therapeutic approach, it is important that you develop and maintain an effective bond with the person seeking help right from the beginning. Consequently, before I deal with the issue of how you respond to the client's initial request for help, I will outline my views on the quality of the bond that I believe you should strive to develop with your clients in brief REBT.

DEVELOPING AND MAINTAINING THE THERAPEUTIC BOND

The bond that develops and deepens between you and your client in brief REBT is the interpersonal context of brief REBT. REBT therapists agree with Carl Rogers (1957) that there are a number of 'core conditions' that need to be established in the client's mind for brief REBT to be a therapeutic experience for the client. However, we disagree with Rogers that these conditions are necessary and sufficient for therapeutic change to occur. Rather, we believe that it is important and highly desirable that the client experience the therapist as understanding, accepting and genuine, but that this is neither necessary nor sufficient for therapeutic change to take place. It is possible for clients to benefit from brief REBT without feeling understood and accepted and without seeing the therapist as genuine, although of course such benefit is more likely to occur when the core conditions are experienced by the client. What are the core conditions from the REBT perspective?

Empathy

In brief REBT it is important that the client experiences you as empathic. As I will discuss later in the chapter, it is important that you show your client at the outset that you understand her problems from her frame of reference. Later, you will show your client a different type of empathy – you will show her that you understand the irrational beliefs that underpin her problems. This type of empathy, which has been called 'philosophical' empathy because it refers to your understanding of the client's underlying philosophies, comes to the fore when you are assessing your client's problems (see Chapter 4).

Unconditional Acceptance

When you show your client unconditional acceptance in brief REBT, you show by your attitude and your words that you accept her as a unique, ongoing, ever-changing, fallible human being who is too complex to merit a single global rating. This does not preclude you from liking certain aspects of her or from disliking her bad behaviour. Indeed, you may, at times, give her feedback on her negative behaviour, for example. But this is done in the context of unconditional acceptance.

During brief therapy, your client may derive enormous benefit from a homework assignment on one occasion and may fail miserably at another assignment at another time. When you offer your client unconditional acceptance you may show your pleasure that she did well in the first case and your disappointment that she failed in the second. But your attitude towards her as a person remains the same. However, despite the value that your client will derive from experiencing that you accept her unconditionally, REBT theory argues that it is more important for you to teach your client how to accept herself unconditionally.

Genuineness

Rogers (1957) argued that it is important for the therapist to be experienced as real in the therapeutic encounter and that it is counter-therapeutic for him or her to hide behind a professional role or other facade. REBT theory would agree with this statement. As will be presently shown, it is important for you to vary your bond with different clients and for some it is important that you emphasize your professionalism more than any other quality. However, it is essential that you do this genuinely.

REBT theory also encourages the use of self-disclosure on the part of the therapist, although this should be done with care (Dryden, 1991). For some clients, to learn that the therapist has struggled with a similar issue to the one they are struggling with and has overcome it can be immensely therapeutic, although for others it is an unwelcome intrusion or worse. As will be shown later, you can attempt to determine the possible value of such techniques with specific clients by eliciting your client's views on preferred therapist behaviour.

The main point of being genuine and with the use of self-disclosure is that you convey to your client that you are also a fallible human being and can accept yourself as such. In this respect, honestly acknowledging the mistakes you make in therapy with your client from a position of unconditional self-acceptance can be a particularly potent therapeutic factor for her.

Humour

Albert Ellis (1977) has said that one way of conceptualizing psychological disturbance is that it is the tendency of humans to take themselves, other people and life conditions TOO seriously. Now, of course, we do need to take negative events seriously, since if we do not we will lack the motivation to change them. However, taking things TOO seriously (e.g. by bringing awfulizing beliefs to a negative event) gets in the way of constructive action and leads to emotional disturbance. Consequently, Ellis argued that the judicious use of humour by the therapist can provide a healthy antidote to the client's tendency to take life *TOO* seriously, and will encourage the client to take a serious, but not *TOO* serious, view on life. Obviously, a great deal of tact and sensitivity is needed here and you should make it quite clear that you are making fun of some of your client's irrational ideas, not ridiculing the client herself. Despite these caveats, therapist humour can be very beneficial for some clients.

Active-directive Style

REBT therapists generally adopt an active-directive therapeutic style in that we tend to be active in directing our clients' attention to the irrational beliefs that we hypothesize are at the core of their emotional and behavioural problems, and to the importance of challenging these beliefs by cognitive, emotive and behavioural means. Having helped our clients to identify a therapeutic focus (which is an important aspect of brief REBT), we are then quite active in encouraging them to keep to this focus until the time is right to move on to a different one. The more your client learns the principles of REBT and the more she shows that she is able to apply these principles to her own life, the less active and directive you need to be in your therapeutic approach. Decreasing the standard active-directive therapeutic style in brief REBT encourages the client to take increasing responsibility for her own therapeutic change which will, in turn, help her to become her own therapist.

Varying the Therapeutic Bond

It is important to recognize that different clients respond to different types of bonds with their therapists. Therefore, if you offer the same kind of bond to all of your clients then accept the fact that more of your clients will drop out of brief REBT than if you tailored your bond to their idiosyncratic requirements. In order to do this you will need to understand the salient bond dimensions along which you may vary your bond behaviour. Let me now outline some of these dimensions.

Formal-informal

Some clients will expect you to be formal in your behaviour towards them and will do better in brief REBT if you do so. To do this you might use surnames and titles, wear formal, professional clothing in therapy sessions and refrain from using profane language.

Other clients, however, will expect you to be informal in your interactional style and will derive more therapeutic benefit from this than if you adopted a more formal style. To be more informal you might wear informal (but not unprofessional) clothing, make suitable adjustments to your seating arrangements (e.g. sitting on floor cushions rather than in chairs) and use non-verbal behaviour to convey informality. In addition, you might use more therapist self-disclosure and humour with such clients than with clients who respond better to greater therapist formality.

Expertise vs Likability

Some clients will pay greater attention to you if they are impressed by your expertise and professional demeanour. Such clients will be impressed by your training and qualifications, by any books or articles that you may have written and by other professional accoutrements. In this case, it is as if the client is saying, 'I'll listen to this person because he seems to know what he is talking about'.

Emphasizing your expertise involves displaying your diplomas and professional qualifications, suggesting to your clients that they read books, chapters or articles that you have written and generally conveying a professional atmosphere by the way you have arranged your office.

Other clients will be more impressed and influenced by your personal and interpersonal qualities. Here, it is as if the client is saying to himself, 'I hope this therapist and I get on . . . If we do, I'll listen to him. If he doesn't then I probably won't.'

Your task, then, is to discover the kind of interpersonal behaviour to which your client will best respond. This may sound to you quite Machiavellian, but this is not the case. In your everyday life you are called upon to make interpersonal adjustments with your friends and relatives, for example. The same is true in therapy. However, you do need to be genuine in whichever interpersonal style you develop with your client. If you are able to do this, then you will be actualizing Arnold Lazarus's (1981) principle of the 'authentic chameleon'. When you believe that you are not able to offer a particular client a particular bond then it is important that you effect a prompt referral to someone whom you consider to be more suitable for that client.

You may be wondering how you can identify the 'relationship of choice' for different clients. Here are some useful suggestions

1. *Ask the client:* George Kelly (1955), the founder of personal construct therapy, has said: 'If you want to know something about your client, ask him. He just might tell you.' Thus, you might ask the person such direct questions as:
   - Do you think that it is more important that your therapist has expertise or is a likable person?
   - Do you think that you would respond better to a therapist who is formal or informal in his or her interactive style?

   In addition, you might ask a number of indirect questions, the answers to which may suggest the kind of therapeutic bond that is best for a particular person. For example:
   - Who are the people in your life who have been naturally therapeutic to you? What were their qualities?

   You can ask the person such questions face to face or put them as items on any questionnaire that you ask the person to complete.

2. *Knowledge of the person's personality style:* Your clients will differ in their personality style and a knowledge of the interpersonal implications of such different styles is important in determining the kind of bond to form with them. Here are a number of suggestions that are worth considering:
   1. Be calm with clients who have a histrionic personality style.
   2. Begin with a formal, intellectual style for clients with an obsessive-compulsive personality, but gradually introduce affect and informality into the therapeutic relationship.
   3. Give a lot of interpersonal freedom to highly reactant clients and consistently emphasize their freedom to choose.
   4. Gently encourage clients with avoidant personality leanings, but do not push them too hard.

Having made these suggestions, I do wish to stress that individual differences do occur within the same personality style and these should be respected when considering the kind of bond to form with a person.

3. *Feedback on bond behaviour:* Later in this chapter (see pp. 68–70), I argue that it is important to develop a channel of communication with your clients in order to discuss your mutual experiences of working together. Part of this process involves you seeking feedback on different aspects of your contribution to the therapeutic process. Since it is important for you to regard the decisions that you make with respect to bond variation as tentative, eliciting feedback from your client on your bond behaviour will help you to calibrate your interpersonal style with that person. Thus, at the end of a therapy session you might ask such questions as:

- How would you describe the way I have been interacting with you? Has this been helpful or unhelpful?
- How would you like me to interact with you? How would this be more helpful to you?

If you are concerned about the impact of any aspect of your bond behaviour, you need to ask directly about this. For example:

- I have been trying to inject some humour into our sessions. How have you responded to this?

You will, of course, wish to evaluate the person's responses to such questions before deciding to modify your bond behaviour. I am not advocating an unthinking consumerism here, but neither do I recommend dispensing with client feedback altogether. Far from it. Adopting a flexible position on this as well as on other issues will help you to become a more effective REBT therapist.

HOW TO RESPOND TO THE INITIAL REQUEST FOR HELP

If you work in a therapy agency, it is likely that you will receive a referral by letter. The referring agent, in writing either to the agency where you work or to you directly, will normally provide a summary of the case from his or her perspective. It may well be that the referrer knows that you or the agency offer brief therapy and has made the judgment that this particular person is a good candidate for brief work. If you or the agency have a brief therapy clinic and regular sources of referrals then it is useful to prepare for these sources a written statement about brief REBT and who is most likely to respond to this approach as well as for whom the approach is not indicated. Summarizing the information presented in Chapter 1 is usually a good way of doing this.

However, even if the referring agent knows about your brief therapy practice and has made a positive 'brief therapy' referral, it is still important that you make your own decision whether or not the person being referred will benefit from this approach.

This will also be your task if you work in private practice. In this setting you may still receive a referral letter about the case, but in my experience it is equally likely that the referrer will give the person your telephone number so that the first you will know about the referral will be in the form of a telephone call from the person herself.

It is important to bear in mind at this point that the person who has been referred to you is not yet your client. Garvin and Seabury (1984) have made the important point that when a person seeks help, she is an 'applicant'. She only becomes a 'client' when she has accepted your offer of help. I consider this to be a useful distinction in brief REBT which prevents me from striving to help someone who has not yet consented to be helped.

Decide What Information You Will Give Before Meeting

Whether you write to offer the person seeking help an appointment or whether you do so in response to a telephone call, you need to decide what information you will give the applicant at that first point of contact. If you are writing to him to offer an appointment, you may wish to avail yourself of the opportunity to tell him something about brief REBT, adding that one of the purposes of the first meeting will be for you both to determine whether the approach is the best one for him. When telling him about brief REBT at this stage it is important that you do so briefly and, in particular, it is important to mention the number of sessions that you will be offering him. If you do this you need to make perfectly clear to the applicant that should brief REBT not be indicated then you will make alternative treatment suggestions.

In your letter you may also wish to inform the applicant about some of the practical aspects of seeing you. Thus, you may wish to tell him about your fee (if any) and whether or not you operate a sliding fee scale. Informing him about your cancellation policy is also useful, as is letting him know of your qualifications and supervision arrangements. Finally, it is important to inform the applicant about the degree of flexibility you have concerning appointment times.

If you are responding to a telephone call, it is a good idea to ask the applicant whether he wishes to know at that time the practicalities of seeing you. If he does then it is important to tell him your standard fee and whether you operate a sliding scale. If you don't do this, you may discover at the end of the first session that the person cannot afford even your lowest fee. If the person asks you about REBT on the phone as Carol did, it is useful to give a short explanation along the following lines:

WINDY: REBT is an approach to therapy which helps you to understand and change the self-defeating attitudes that lie at the bottom of your problems. You and I will work together in an active way to help you do this so you can overcome your problems and live a more satisfying life.

If your client asks you to elaborate (as Carol did), it is best not to do so otherwise you may get drawn into counselling the person, which is not appropriate over the telephone. Thus:

CAROL: That sounds interesting. Can you tell me more?

WINDY: I will be pleased to do so at our first meeting if you wish to make an appointment.

Alternatively, you might offer to send the person a brief informational sheet which she can read before she decides whether to make an appointment (see p. 51).

Some REBT therapists send applicants much longer descriptive material about REBT and I have included an example in Appendix 1. If you do send the applicant information about REBT, then it is worthwhile asking her whether she would also appreciate receiving written information about the practicalities of seeing you.

Whether you write to the person seeking help or whether you speak to her on the telephone you should be polite and professional, and communicate that you are genuinely interested in helping her should she decide to make an appointment. Never forget that building a working alliance begins at the very first contact between you and your potential client.

A GUIDE TO CONDUCTING THE FIRST SESSION

In this part of the chapter I will consider how to conduct the first session in brief REBT. First, I stress the importance of setting an agenda at the beginning of the session. Then I discuss the tasks that you need to complete in that first session if possible.

Set an Agenda for the Session

When you meet the applicant for the first time, you have a number of tasks to accomplish. REBT is an approach to therapy which holds that the therapist should be open about her therapeutic tasks. It is also an approach which stresses the therapeutic value of structure. Setting an agenda at the beginning of the first session allows you to combine both these therapeutic virtues. Here is how I set the agenda for the first session with Carol. In doing so I will state the issues which I will consider in greater detail later in the chapter.

Information Sheet on REBT for Potential Clients

RATIONAL EMOTIVE BEHAVIOUR THERAPY (REBT)

What is REBT?

REBT is a brief form of psychotherapy which holds that our emotional problems are determined not by events, but largely by the self-defeating beliefs that we have about these events.

For example, if you are anxious about speaking in public, the REBT position would be that your anxiety stems from a belief such as: 'I must give a good speech and I am worthless if I don't.'

How Does REBT Work?

REBT works by teaching you to recognize and change those beliefs that result in emotional problems such as anxiety, guilt, anger and depression. The application of REBT will enable you to make greater use of your potential and help you to achieve your long-term goals.

Collaborative Teamwork

You and I will work closely together as a team identifying your problems, defining your goals and finding the means to achieve those goals. As a therapist, I will be responsible for providing structure and direction within the framework of therapy. As a client, your role in the process will be to describe your problems as clearly as you can, to be open to alternative ways of looking at these problems and to commit yourself to trying out new ways of thinking and acting in your everyday life by putting into practice the skills you develop within therapy sessions.

I want to stress that therapy involves working together as a team.

WINDY: In this first session, I want to spend most of the time giving you an opportunity to tell me what problems you have that you want help with. I also want to understand what you wish to achieve from therapy. For my part, I want to tell you something about the therapeutic approach that I practise which is known as Rational Emotive Behaviour Therapy or REBT for short. It was suggested by your doctor that you might benefit from what is known as brief therapy which, as I practise it, lasts for 11 sessions. So, I want to assess whether or not that is the case. If it is then we can discuss what this involves. If not, I will tell you what I think may be more helpful for you. Does that make sense?

CAROL: Yes, that sounds fine.

WINDY: What I have just done is to put items that I want to cover today on what is called a therapeutic agenda for the session. I'll ask you in a moment what items you would like to put on the agenda for today's session. The purpose of an agenda is to ensure that we make the best use of the time that we have together and to ensure that we are on the same wavelength. Now what items would you like to place on the agenda?

CAROL: (*hesitantly*) . . . I'm not sure.

WINDY: Well. Do you have any questions about therapy or about me as a therapist that you want to ask, for example?

CAROL: Well, I don't know much about therapy, so I'm glad you will be explaining it to me. Perhaps you can also tell me about your qualifications?

WINDY: I'll be pleased to. Does it make sense for us to start by you telling me about your problems and what you want to achieve from therapy and then we can discuss the other matters later?

CAROL: Fine.

Having set the agenda, it is your responsibility to ensure that you and the applicant deal with all the items. If you run out of time before you have done so, make sure that you make a note of the remaining items and put them on the agenda for the following session. It is for this reason that you need to decide how many items you and the applicant can realistically cover in the first session. If you consider that there are too many items on the agenda say so and help the client to prioritize the items that she particularly wants to discuss. Of course, you can never be sure that you have enough time for the prioritized items, but at least you can make an educated guess at the outset.

Let the Person Tell You her Problems in her Own Way

Although brief REBT is a structured approach to therapy, it is important that at this point you give the applicant an opportunity to tell you about her problems in her own way. Don't forget that she has probably been holding in her feelings and rehearsing in her mind what she wants to tell you. She is also probably concerned about whether or not you will be understanding. So let her tell you about her problems in her own way. In doing so, your major task is to communicate that you understand her problems from her frame of reference. You do this by using basic coun-selling skills and in particular asking her to confirm or disconfirm your attempts to understand. For example:

CAROL: Whenever I meet a man that I like, I find it very difficult to be friendly to him. I'm OK with men whom I don't fancy, but for some reason I show an 'I don't care attitude' to the ones whom I am attracted to.

WINDY: So have I got this right? You want to respond to the men that you like, but for some reason that you don't yet understand you are indifferent to them instead.

CAROL: Yes, that's right.

Develop a Problem List

Another task that you have in the first session is to help the person to develop a problem list. A problem list contains exactly what it says it does – a list of your client's problems in summary form. These are the problems that your client hopes to overcome as a result of therapy. As we shall see later, you may not be able to address all the problems on the person's list in brief REBT, but at this point it is best to develop a list which contains all her problems. Here is a list of problems that I developed with Carol.

- I find it difficult responding to men that I find attractive.
- I am in trouble at work because I am often late in the morning.
- I get used by my friends.
- I am overweight.
- I am oversensitive and easily hurt when criticized.
- I am always in debt.

In drawing up a problem list with the person, it is important to follow a few simple guidelines.

1. Keep the description of the problems short.
2. Use the person's own words in defining her problems.
3. Ensure that the person agrees with the description of each problem and in doing so has the opportunity of correcting your wording.

Remember that the problem descriptions should reflect the problems as the person sees them. These descriptions will probably change after you have assessed the problems using the ABCs of REBT (see Chapter 2). However, they are sufficient at this point and will serve two purposes: first, they indicate to the applicant that you understand her from her frame of reference and second, by helping her to describe her problems in a succinct manner you are beginning to bring some order to the often chaotic nature of her experience.

Help the Person to Set Goals in Line with her Defined Problems

Once you have helped the person to define her problems, the next step is to help her to set goals in line with each of the defined problems. Again, remember that you have not assessed these defined problems yet. When you do so the person's goals may well change in line with each of her now assessed problems. Notwithstanding this point, it is helpful to encourage the person to set goals for each of her defined problems since this will make brief REBT forward looking and will show your client that you take her objectives seriously.

REBT therapists agree with their behaviour therapy colleagues concerning the nature of therapeutic goals. Amongst others, these should be:

1. *Within the person's control:* Here, only accept as therapeutic goals those which are within the direct control of the person. Do not accept as therapeutic goals statements which desire a change in the behaviour of other people or life conditions since these lie outside the person's control. You can, of course, accept goal statements which point to the person's attempts to influence the behaviour of other people or the existence of a set of life conditions. The difference here is that such influence attempts are within the person's direct control while the behaviour of other people, for example, certainly is not.
2. *Stated positively:* When you ask applicants at this beginning stage of brief REBT what they want to achieve from therapy, it is likely that their reply will refer to the absence of a negative state. Thus, a client, in reply, might say that she doesn't want to feel anxious when she speaks

in public. 'Not wanting to feel anxious' is the absence of a negative state – in this case anxiety. However, goals are best achieved when they point to the presence of a state rather than the absence of a negative state. In this example, 'feeling concerned' points to the presence of an emotional state.

3. *Observable:* Whenever possible, therapeutic goals need to be observable. If they cannot be directly observed, the person needs to point to an observable referent of a desired emotional goal. For example, in response to a person's goal that she wants to feel concerned rather than anxious about public speaking, the therapist might ask something like: 'How would other people know that you were concerned rather than anxious about speaking in public?'

4. *Achievable:* It is important that the person's goals are achievable. Otherwise, she will quickly become demoralized as she says that she has little or no chance of meeting these goals. People with strong perfectionistic leanings tend to set goals which are unachievable and often people with an introverted temperament set what for them are unachievable extroverted-type goals. If the person sets goals which are, in your opinion, unobtainable you do need to voice your opinion and discuss this with the applicant.

5. *Health-promoting:* It is also important that you ensure that the applicant's goals are in her healthy best interests, particularly from a long-term perspective. If the person discloses goals that are not, in your opinion, in her long-term healthy interests, then it is important that you voice your concerns openly with the person and resolve the situation (hopefully in your favour!).

When your client clings to goals that are clearly unhealthy you can do the following. First, you can decide that she is not a good candidate for brief REBT and recommend longer term REBT or some other form of long-term treatment. Second, you can view her unhealthy goals as being based on a set of irrational beliefs. In which case, you might accept the person into brief REBT, target these irrational beliefs for change during treatment and hope that the client's goals will change in a healthier direction as a result.

When the person's unhealthy goals are rigidly held or when they are life-threatening, I regard these two situations as contraindications for brief REBT since they are normally signs that the person requires more than the 11 sessions that comprise my approach to this brief therapeutic approach.

6. *Ethical and legal:* Finally, acceptable goals (in line with problems as defined) are consistent with the person's ethical code, do not harm the person or other people, and do not contravene the law of the land.

In working with Carol, I helped her to set the following goals in relation to her problems as defined.

Problem: I find it difficult responding to men whom I find attractive.
Goal: To show interest and respond emotionally to men whom I find attractive.

Problem: I am in trouble at work because I am often late in the morning.
Goal: To arrive at work on time.

Problem: I get used by my friends.
Goal: To assert myself with my friends whenever I consider that they are using me.

Problem: I am overweight.
Goal: To get down to 9 stone and maintain this weight.

Problem: I am oversensitive and easily hurt when criticized.
Goal: To accept criticism when it is fair and assert myself when it is not.

Problem: I am always in debt.
Goal: To develop a financial plan and keep to it so that I remain in the black.

Encourage the Person to Select Two Problems for Particular Attention

Given that brief REBT (as I practise it) lasts 11 sessions, it may not be possible for you to help the applicant to achieve her goals on all of her problems. Consequently, it is important that you help her to select two problems which have particular priority for her. Now in dealing with these two problems you can then help her to generalize her learning to her other problems and you should certainly aim to do this if at all possible. However, don't forget that in brief therapy you are constrained by the limited amount of time you have with the person. Consequently, even if you can only help her with her two prioritized problems you will have helped her a great deal. Helping the applicant to have similar expectations from brief REBT is also important, as the following dialogue with Carol shows.

WINDY: Now, Carol, so far we have developed a problem list which has six problems on it. One of the things that we need to consider is whether or not you would benefit from a brief period of 11 sessions of therapy.

CAROL: Well, my doctor thought I would.

WINDY: And she may well be right. Since brief therapy takes 11 sessions, we have to be realistic and conclude that we may not have time to deal with all of your problems in that time. So I would like to ask you this question. If we could only deal with two of your problems, which two would you like to focus on?

CAROL: That's a difficult one. Well, the most immediate problem is arriving late at work. So that would be one. But the one that causes me most distress is being oversensitive.

WINDY: Which one of these two problems should we start with?

CAROL: The work situation.

WINDY: Fine. If we decide to work together in brief therapy and we don't have time to deal with all six of your problems, I will help you to discover any links between your two prioritized problems and the remaining problems on your list. If there are such links, then I will help you to transfer what you learn on the two target problems to the remaining four.

CAROL: What if I opt for brief therapy and at the end of the 11 sessions I still have one of my problems and there are no links between that problem and the ones we have dealt with?

WINDY: That's an important and a tricky question. First of all, let me say that in focusing on your two target problems I hope to show you a way of dealing with these problems which is general enough to help you deal with a broad range of emotional problems. That's the first point. The second point is that if you are still struggling with a problem at the end of brief therapy and you still wish therapeutic help with it, we will discuss the situation then. We won't be able to extend the sessions beyond 11, but I'll make a few recommendations then.

However, let me say that brief Rational Emotive Behaviour Therapy is not designed to help you overcome all your problems. It is designed to help you get to grips with your major problems and for you to learn a way of dealing with emotional problems so that in future you can become your own therapist. So, to be frank, you MAY end therapy still with one of your problems intact.

CAROL: I understand. That gives me a clearer idea about the scope of brief therapy.

[It was my intention to raise this issue with Carol, but she brought it up first. It is important to let the applicant know the scope of brief REBT (as Carol nicely put it) even if she does not raise it herself. A good time to do so is when you come to help the person to select two target problems. The point to stress is what I put to Carol: brief REBT is designed to help clients deal with two specific problems and learn a general methodology of emotional self-help that they can apply both to the other problems on their problem list (with the therapist helping them to make the relevant links) and to any future problems that they might experience. You also need to stress that brief REBT is not designed to cover all the problems on the client's problem list, although occasionally this does happen.]

WINDY: Now, I would like to give you a clear idea of how the therapy that I use approaches emotional problems. Does that make sense?

CAROL: Yes, that is one of the things I wanted to know.

Explain the ABCDEs of REBT

Bordin (1979) has stressed that you and your client have tasks to do in therapy. One of the most important tasks that you have is to agree on a way of conceptualizing and dealing with the person's problems and to use this throughout therapy. This process can either occur explicitly where you explain your approach or it is done implicitly where you practise your approach and your client makes inferences about your problem conceptualization and treatment approach.

In brief REBT, in line with its views on the importance of therapist openness, this means that you will often choose to explain to the person the ABCDEs of REBT. This needs to be done quite early in the process so that the applicant can make an informed choice concerning whether or not she wishes to make use of brief REBT. If brief REBT is suitable to her therapeutic needs and if she decides that she does wish to commit herself to it, at this point she becomes a client rather than an applicant.

Let me now show you one way of explaining the ABCDEs of REBT. I will do so by illustrating the 'money' example in my work with Carol. You will recall from Chapter 1, that A stands for the critical activating event which triggers the client's irrational beliefs (in this case) at B which in turn underpin his emotional and behavioural responses at C. D stands for disputing irrational beliefs while E refers to the effects of disputing.

WINDY: I would like to outline the approach I will be taking to your problems so that you can judge whether or not it makes sense to you and whether or not you think it will be helpful. Would you like to understand one way of making sense of and dealing with your problems?

CAROL: Yes, that would be useful.

WINDY: Fine. Now this explanation has four parts and I'll take you through each part slowly. OK?

CAROL: OK.

WINDY: Here is part one. I want you to imagine that you hold the following belief: 'I would like to have a minimum of £11 on me at all times, but it is not absolutely necessary that I do so. If I have less than £10 it would be bad, but not the end of the world'. Now can you imagine having that belief?

CAROL: Yes.

WINDY: Good. Now with that belief you look in your pocket or purse and discover that you have only £10. How would you feel about having £10 when you believe that you want, but don't absolutely need £11?

CAROL: I'd feel somewhat concerned about it.

WINDY: But you wouldn't want to commit suicide.

CAROL: No, I wouldn't.

WINDY: Right, you wouldn't. Now let's go to part two. This time I want you to imagine that you hold a different belief. This time you believe the following: 'I absolutely must have a minimum of £11 on me at all times. It is absolutely necessary that I have a minimum of £11 and it would be the end of the world if I didn't'. Now can you imagine having that belief?

CAROL: Yes.

WINDY: Now again with this belief that you absolutely have to have a minimum of £11 on you at all times, you look in your pocket or purse and realize that you have only £10. Now how would you feel?

CAROL: Panicked.

WINDY: That's exactly right. Now note something really important. So far we have had two very different reactions to the same situation and those different reactions were each based on a different belief or attitude that you had towards the situation. Do you see that?

CAROL: Yes, I do.

WINDY: Now here's part three. You still believe: 'I absolutely must have a minimum of £11 on me at all times. It is absolutely necessary that I do have a minimum of £11 and it would be the end of the world if I didn't.' But on rechecking your money you discover that nestling under the £10 note are two £1 coins and you now have £12. Now, how do you feel?

CAROL: Very relieved.

WINDY: That's right. Now here's the fourth and final part. You now have £12 and you still believe: 'I absolutely must have a minimum of £11 on me at all times. It is absolutely necessary that I do have a minimum of £11 and it would be the end of the world if I didn't.' One thing would occur to you which would lead you to feel panicky again. What do you think that would be?

CAROL: That I might lose £2?

WINDY: Correct. Or that you might spend the £2 or get mugged. Now the point of this example is this. All human beings, male or female, black or white, old or young, make themselves emotionally disturbed when they don't get what they believe they must get, and are vulnerable to making themselves emotionally disturbed when they do get what they believe they must get because they could always lose it. But if they stick to their flexible desires and don't change these into dogmatic musts, then they will feel healthily concerned, for example, when they don't get what they want, and this will help them to take whatever constructive action is appropriate. Does this explanation make sense to you?

CAROL: Yes, it does. It sounds like when your beliefs are rigid, then that's when you're in trouble.

WINDY: That's an excellent way of putting it. My job is to help you to take the rigidity out of your beliefs and to keep them flexible. So that's an example of the model that I will be using to help us to make sense of your problems, and in particular to identify and help you to change the rigid beliefs that are probably at the bottom of your problems. Now, do you think that this framework could be useful to you?

CAROL: Yes. It sounds like it is down to earth which I like.

To summarize how to use the money example consider these seven steps:

Step 1.   Ask the person if he is interested in an explanation of emotional problems.

Step 2. Present part 1 of the model. Stress that the person has less money than he prefers (rational belief). Enquire about his feeling. If he doesn't give you a healthy negative emotion, explain why this would be his emotional response.

Step 3. Present part 2 of the model. Stress that the person has less money than he demands (irrational belief). Enquire about his feeling. If he doesn't give you an unhealthy negative emotion, explain why this would be his emotional response.

Step 4. Emphasize that different beliefs about the same situation lead to different feelings.

Step 5. Present part 3 of the model. Stress that the person has more money than he demands (irrational belief). Enquire about his feeling. Prompt, if necessary.

Step 6. Present part 4 of the model. Stress that he still has more money than he demands (irrational belief), but that he has a thought that leads him to feel disturbed again. Enquire about the nature of this thought. Encourage him to identify possible thoughts for himself, but give suggestions if he is stuck.

Step 7. Summarize all the information, emphasizing the importance of distinguishing between rational and irrational beliefs and showing their differential effects.

Spelling Out your Tasks and your Client's Tasks in Brief REBT

Having carried out these seven steps, I suggest that you continue by outlining your tasks as an REBT therapist and the other person's tasks if she decides to become a client. Many ethical codes stipulate that in order for clients to give their informed consent to a therapeutic procedure, they first have to understand its nature and what it demands of them. In brief REBT this means that you first need to help the applicant to understand how REBT conceptualizes emotional problems (which is the purpose of the 'money' example). Second, you need to spell out to the applicant what REBT requires of you both during therapy. Once the applicant has fully understood these points, when you ask her whether or not she wishes to commit herself to brief REBT and become a client, if she agrees then she can be said to have given her informed consent.

The following is how I explained our respective tasks in brief REBT to Carol.

WINDY: Now before I ask you whether or not you wish to commit yourself to brief REBT, let me tell you a little about what I will be doing in therapy and what I will expect from you. Would that be helpful?

CAROL: Yes, that would be very useful.

WINDY: Let me start by outlining my tasks.

First, I will help you to identify your problems and to set goals that are based on our understanding of your problems as we have defined them. We've already made a start by doing this.

Second, I will help you to assess your problems and in particular help you to identify the self-defeating irrational beliefs that underpin your problems. If necessary, we'll take another look at your goals since sometimes goals change once problems have been assessed.

Third, I will help you to question your self-defeating beliefs and to replace them with beliefs that are more healthy for you, in the sense that they will help you to achieve your goals. During this process I will be asking you a lot of questions and explaining any issues that aren't clear to you.

Fourth, I will help you to identify things that you can do to practise and strengthen these new, more healthy beliefs. Fifth, since therapy doesn't always go smoothly, it may be that this will be the case in our work. If that happens, I will initiate a discussion so that we can identify and overcome any obstacles we find that may be interfering with your making progress in therapy.

So, these are my major tasks as I see them. How does that sound to you?

CAROL: That sounds fine. I thought, though, that therapy involves going into your past.

WINDY: We'll do that if it's necessary, but it may not be necessary. In Rational Emotive Behaviour Therapy our view is that you may have learned some self-defeating beliefs in your childhood, but the reason why you are emotionally disturbed today is because you still have the same beliefs. You have carried them forward as it were, and given this, I need to help you by encouraging you to identify, challenge and change those beliefs that you currently hold. Does that answer your question?

CAROL: Yes.

WINDY: Good. Now, shall I outline what I think your tasks in therapy are?

CAROL: Fine.

WINDY: Your first task, which you have already done, is to tell me what your problems are in as specific a manner as you can. Brief Rational Emotive Behaviour Therapy is a therapeutic approach which works best in helping you to deal with and overcome problems that can be specified. Ordinarily, it does not give us enough time to deal with problems that can only be vaguely expressed. That's why I asked you to list the problems that you want help with and to do this as specifically as you could. Also, remember that I asked you to specify your goals as they relate to each of your problems.

CAROL: So that's my first task and I've already done that?

WINDY: Yes. Your second task as I see it is to listen to what I have to say with an open mind. I don't expect that you will always agree with me, but at least listen to me without prejudging what I am saying. Now, related to being open-minded, it is important that you tell me honestly what you think of what I have to say. It's no good you saying that you accept any points that I make when privately you disagree with my viewpoint. So, I will be looking for an honest response from you. If you disagree with me, please say so and we will then discuss our differing opinions and resolve any disagreements.

So can I count on you to be open-minded and give me an honest reaction to any points that I put to you?

CAROL: Yes, that's reasonable and I'll do my best on both counts.

WINDY: Excellent. Now, let's suppose that you agree with the REBT viewpoint that I outlined to you in the money example and you can see how it helps to explain your problems. Your next task is to participate actively with me as I strive to assess your problems and take steps in the sessions to help you overcome them. The more active you can be here, the better.

CAROL: What do you mean by being active?

WINDY: Good question. By being active in the assessment phase, I mean answering my questions as fully as possible, correcting me when I seem to have gotten the wrong end of the stick and pointing me in the right direction. Once we have accurately assessed your problems, then I will suggest certain ways of overcoming them. If these make sense to you there are two ways of involving yourself in the techniques and procedures that I suggest. If you do so passively, it's as if you think it is basically my responsibility to change you and you will go along with me. By taking an active stance you realize that therapeutic change is based on what you do for yourself rather than what I do in the session. So the more you can throw yourself into the techniques that make sense to you the more benefit you will derive from therapy.

CAROL: I see. That's much clearer now.

WINDY: Your final task in therapy as I see it is to practise in your everyday life what you learn in therapy sessions. I'll help you to set useful assignments that you can do between therapy sessions, but you are responsible for actually doing them. Is that reasonable?

CAROL: So, coming to therapy sessions isn't enough for me to deal with my problems.

WINDY: That's right. I think of therapy as a unique kind of educational experience. You are coming to me to learn about what determines your problems and what you can do about them and I will be teaching you about how one approach to therapy can be helpful to you. It's a bit like learning to play the piano. I can teach you how to play in my conservatory, but unless you practise on your own piano at home, you won't learn. In therapy, without going over the top, the more you put into practice what you learn in my office the more progress you will make.

CAROL: I hadn't looked at it like that before, but I can see that you are right.

WINDY: Now, of course, I will help you to set suitable assignments, that's my bit. But your responsibility is to do the assignments once they have made sense to you and once you have agreed to do them.

CAROL: That's fair.

WINDY: Are you willing to commit yourself to your tasks as I've outlined them?

CAROL: I am.

WINDY: And do you think doing our respective tasks will be helpful to you?

CAROL: As you've described them, yes. In particular, I can see the value of doing something to help myself between therapy sessions.

WINDY: Excellent.

Let me summarize the points made in the above interchange.

The therapist's tasks in brief REBT are as follows:

1. To identify the person's problems and to set goals (as these relate to the problems as defined).
2. To assess the person's problems and in particular help her to identify her irrational beliefs (and to set goals in line with each assessed problem).
3. To dispute the person's irrational beliefs.
4. To help the person identify and strengthen her rational beliefs.
5. To identify and deal with any obstacles to client change.

Similarly, the client's tasks in brief REBT are as follows:

1. To specify her problems and goals.
2. To be open-minded about the therapist's viewpoint.
3. To give the therapist honest feedback about different aspects of the therapeutic process.
4. To participate actively in the assessment of her problems and in-session attempts to facilitate change.
5. To practise in her everyday life what she learns in therapy sessions.

Deciding Whether or Not the Person is a Good Candidate for Brief REBT

By now you should have gained enough information to judge whether or not the person is a good candidate for brief REBT. In Chapter 1, I outlined seven criteria which I use to judge whether or not a person is suitable for brief REBT. My assessment of Carol led me to the conclusion that she met all seven criteria. I thus considered her to be an excellent candidate for brief REBT, and consequently I offered a therapeutic contract on this basis. More specifically:

1. Carol was able and willing to present her problems in a specific form and set goals that were concrete and achievable.
2. Her problems were of the type that could be dealt with in 11 sessions.
3. She was able and willing to target two problems that she particularly wanted to work on during therapy.
4. She understood the ABCDEs of REBT and indicated that this way of conceptualizing and dealing with her problems made sense and was potentially helpful to her.
5. She understood the therapist's and her own tasks in brief REBT and indicated that these would be helpful to her. She also agreed to carry out her tasks which, in my judgment, she was capable of doing.

6. Her level of functioning in her everyday life was sufficiently high to enable her to carry out her tasks both inside and outside therapy sessions.
7. From my experience of working with Carol in this first session, I concluded that we had developed a good rapport and that the prospect of our developing a strong working alliance was good.

Ask the Person if She Wishes to Commit Herself to Brief REBT

You have now done the following things in the first session:

1. Set an agenda for the session.
2. Allowed the person to talk about her problems.
3. Helped her to develop a problem list.
4. Helped her to set goals in line with these defined problems (in a way that met the criteria for workable goals discussed on pp. 54–56).
5. Helped her to select two problems for particular therapeutic attention.
6. Taught her the ABCDEs of REBT.
7. Explained your respective tasks in brief REBT.
8. Judged that the applicant is a good candidate for brief REBT.

Before I proceed, you may be wondering at this point whether you can accomplish all these tasks in one session. My experience is that with the majority of clients who are suitable for brief REBT you can. However, I am well aware of saying this as a seasoned REBT practitioner. Given that you may be new to REBT, I would say that a more realistic goal for you is to spend two sessions carrying out the aforementioned tasks until you gain more experience in REBT. If, as a novice REBT therapist, you need to spend more than three sessions with a person over these tasks, then this is evidence that the person is not a good candidate for brief, 11-session REBT. However, if you are more experienced and you need more than two sessions to accomplish these tasks, then the person is not a good candidate for brief REBT.

Having made that point, I will now deal with the situation where you have completed the aforementioned tasks and you are ready to ask the person if she wishes to commit herself to REBT. If she agrees, then at that point she ceases to be an applicant and becomes a client.

Here is how I broached this subject with Carol.

WINDY: So far we have identified some problems that you wish to work on and set some goals in line with these problems. You have selected two problems that have a high priority for you. I have explained a little about REBT and in particular have outlined REBT's stance on emotional problems and how these can be dealt with. Finally, I've discussed with you the tasks that you and I need to accomplish in therapy together. Now the time is right for me to ask you an important question. Would you like to commit yourself to a course of brief REBT? This would involve seeing me for ten more sessions, initially weekly, but as things improve we can think of increasing the time between sessions.

CAROL: Yes, I would like to do that.

WINDY: Do you have any questions about brief REBT that I can answer at this point?

CAROL: How long does each session last for?

WINDY: Each session lasts for 50 minutes. Any other questions?

CAROL: Not that I can think of at the moment.

Suggesting the First Homework Assignment

WINDY: Now as I said earlier, to get the most out of brief REBT, it is important for you to put into practice what you learn in therapy sessions. Do you remember that?

CAROL: Yes.

WINDY: As you know we haven't started to deal with your problems yet other than developing a list of them and setting some goals. So, I'd like to suggest that you do some reading which will refresh your memory about the REBT approach to dealing with emotional problems in general. Would that be useful to you?

CAROL: Yes. I'd welcome that.

WINDY: Good. I suggest that you read Chapter 1 of a book that I wrote with a colleague entitled *Think Your Way to Happiness* (Dryden & Gordon, 1990). Then we can discuss your impressions next week. It will be particularly useful if you would write down points that are especially relevant to you and points that you disagree with. OK?

CAROL: Fine.

WINDY: It's a good idea if we both keep a note of assignments like this one so neither of us forget.

CAROL: Good idea.

Establish the Reflection Process

It is my view that in any approach to psychotherapy, whether brief or long-term, it is important for the therapist to establish what I call the reflection process with his or her client. The reflection process is the name that I have given to a process whereby therapist and client stand back from the action as it were, and reflect on what they are experiencing or have experienced in therapy. It is also an opportunity for them to reflect and discuss the possible future direction of their work together. In brief REBT there are four main established opportunities for such reflection to occur.

At the End of the Session

This is an opportunity for the therapist and client to discuss their re-actions to the session that they have just experienced and an occasion, in particular, for the therapist to discover how he might calibrate his thera-peutic approach to the client, based on the latter's feedback.

Here is how I initiated such feedback with Carol at the end of our first session. Note how I used this opportunity to raise the general issue of the importance of the reflection process.

WINDY: We are almost at the end of the session. Before we finish I'd like to ask you for your feedback on the session. I am particularly inter-ested in what you found helpful about it and what was unhelpful for you. This is an opportunity for us to reflect on the work we have done together and is part of a wider process that I call the reflection process. This process involves us standing back and reflecting on the work we have done together. While there will be set opportunities for us to reflect on our work, such as at the end of a therapy session and at the beginning of the following one, I would like to suggest that either of us may at any time invoke the reflection process to discuss what has just gone on between us. What do you think of that idea?

CAROL: Yes. I like that idea. But how might we do this practically?

WINDY: How about if we say something like, 'I think we need to stand back for a moment?'

CAROL: That's a good idea.

WINDY: Good. Now let's proceed with the end of session feedback. What was helpful about this session?

CAROL: Well, I liked the logical, step-by-step way that you helped me to list my problems and set goals. I also thought it was very useful that you helped me understand the role of beliefs in people's problems and our roles in therapy. I generally like to have a lot of information about something before I decide to opt for it so that was very useful . . .

WINDY: What about unhelpful factors?

CAROL: Well, there were no outright factors, but – and I hope you don't think I'm being rude when I say this – when I was given your name, I thought Windy was a woman and when I found out you were a man, I was disappointed.

WINDY: Why was that?

CAROL: Because in my experience women are more understanding than men on emotional issues and I wondered whether you would understand my problems.

WINDY: Have you experienced me as lacking understanding of what you've said today?

CAROL: No, not today. But we really haven't gone very deeply into problems today.

WINDY: That's right. But you are concerned that as a man I might not understand you and I do appreciate that. Do you think it would be useful for you to tell me when you sense that I don't understand you? I would certainly appreciate such feedback.

CAROL: Yes, that would be useful.

WINDY: Do you think that you would be able to do that?

CAROL: I think so.

WINDY: Let's agree on that then.

At the Beginning of the Following Session

This is an opportunity for the therapist to elicit the client's considered reaction to the previous session. When the therapist asks the client for her reactions to the session that they have just finished, it may be that the client is too close to the session to give a considered reaction to it. At the following session, the client has had a week to digest her experience of the session and it is important for the therapist to learn from the client's considered response since this may have affected what she has taken away from the session.

At a Mid-therapy Progress Review

This is an opportunity for you and your client to conduct an extensive review of the therapy up to that point. I suggest that you schedule it for session 6 and review your client's experiences of the helpful and unhelpful aspects of the therapy. As with other shorter reviews, it is important that you evaluate your client's responses and modify your therapeutic stance accordingly, if in your view it is in your client's best interests to do so.

The mid-therapy review which should not, if possible, take up more than half of session 6, is also an opportunity for you to ascertain the degree of progress that your client has made in achieving her goals with respect to her two prioritized problems and how much can be realistically achieved in the remaining sessions.

At the End of Therapy

The final, formal opportunity for you and your client to reflect on your work together is at the end of therapy. This is also an opportunity for you both to raise and complete any unfinished business that either of you may have.

In addition, as I mentioned to Carol, I suggest that both you and your client can refer to the reflection process at any point in therapy where one of you wishes to initiate a brief period of reflection on what has just transpired between you.

By now, if you have followed the steps that I have outlined, you should have established a good alliance with your client. The next step is for you to assess her target problems using the ABCs of REBT. This is the focus of the next chapter.

4

ASSESSING PROBLEMS

INTRODUCTION

In this chapter, I will consider an important part of brief REBT – assessing your client's problems. Making an accurate assessment of your client's two target problems is crucial if you are going to help her to overcome these problems successfully. Thus, it is important for you to take your time working with your client in making an assessment of her problems. More specifically, I will deal with the following issues: (i) working with specific examples of the target problem; (ii) assessing the ABCs of the client's problem; (iii) helping the client to set a goal in line with the problem as assessed; and (iv) assessing meta-emotional problems.

Before I start, let me remind you of Carol's two defined target problems and their associated goals. If you recall, she decided to begin by focusing on her problem of turning up late at work.

Carol's Problems and Goals

Problem 1: I am in trouble at work because I am often late in the morning.
Goal: To arrive at work on time.

Problem 2: I am oversensitive and easily hurt when criticized.
Goal: To accept the criticism when it is fair and to assert myself when it is not.

ASKING FOR A SPECIFIC EXAMPLE OF A TARGET PROBLEM

If you are to assess your client's target problem accurately you need to have a specific example of this problem. The reason for this is that the client is more likely to give you accurate information about her emotions, thoughts and actions when describing a specific situation than when describing her problem in general terms without reference to an actual context in which this problem occurred.

Ideally, when your client gives you a specific example, it should either be a recent example of the problem, a typical example of the problem, or a vivid or memorable example of the problem. Whichever your client chooses, it is preferable that the example is affect-laden. If you recall, Carol's primary target problem (i.e. the problem she selected for initial attention) related to her being late for work. Here is how I helped her to identify a real and specific example of the target problem.

Asking Carol for a Specific Example of her Problem

WINDY: So your main problem is 'being late for work' and your goal is be on time. Is that it?

CAROL: Yes, that puts it quite nicely.

WINDY: Good. Now can you think of a specific example of this problem which will help us to find out what is going on to stop you from arriving at your work on time?

CAROL: Yes I can.

WINDY: Please tell me about it.

CAROL: Well, it happened only last Thursday. I remember saying to myself that I needed to get an early start the next day, but it didn't happen like that. I stayed up that night until the small hours of the morning and when the alarm clock went off the next morning, I slept right through it.

WINDY: Are you clear about the importance *FOR YOU*, rather than for anyone else, of being punctual for work?

[Here I am taking particular care to check that Carol's goal of being on time for work is in her best interests as determined by Carol herself rather than by anyone else. If Carol's goal is what she truly wants then we will make far easier progress than if her stated goal has been determined by someone else and has been introjected by her.]

CAROL: Yes, I am clear about that. In our company it is made quite clear that punctuality will be recognized and rewarded whereas poor time-keeping will be penalized.

WINDY: But that is what your company wants from you. I'm more interested in what you want for yourself on this issue.

CAROL: Well, ideally I'd like to stay in bed till noon, but that's totally unrealistic.

WINDY: So in an ideal world you'd like to turn up at work at a time determined by yourself, but this isn't an ideal world. Let me put it like this. It sounds as if your goal is to do something that you don't really want to do because it is in your interests to do it. Is that close?

CAROL: Exactly. I've put it like that to my friends before now.

[If I had considered that Carol was more ambivalent about this goal I would have initiated a cost-benefit analysis of the problem behaviour (turning up at work late) and the stated goal (arriving at work on time) – see Appendix 2.]

WINDY: Since you wanted to turn up at work on time last Friday and yet you didn't do that, because you stayed up very late last Thursday night, then there must have been a restraining force of some power with which you stopped yourself from going to bed at a reasonable time on Thursday night. Would you agree with that?

CAROL: Yes, I would.

WINDY: Let's see if we can discover what this restraining force was.

ASSESSING THE SPECIFIC EXAMPLE USING THE ABCs OF REBT

Once your client has given you a specific example of her problem, then the next step is for you to assess it using the ABCs of REBT. The order in which you do this is important. REBT therapists generally assess A and C before B. Sometimes you may wish to assess C before A and at other times you will wish to assess A before C. However, in whichever order you decide to proceed, refrain from assessing B until you have elicited the client's main disturbed emotion and/or self-defeating behaviour at C and her critical A (see Chapter 2, p. 33). Most often you will find yourself assessing emotional Cs although as I discussed in Chapter 2, you will also be called upon to assess behavioural Cs when seemingly there are no emotional Cs or when the behavioural Cs have value in 'warding off' disturbed emotional Cs. Let me now consider the important issues that emerge when you endeavour to assess your client's ABC of a specific example.

Assessing C

In this section, I will discuss the assessment of emotional and behavioural Cs.

Assessing the Emotional C

Let me take the situation first where C is an emotion. When enquiring about the nature of this emotion, remember that you are looking for an unhealthy negative emotion. In doing so, it is important to guard against working with the following situations:

- Where the emotion given is not an unhealthy negative emotion.

Here you need to help your client to formulate an unhealthy negative feeling or, if he really does have a healthy negative emotion, then you either need to educate him about the constructive features of the healthy negative emotion or you need to assess whether or not he is condemning himself for having this healthy emotion in the first place. In this case, switch to the client's meta-emotional problem (see pp. 92–96).

- Where the emotion given is too vague.

Here, your client might say that she felt 'upset' about a certain event, for example. In response, you need to explain the importance of identifying a specific unhealthy negative emotion and to outline what you are looking for. If you are still in doubt when your client responds, you might enquire about the cognitive consequences of the emotion and about her action tendencies. From this information you may be able to infer what emotion your client experienced in the event under investigation.

- Where the emotion given is really an inference.

Here, your client provides you with what is really an inference rather than an emotion. For example, your client might say that she felt 'rejected', 'criticized' or 'unloved'. As you can see, none of these are emotions; rather, they are inferences about certain events. In this case you need to acknowledge that it might be true that she was rejected, for example, but then enquire what her major emotion was about the rejection. Proceed in this way until your client understands the difference between her inference and the emotion she experienced about the inferred A.

Once you and your client have identified an unhealthy negative emotion, it is important that you assess your client's motivation to change this emotion. This is important even though you have identified a goal which relates to your client's problem as he defined it. In this regard, it is important to recognize that the problem as the client has defined it may change in character once you have assessed it. In addition, it may be the case that the problem-as-defined may not contain an unhealthy negative emotion whereas the problem-as-assessed will more frequently do so. Thus, if the problem-as-assessed does contain an unhealthy negative C, then you do not know at this point whether he is motivated to change this C now you have assessed its presence. This is why it is important that you assess your client's motivation to change C.

In my own experience and that of other REBT therapists, anger and guilt are unhealthy negative emotions which clients are likely to be particularly ambivalent about changing. In which case, it is important for you to help your client to do a cost-benefit analysis of the advantages and disadvantages of the unhealthy negative emotion and its healthy counterpart (see Appendix 2). You may have to spend quite a long time with your client before he commits himself to changing his unhealthy negative emotion, but such time is usually well spent.

Assessing the Behavioural C

When you come to assess a behavioural C, it is important to bear in mind the following points:

1. Frequently, unhealthy behavioural Cs stem from unhealthy negative emotions. When this occurs, we might say that the behavioural C is a direct expression of an action tendency related to the emotion under consideration (see Table 2.2, for a list of the most common unhealthy negative emotions and their associated action tendencies). In this situation it is best to work with the emotional C to the forefront of the discussion. For example, Donald experienced guilt about shouting at his neighbour. He then started to buy his neighbour gifts to try and make amends for his behaviour. In this scenario, Donald's REBT therapist realized that Donald's behaviour stemmed from and was a direct expression of his guilt, and he would use the guilt to help him assess the A and B components of the emotional episode.

2. Sometimes, unhealthy behavioural Cs are initiated by your client to help prevent her from experiencing an unhealthy negative emotion. In these cases, it is important to ask the client what she thinks she would experience if she did not initiate the behaviour. Once you have identified this 'warded-off' emotion, you would then keep it to the fore when assessing A and B. For example, Sulamuth would eat chocolates whenever her

family or friends seemed to criticize her. On further enquiry, it became apparent that Sulamuth thought that she would feel hurt and anger if she did not eat chocolates. In this case, having ascertained that hurt was the emotion that Sulamuth tended to find more distressing than anger, her therapist used hurt as the target C and proceeded to assess the A and B components of Sulamuth's chosen emotional episode.

At other times, unhealthy behavioural Cs can be directly targeted for change even though they are initiated by clients to ward off emotional states that they find difficult to tolerate. This is usually done when the client cannot identify the warded-off emotional state (and you are reasonably certain that one exists) or when the client particularly wants to change the dysfunctional behaviour. This often happens when procrastination is the self-defeating behaviour.

3. Sometimes unhealthy negative behavioural Cs exist in their own right, do not have unhealthy negative emotions associated with them, and do not serve the purpose of warding off disturbed negative emotional Cs. In this case they can be treated as the C in the ABC episode and you can proceed to assess A and C accordingly.

Assessing Carol's C

You will recall that Carol's problem as she defined it was: 'I am in trouble at work because I am often late in the morning'. As discussed on pp. 72–73, I asked Carol to give me a specific example of her problem and she told me about a situation where she was late for work because she had stayed up into the 'small hours of the morning', as she put it, with the result that she slept through the ringing of her alarm clock the next day. The dialogue below indicated how I went about assessing her most relevant C in this episode.

WINDY: Now, Carol, what time do you think you needed to go to bed in order to give yourself a good chance of being awoken by your alarm clock?

CAROL: 11 o'clock. I remember making a pact with myself that I would go to bed at 11 o'clock.

WINDY: And did you notice when 11 o'clock arrived?

CAROL: I did.

WINDY: Now, this is an important question. What do you think you would have experienced if you had decided to go to bed?

[Here I am endeavouring to identify Carol's 'warded-off' unhealthy negative emotion. However, as Carol's response shows, my question does not elicit what I'm looking for.]

CAROL: I would have been pleased.

[Given this response, I decide to take a slightly different tack.]

WINDY: You would have been pleased, I agree, but if that was the case you would have gone to bed. But we know that you stayed up. Let me approach this in a different way. What were you doing at 11 o'clock?

CAROL: I was doing some knitting.

WINDY: And were you enjoying it?

CAROL: Not particularly.

WINDY: So why didn't you put it down and go to bed?

CAROL: Because I was in the middle of it.

[This is a very revealing response. It showed me that there probably was a negative emotional experience that Carol was avoiding: namely the great discomfort she would have experienced in stopping doing something before she had finished it. However, I doubted whether I could help her to see this at this point so I decided to go along with her behavioural C which in this case was 'continuing to knit'.]

WINDY: That is what we call a behavioural C. So the C in the ABC analysis of this episode was 'continuing to knit' and I would add 'at a time when you ideally wanted to go bed'. Is that correct?

CAROL: Yes it is.

It is important to note at this point that Carol's C was difficult to identify. In most cases, particularly when emotional Cs are present, the assessment of C is relatively straightforward, especially if you bear in mind the points I made on pp. 74–75.

ASSESSING A

You will recall from Chapter 2, that in relation to your client's emotional or behavioural problem, an A can be an actual event such as the death of a parent, or an inference of an actual event such as predicting that one won't be able to cope with the death of a parent.

When assessing the A in your client's specific example of her problem, it is your job to identify the A that actually triggered the irrational beliefs that explain the presence of the C that you have already identified. In REBT theory, this A is called the critical A.

Sometimes this is no easy matter since the critical A might exist in a network of competing actual and inferred As. Your job is to discover, with your client's help, the critical A by using one of a number of techniques that have been devised for this purpose. In this chapter I will focus on inference chaining – one particularly potent technique for identifying the critical A – and refer the interested reader to Dryden (1995) for a discussion of other methods.

However, before describing and illustrating inference chaining, I do wish to stress that sometimes identifying the critical A can be a straightforward matter, as the following examples show.

Example 1:   Fiona has sought brief therapy for her fear of being rejected. I ask her for a specific example and she relates the following. She recently met Bob, whom she has been dating for a month. On each date she is anxious (C) because she thinks Bob will reject her at the end of the date (A). How did I know that 'rejection' was Fiona's critical A? Because when I asked her what was scary about being rejected, she expressed, with affect, an irrational belief which is one of the most reliable indicators that you have identified a critical A.

Example 2:   George was referred to me for guilt problems. In response to my request for an example, George told me of a recent episode when he had to cancel Sunday lunch with his parents because there was an emergency at work. George said that he felt guilty (C) about hurting his parents' feelings (A); the latter was said with some degree of affect. When asked what was guilt-provoking about hurting his parents' feelings, George could not elaborate further, another sign that a critical A had been identified.

Inference Chaining

The method of inference chaining is based on the idea that inferences are often linked together in the person's mind and given this, your task as an REBT therapist is to assess the chain of inferences in order to identify the inference in the chain that has triggered the client's irrational belief (i.e. his critical A). Inference chaining can be used with any emotional episode, but is particularly useful in situations where the client's A is not apparently clear and there are likely to be a number of possible As that the client could be disturbed about. Here are some rules concerning the use of inference chaining. In outlining these rules I will take an example where the client's target C is anxiety.

1. Use the target emotional C to make an initial enquiry about A (e.g. 'What were you most anxious about in this situation?')
2. Take the A that the client has given you (in this case 'the person sitting next to me is looking at what I am typing') and assume temporarily that it is true even if it is an obvious distortion. This is important because it will help you to identify the client's irrational beliefs. If you challenge the inference at this point you will interfere with this process.
3. Continue your questioning, using the targeted emotional C as the driving force (e.g. 'what's anxiety-provoking in your mind about the person looking at what you are typing?')
4. Continue in this way until the client expresses an irrational belief.
5. Review the inferences in the chain with the client and ask her which A she was most anxious about. Treat this as the critical A unless you have a different idea. In which case discuss your view with the client and negotiate the critical A.

Inference chaining is a skill that is difficult to learn and I suggest that you consult Moore (1988) and Dryden (1995) for further information. However, there are three situations which are particularly difficult to deal with.

When Your Client Gives You a C

It may well happen that your client will give you a C in response to one of your questions. For example:

THERAPIST: What were you anxious about?

CLIENT: I was anxious that the person sitting next to me would look at what I was typing.

THERAPIST: And if he did look at what you were typing, what would be scary about that for you?

CLIENT: I might shake.

[Now this response might be an A or a C. You can tell which by asking the question 'why?']

THERAPIST: Why?

CLIENT: Because I wouldn't want him to criticize what he might read.

[This response indicates that the client's 'shaking' was a C because it was related to another inference. In the following interchange the client's shaking turned out to be an A because on being asked the question 'why?', the client could not provide an answer.]

CLIENT: I might shake.

Therapist: Why?

CLIENT: I'm not sure.

[In this case, since it is likely that the client's shaking is an A, the therapist can resume with the previous line of questioning.]

THERAPIST: And what would be anxiety-provoking about shaking?

CLIENT: If I shook, then people might notice . . .

When You Sense that the Client's Target Emotion has Changed

I have already suggested that you keep your client's target emotion to the fore when conducting inference chaining. Thus if the client's emotion is anxiety, it is useful to keep asking questions such as 'what was anxiety-provoking about . . .?' in order to identify the client's critical A. However, sometimes when you do this the client will reveal an A which indicates that her target emotion has changed. When you think that this has happened, it is worthwhile checking with your client by asking her how she felt (or would feel) confronting the A that she has just revealed. One major clue that this has happened is when your client reveals an inference, the theme of which is associated with a different emotion. This is why I suggest that you thoroughly familiarize yourself with the material that I presented in Table 2.2.

This change in your client's target emotion also particularly occurs when her initial target emotion is anxiety. Remember that anxiety is usually to do with a future threat. If, in the course of inference chaining, you encourage your client to assume that a particular event has happened, then your client's target emotion may well change. Let me give you an example when during the course of inference chaining the client's target emotion changes.

THERAPIST: What were you most anxious about in that situation?

CLIENT: I was scared that I might say something to upset Gloria.

THERAPIST: And if you did what would be anxiety-provoking in your mind about doing that?

CLIENT: Well, Gloria is well known for her tongue. So I was scared that she would criticize me unfairly.

[At this point the therapist senses that the client's target emotion might have changed – being criticized unfairly is usually associated with 'hurt' (see Table 2.2). So he decides to encourage a change of time frame from the future to the present.]

THERAPIST: Let's suppose that Gloria does criticize you unfairly, how would you feel while she is doing this?

CLIENT: Very hurt.

[You can now continue the inference chain with hurt as the driving emotion, e.g. 'What would be hurtful for you about her unfair criticism?'. Once you have identified the client's critical A that best accounts for her hurt, you can then ask her if this A was also critical in accounting for her original anxiety. This will often be the case. Then you have a choice. The ABC that you are helping your client to construct can either be formulated with C as anxiety and A representing the prospect of the critical event happening (A = future event), or with C as hurt and A representing the critical event either currently happening or having just happened (A = current or past event). Discuss this with your client before you decide which one of these routes to take.]

When Your Client Gives You Theoretical Inferences

Sometimes during inference chaining, you begin to sense that the inferences that your client is identifying are more apparent than real. In other words, the client may not be scared that a particular event is happening, but discloses it because she interprets your continued questioning to mean that she is expected to find another event. When your client discloses inferred As that she is *NOT* scared may happen, but says that she is, she is disclosing what I call theoretical inferences. These refer to events that possibly may follow from inferences that the client did make (which I call 'experiential' inferences), but your client is not scared of them, probably because she doubts that they will, in fact, happen.

I first discovered the fact that clients will disclose theoretical inferences if you keep asking questions of the 'what would be scary about that . . .?' variety, when I was working in a mood clinic in North America in 1981. I found that either a majority of my anxious female clients had a dire fear of becoming a 'bag lady' or I was doing something wrong. I discovered that the latter was the case and it stemmed from the *false* idea that I held at the time that the critical A was *always* to be found at the end of the chain. I now know that this is not the case. Rather, the critical A can be found at any point in the chain. Its existence is established by its proximity to the client's irrational belief and its discovery is often accompanied by displays of affect. By contrast, my clients would disclose their 'false' fears of becoming a bag lady without affect, in a haltering fashion and after a long period had elapsed between my question and their answer. These three signs are clues that you are assessing theoretical rather than experiential inferences.

Assessing Carol's A

When I assessed Carol's C (see pp. 76–77), it was behavioural nature ('continuing to knit when ideally I would have liked to have gone to bed'). My next task was to help her to identify her critical A.

WINDY: So, you continued to knit even though you knew it was 11 o'clock, because you were in the middle of the knitting. Is that right?

CAROL: Yes.

WINDY: Now, what was it about being in the middle of your knitting that you found difficult to stop?

CAROL: I have always found it almost impossible to stop half way through doing something.

WINDY: So it was just being in the middle of the knitting that was the event that you found difficult to cope with.

CAROL: It doesn't feel like that, but you're right.

WINDY: My guess is that it didn't feel difficult because, in fact, you didn't stop at 11 o'clock.

CAROL: That's exactly right. I went on until I had finished the section I was working on.

WINDY: And what time was that?

CAROL: I hate to admit it . . . but it was 3.30.

So far, then, my assessment of Carol's specific example looks like this:

    A = 11 o'clock – in the middle of a piece of knitting
    B = ?
    C = Continue to knit

My next task is to help Carol to identify the irrational beliefs that prompted her to continue to knit at a time when she wanted to go to bed. This is the subject of the next section: assessing irrational beliefs.

Assessing Irrational Beliefs (B)

As I have pointed out elsewhere, there are two basic approaches to assessing clients' irrational beliefs: (i) the theory-driven approach and (ii) the open-ended approach (Dryden, 1990).

The Theory-Driven Approach to Assessing Irrational Beliefs

In this approach you teach your client the four irrational beliefs advocated by REBT theory to be at the core of much psychological disturbance and contrast these with the four rational beliefs thought to be at the core of psychological health (see Chapter 2 for a review of rational and irrational beliefs). It is worth remembering that you have already taught your client the central role that musts play in psychological problems and in doing so you alluded to one of the other irrational beliefs. At this point you build upon this and introduce your client to all four irrational beliefs and their rational alternatives.

After you have taught your client in particular to recognize all four irrational beliefs, you then help her to apply this knowledge so that she can recognize the irrational beliefs that were present in the example that you are assessing. This is what is meant by the theory-driven approach to assessment. You use REBT theory with your client to identify her irrational beliefs. This is the approach to assessment that I prefer in brief REBT because in the long run it saves time. Here is how I used it with Carol.

Assessing Carol's Irrational Beliefs

The following dialogue shows what happened when I used the theory-driven approach to assess Carol's irrational beliefs.

WINDY: So far we have discovered that your C was 'continuing to knit' and the critical A was being in the middle of knitting the section that you were working on. Now, do you remember the money model that I taught you in our first session?

CAROL: Yes I do.

WINDY: What was the point of that model?

CAROL: That when we have emotional problems we think in terms of musts.

WINDY: Correct. Now before I help you to identify the beliefs that you held which explained why you continued to knit until the early hours instead of going to bed at 11 o'clock, let me teach you the four irrational beliefs that underpin most psychological problems and their rational alternatives. Then we can apply this to the example that we are discussing and to other examples later on. Does that make sense to you?

CAROL: Yes, that would be useful.

WINDY: First, let me review what I showed you in our first session. Human beings disturb themselves when they believe that they absolutely must get what they want, or when they believe that they absolutely must not get what they don't want. However, when they stick rigorously to their non-rigid preferences and don't change these to dogmatic musts they feel healthily bad when their desires aren't met, and this encourages them to change what can be changed and to make a healthy adjustment when things can't be changed.

CAROL: Right. I remember that and it makes a good deal of sense to me.

WINDY: Excellent. That is really the most important part of Rational Emotive Behaviour Theory. Musts are the core of much psychological disturbance, whereas preferences are the core of psychological well-being.

Now REBT theory argues that there are three irrational beliefs that stem from dogmatic musts and three rational beliefs that stem from flexible preferences. Let me go over these one set at a time. OK?

CAROL: OK.

WINDY: When you believe that you must get something that you dearly want, for example, REBT theory states that you are further likely to believe that it would be *AWFUL* if you didn't get what you demand. Here awful means the 'end of the world', more than 100 per cent bad if you will and worse than it absolutely must be.

CAROL: (*with irony*) That sounds pretty bad.

WINDY: It does, doesn't it? However, when you believe that you prefer to get something that you dearly want, but that you don't have to get it, then REBT theory states that you are likely to believe that it would be very bad, but *NOT AWFUL* if you don't get what you want. Here very bad means just that. Note here that when your preferences aren't met you aren't concluding that it doesn't matter. It does matter and that's healthy.

CAROL: I see. Yes, I'm glad you said that. My friends try to help me by telling me either to forget whatever I'm worried about or it will pass.

WINDY: That advice won't work because it means trying to convince yourself that what is really important to you is, in fact, not important to you.

So, 'awfulizing', as we jokingly call it, means that you think in end-of-the-world extremes, while 'anti-awfulizing' involves recognizing that not getting what you desire *IS* very bad, but *NOT* the end of the world. Is that clear?

CAROL: Very. When you awfulize you exaggerate out of all proportion, but when you don't awfulize you are accepting that something very bad has occurred . . .

WINDY: And feel suitably and healthily negative as a result.

Now the second set of beliefs that stem from musts and preferences respectively are as follows. When you believe that you must get something that you dearly want, REBT theory states that you are further likely to believe that you *could not stand it* if you didn't get what you demand. This is known as a philosophy of low frustration tolerance and means either that you would disintegrate or that you would never experience any happiness as long as you are deprived of what you must have.

CAROL: So, it's like an 'I can't cope' attitude.

WINDY: Actually, it's more than that. It's more of an 'I can't bear it' attitude. When you tell yourself that you can't cope, you don't necessarily mean that you can't bear it.

CAROL: But isn't that semantic?

WINDY: That is precisely the point. We disturb ourselves as humans precisely because we profoundly believe the semantic meaning of the disturbing statements that we tell ourselves. So you're right, I am talking semantics here but not in the sense that I think you mean by the term, i.e. nitpicking over words. I'm using it in the sense that if we believe in the semantics of rational beliefs, we won't disturb ourselves, but if we believe in the semantics of irrational beliefs, then we will. Do you see what I'm saying?

CAROL: Yes I think so. I think you're saying that it is important to distinguish between different terms because if we believe them then they have the power either to disturb us or not.

WINDY: Exactly. So to recap, an '*I can't stand it*' attitude stems from a must. Now returning to our example, when you believe that you prefer to get something that you dearly want, but that you don't have to get it, then REBT theory states that you are likely to believe that it would be difficult to tolerate not getting what you want, *but that you can stand it*. Believing that you can stand something will help you to take constructive action, while believing that you can't stand that same thing will largely prevent you from taking constructive action.

CAROL: Right, that again makes sense.

WINDY: Now the final set of beliefs that I want to introduce to you concern beliefs about the self. Thus, when you believe that you must get something that you dearly want, and you consider that not getting it says something about you, for example, REBT theory states that you are likely to believe that you are *no good* if you don't get what you demand.

If you have such a demand and another person blocks you from getting what you demand, then you are likely to believe that he or she is no good for obstructing you.

These two beliefs are called self- and other-downing respectively and involve you giving yourself or the other person a negative global rating. Is that clear?

CAROL: So you condemn the sinner for committing the sin. Is that what you mean?

WINDY: That is what I mean. Good. Alternatively, when you believe that you prefer to get something that you dearly want, but that you don't have to get it, and you consider that not getting it says something about you, REBT theory states that you are more likely to accept yourself as a fallible human being who has done the wrong thing than you are to condemn yourself.

Also if you have such a preference and another person blocks you from getting what you want then you are more likely to believe that he or she is a fallible human being who has done the wrong thing by obstructing you than that he or she is no damn good for doing so.

These two beliefs are called self- and other-acceptance respectively and involve your acknowledging that humans are fallible and far too complex to merit a single global rating. However, in doing so you don't condone bad behaviour. Have I made myself clear?

CAROL: So that's like accepting the sinner, but not the sin.

WINDY: Correct, although in REBT we say that people who sin are fallible human beings rather than sinners, but the principle is the same.

Now are you ready to apply this to identifying the beliefs you held about being in the middle of your knitting which led you to continue knitting into the early hours rather than going to bed at 11 o'clock?

CAROL: Fine.

WINDY: Just to recap, your A or activating event was realizing that you were in the middle of a section of knitting and your behavioural C was continuing to knit rather than going to bed at 11. Now what demand did you make about being in the middle of the knitting that led you to continue knitting well past 11?

[You will note that I asked Carol *what* her demand was rather than *whether* or not she had one. Here I am assuming on theoretical grounds that she did make a demand because her behaviour was self-defeating. As you will see, later I ask her *whether or not* she had awfulizing, LFT and self-downing beliefs. I do so because REBT theory predicts that clients will not always have all three irrational derivatives from the must.]

CAROL: I must finish it.

WINDY: Right. Now do you think you had an awfulizing belief in there?

CAROL: No, I don't think so.

WINDY: So you don't think you believed at the time that it would be terrible to stop with the knitting section unfinished?

CAROL: Well put like that I'm not sure.

WINDY: That's OK. You don't have to have all four of the irrational beliefs in any episode. Now what about low frustration tolerance. Was there anything that you believed you couldn't bear?

CAROL: Yes, I couldn't bear leaving the section unfinished.

WINDY: Finally, do you think you would have put yourself down if you had stopped with the knitting unfinished?

CAROL: No, I don't think so.

[Carol's answer here is strong evidence that her problem is an example of discomfort disturbance rather than ego disturbance – see Chapter 2.]

WINDY: So to sum up, the reason why you continued knitting beyond 11 o'clock rather than going to bed was because you believed at the time that you must finish the knitting section and you couldn't bear going to bed with it unfinished. Is that right?

CAROL: Yes it is. I wasn't aware of thinking that way at the time, but it certainly explains my behaviour.

[This is a common response when the client's C is behavioural. Carol would have only been able to identify her two irrational beliefs at the time if she had stopped knitting at 11 o'clock. If she had stopped at that time she would have experienced a lot of discomfort which her behaviour was partly designed to prevent her from experiencing. Thus her knitting beyond 11, was, in part, an example of behaviour designed to ward off unhealthy negative emotions, even though at present she cannot see it as such.]

The Open-ended Approach to Assessing Irrational Beliefs

The open-ended approach to assessing irrational beliefs differs from the theory-driven approach in that you do not teach your client the role of irrational beliefs and their rational alternatives in psychological disturbance and health respectively before assessing her irrational beliefs. Rather, you use Socratic questioning to help your client to identify these irrational beliefs. When your client gives the wrong answer in response to your questions, you briefly explain why the answer is incorrect and then ask her further Socratic questions. You proceed in this way until your client provides the irrational beliefs that account for her target C and understands why these beliefs do indeed explain the existence of her disturbed emotion.

Although I did not in fact utilize the open-ended approach to assessing irrational beliefs with Carol, the following constructed dialogue outlines how I imagine our conversation would have proceeded if I had used the open-ended approach with her.

WINDY: Just to recap, your A or activating event was realizing that you were in the middle of a section of knitting and your behavioural C was continuing to knit rather than going to bed at 11. Now what were you telling yourself at B – which as you now know is your belief system – about being in the middle of the knitting that led you to continue knitting well past 11?

CAROL: That I really want to get it finished.

[I know on theoretical grounds that this belief is insufficient to explain Carol's behaviour. Thus, she could believe 'I really want to get it finished' but then go on to say, ' . . . however, I don't have to get it finished and I'm not going to do any more knitting now because I want to go to bed early because I want to get to work on time'. This will form the basis of my response to Carol on this point.]

WINDY: Right, but if you only said that, you might still have gone to bed because you would have added, ' . . . even though I really want to get the knitting finished, I also really want to get up early in the morning and since I don't *HAVE TO* finish the knitting, then I will do what I don't want to do now so that I can have what I want more later'. Now if you had believed that what would you have done?

CAROL: I would have gone to bed.

WINDY: But, we know that you didn't go to bed; so just telling yourself that you really wanted to get the knitting finished isn't enough to explain your behaviour. Now what do you think that you added to your strong desire that led you to act against your longer term interests?

CAROL: That I have to finish it.

[For reasons of brevity I have described a notional dialogue where the client saw quite quickly that her demand accounted for her self-defeating behaviour. Other clients will take much longer to understand this point. If this occurs, the principle is the same: you show the client that her response is insufficient to account for her C, you help her to understand why this is the case and you again ask for the belief which does account for the existence of the C. This will almost always be an irrational belief.]

It is important to realize that when you are using the open-ended approach to irrational belief assessment, you are very much theory-driven in what you do. However, in this approach you use the theory covertly, while in the 'theory-driven approach' discussed earlier, you use the theory overtly with your client.

Finally, in practice, you may well use a combination of both approaches to assessing your client's irrational beliefs.

SETTING A GOAL IN LINE WITH THE PROBLEM AS ASSESSED

You will recall that you have already encouraged your client to develop a problem list and set goals in line with her problems as she has defined them. This is an important strategy since it not only shows your client that you are taking her problems seriously, but also that you are taking her healthy goals seriously (see Chapter 3 for a discussion of what constitutes acceptable client goals in brief REBT), and that therapy will be forward looking.

Goals which are based on your client's problems as assessed stem from your assessment of specific examples of your client's broader problems.

These goals have two main characteristics: (i) they will be more influenced by REBT theory than goals based on defined problems and (ii) they will often have to be achieved first before goals based on defined problems can be achieved.

Before I illustrate these points with material from my work with Carol, let me show how I elicited her goal with respect to my assessment of the knitting example.

WINDY: So, Carol, I think we now understand why you continued to knit until the early hours of the morning when you at last finished the section that you were working on. Now what would your goal be if you were faced with the situation again?

CAROL: To go to bed at 11 o'clock.

WINDY: Right, but let's expand that a little. If you do decide to go bed at 11 o'clock wouldn't that also involve leaving the knitting unfinished and putting up with the discomfort that would involve?

CAROL: I see what you mean. Yes, it would involve doing those other things.

WINDY: How typical is it that you continue doing something until it's finished rather than stopping at a time that is better for you in the longer term?

[This is an important point. Once you have assessed an example of the client's problem and it turns out to be somewhat different from the problem as defined, then it is important to check with your client whether or not the assessed problem is typical of her behaviour. If it is, as it will normally be, then the goal that you will set with respect to the specific problem as assessed will be generalizable to other situations. This is important in brief therapy since you need to use every opportunity to help your client generalize her learning from the specific to the general.]

CAROL: Very typical.

WINDY: So is it worth broadening the goal to something like: 'Whenever it is in my longer term interests to do so, I will stop doing a task even though I might be in the middle of it and I will put up with the discomfort of so doing'. Is that an accurate representation of your goal?

CAROL: It is, yes. But I have a question.

WINDY: Yes?

CAROL: How can I do that?

WINDY: I predict that you will be in a position to do that once I have helped you to challenge and change the beliefs that lead you to continue working at a task like knitting until you have finished it, no matter what the time is.

[Carol's question is fortuitous in that it provides me with an opportunity to build a bridge between the assessment of her problem and associated goal and the intervention work that I will soon be doing to help her to dispute her irrational beliefs.]

Before I leave the issue of goals, let me remind you of the goal that I helped Carol set with respect to her target problem as defined and compare this with the goal that I have just now elicited with respect to her target problem as assessed.

If you recall, Carol's target problem as defined was as follows:

'I am in trouble at work because I am often late in the morning.'

The goal that I helped Carol to set in line with this problem was:

'To arrive at work on time.'

Taking a specific example of Carol's difficulty in arriving at work on time, we traced this to her difficulty in leaving things unfinished, which can be viewed from the assessment that I carried out as a general problem and one which interferes with Carol arriving at work on time.

In relation to her problem as assessed, I elicited the following goal:

'Whenever it is in my longer term interests to do so, I will stop doing a task even though I might be in the middle of it and I will put up with the discomfort of so doing.'

As you can see, this goal meets the two major criteria for a goal in line with the problem as assessed:

1 It is informed by REBT theory – it clearly recognizes the problem as an example of discomfort disturbance and suggests that the behavioural goal can be achieved by tolerating discomfort.
2. Its achievement will help the client to achieve the goal in line with the problem as defined. Carol needs to leave things unfinished and tolerate the discomfort of so doing before she can consistently turn up at work on time.

Defer Requesting Commitment to the Goal until You have Helped Your Client to Dispute Her Irrational Beliefs

You might think at this point that it is logical to ask your client to commit herself to this goal. Indeed, you can do this and if your client shows any ambivalence about doing so, you can use the cost-benefit analysis form (see Appendix 2) to identify and challenge any advantages that the client sees in remaining with the problem as assessed and any disadvantages that she sees with her goal.

However, I have found it useful to defer asking clients for such a commitment until after I have helped them to dispute the irrational beliefs that account for the existence of their problems as assessed. It has been my experience that once I have helped my clients to see clearly that their irrational beliefs are rigid, self-defeating, inconsistent with reality and illogical, and that their alternative rational beliefs are flexible, serve their interests better, are more consistent with reality and are logical, then they are prepared to commit themselves to their goals more fully than before disputing has taken place. I will return to the issue of asking your client to commit herself to her goals in line with the problem as assessed in Chapter 5.

ASSESSING META-EMOTIONAL PROBLEMS

REBT theory states that when clients have emotional and/or behavioural problems, they often disturb themselves about these primary problems. I call these second-order problems 'meta-emotional problems' because they are literally problems about problems.

Let me give you a few examples using the ABC framework of REBT. In doing so I will provide common examples that are frequently encountered in therapeutic practice.

Example 1:

      A1 = Prediction of being rejected
      B1 = I must not be rejected
      C1 = Anxiety

        |
        |
        |

      A2 = Anxiety
      B2 = I must not be anxious
      C2 = Increased Anxiety

Clients frequently make themselves anxious about being anxious, thus increasing their anxious feelings. Anxiety about anxiety often occurs in panic disorder and generalized anxiety disorder (GAD).

Example 2:

> A1 = Being treated unfairly by boss
> B1 = He absolutely should not have treated me unfairly
> C1 = Anger
>
> |
> |
> |
>
> A2 = Anger is wrong
> B2 = I must not be angry
> C2 = Guilt

Here the client infers that being angry is wrong and then condemns himself for doing what in his mind is the wrong thing.

Example 3:

> A1 = My tutor may criticize me
> B1 = I can't stand being criticized
> C1 = Avoidance
>
> |
> |
> |
>
> A2 = Avoidance is weakness
> B2 = I am inadequate for not facing up to my problems
> C2 = Shame

Here the client infers that avoiding an anxiety-provoking situation is evidence of personal weakness and then proceeds to condemn himself as inadequate for having such a weakness.

It is worth noting that in the second and third examples, the client made an inference about the original emotional or behavioural C and then proceeded to think irrationally about this inference, leading to the meta-emotional problem.

When to Deal with the Meta-emotional Problem before the Primary One

Once you have established that the client has a meta-emotional problem about the target problem you have been assessing, you are faced with the question of which problem to deal with first. Here are some guidelines to help you. Deal with your client's meta-emotional problem first:

1. When the presence of the meta-emotional problem interferes with the work that you are trying to do on his primary problem in the session.

Thus, in the third example above, you would deal with your client's feelings of shame first when the presence of this emotion distracts him from focusing on his avoidant behaviour.

2. When the presence of the meta-emotional problem interferes with the work that the client is trying to do on his primary problem outside the session.

Thus, in the second example you would deal with your client's guilt when he considers that he would feel guilty whenever he attempted to work on his anger.

3. When the meta-emotional problem is clinically more important than his primary problem.

Thus, in the first example, you would often work on your client's anxiety about his anxiety before dealing with his original anxiety, especially in generalized anxiety disorder.

4. When the client sees the sense of addressing his meta-emotional problem before his primary problem.

In brief REBT it is important not to threaten the working alliance between you and your client. Thus, only work on the meta-emotional problem first when the client sees the sense in doing so.

Assessing Whether or Not Carol has a Meta-emotional Problem

The following is how I checked whether or not Carol had a meta-emotional problem about continuing to knit beyond the time when she had promised herself that she would go to bed.

WINDY: Now, Carol, I want to check one thing out with you. Sometimes when people have emotional or behavioural problems and they become aware of these problems, they disturb themselves in some way about having them. Now when you focused on the fact that you hadn't gone to bed at 11 o'clock and that you had continued to knit into the early hours of the morning, how did you feel?

CAROL: Annoyed that once again I hadn't managed to do what I set out to do.

[This response seems to indicate that Carol experienced a healthy negative emotion about not doing what she had planned. However, I wanted to make sure that this was in fact the case. So I questioned her further on this point.]

WINDY: So, if I understand you correctly, you were annoyed about the fact that you hadn't managed to do what you had planned to do. Were you also angry with yourself and putting yourself down in some way for once again failing to have an early night?

CAROL: No, I didn't put myself down. I was annoyed rather than angry with myself.

[Here it is clear that Carol does not have a meta-emotional problem. But what if she did? The following shows how I would have dealt with this situation.]

WINDY: . . . when you focused on the fact that you hadn't gone to bed at 11 o'clock and that you had continued to knit into the early hours of the morning how did you feel?

CAROL: I felt really angry at myself.

WINDY: Do you think that your anger with yourself will interfere with the work that we need to do to help you deal with your difficulty in leaving things unfinished?

CAROL: I'm not sure.

WINDY: Well, have you felt angry with yourself as we have been talking about this problem?

CAROL: Not really.

WINDY: And when you recognize the existence of the problem when you identify it in your everyday life, do you think that your anger with yourself will interfere with your identifying and evaluating the irrational beliefs that lead you to have the problem?

CAROL: I don't think it would, now I come to think of it.

[Carol's answers to my questions would lead me to the tentative conclusion that we could safely start working on her primary problem. If, however, Carol found that her self-anger in reality did interfere with the work that she needed to do in the situation to overcome her primary problem, then I would switch to dealing with the meta-emotional problem. I would then return to the primary problem when the meta-emotional problem had been dealt with.]

Encouraging your Client to Take the Lead in Assessment

In this chapter, I have dealt with the major issues concerning the assessment of your client's target problems and have illustrated these principles with excerpts from my work with Carol. However, as your client becomes more familiar with REBT ideas, then you should encourage her to take a more active lead in the assessment of other examples of her target problem and with specific examples of a new target problem. Don't forget that your aim is not only to help your client to overcome her problems, but also to help her to become her own therapist. Here is an example of what I mean. In the following excerpt taken from the halfway point in our work together, Carol discusses another incident when she failed to get to work on time.

CAROL: I turned up late at work again today.

WINDY: Based on what we've already discussed, how do you think you stopped yourself from turning up on time?

CAROL: Well, I went to bed at 11 o'clock and I got up on time, but then my favourite magazine arrived and I got involved in reading a long article on sewing which I couldn't put down.

WINDY: What was your behavioural C?

CAROL: Continuing to read the article beyond 8 o'clock which was when I needed to leave to get to work on time.

WINDY: And what was the activating event?

CAROL: Being half way through the article at 8 o'clock.

WINDY: And what was your irrational belief that led you to continue reading?

CAROL: I have to finish the article.

As this dialogue shows, Carol has learned to assess her own problem with minimal prompting from me.

In the next chapter I will discuss helping clients to understand the rational solution to their problems. I will again illustrate how to do this referring to my work with Carol.

5

HELPING CLIENTS TO UNDERSTAND THE RATIONAL SOLUTION TO PROBLEMS

In this chapter, I will discuss how to encourage your client to understand the rational solution to her problems. First, I will distinguish between helping your client to understand the rational solution and helping her to implement it so that she can integrate it into her belief system, with the result that it makes a real difference to the way that she thinks, feels and acts. Second, I will consider the key task of disputing irrational beliefs. In the view of many REBT therapists, disputing irrational beliefs lies at the core of this therapeutic approach so it warrants the detailed coverage which it receives in this chapter. Finally, I will introduce you to the self-help form that I use to help clients gain practice in assessing their own problems and disputing for themselves the irrational beliefs that lie at the root of these problems.

DIFFERENCES BETWEEN UNDERSTANDING AND INTEGRATION

In the early 1960s, Albert Ellis wrote an important paper contrasting intellectual insight with emotional insight in therapeutic change (Ellis, 1963). While the terms 'intellectual insight' and 'emotional insight' are in common use in the psychotherapy literature, they are often taken to refer to two different types of cognition (the term 'insight' itself strongly suggests cognitive activity). Due to this confusion, I now prefer to distinguish between a client's understanding of the rational solution to his problems (which is equivalent to intellectual insight), and that client being able to integrate the rational solution into his belief system so that it makes a significant difference to the way he thinks, feels and acts in areas where he previously experienced problems (this is equivalent to emotional insight).

Understanding the Rational Solution

When your client understands the rational solution to his problems, but has not yet been able to integrate this understanding into his belief system, he knows why his irrational beliefs are irrational and why his rational beliefs are rational and can see that operating on the latter will help him to achieve his goals. However, his conviction in his rational beliefs is light and occasionally held. When your client understands only the rational solution to his problems, he will say such things to you as:

- 'I understand what you are saying . . .' (here there is often an implied '. . . but I don't believe it yet').
- 'I understand what you are saying in my head, but not in my heart.'

Integrating the Rational Solution into one's Belief System

When your client both understands the rational solution to his problems and is able to integrate this understanding into his belief system, he also knows why his irrational beliefs are irrational and why his rational beliefs are rational and can see that operating on the latter will help him to achieve his goals. Furthermore, his conviction in his rational beliefs is strong and frequently held. Because he has been able to integrate the rational solution into his belief system, he is able to act on it and it will have an effect on the way he thinks and feels.

When your client understands the rational solution to his problems and has integrated it into his belief system, he will say such things to you as:

- 'I understand what you are saying and I truly believe it.'
- 'I understand what you are saying both in my head and in my heart.'

Understanding Precedes Integration

In the REBT theory of therapeutic change, it is important to realize that understanding the rational solution precedes being able to integrate it into one's belief system. Thus, when your client says things like: 'I understand what you say in my head, but I don't believe it', it is important not to be discouraged. Indeed, it is helpful for you to explain to your client why such understanding precedes integration and what he needs to do to promote such integration. I will return to this issue in the following chapter.

DISPUTING IRRATIONAL BELIEFS

Disputing irrational beliefs is perhaps the most well-known therapist task in REBT, and some would say the most controversial (DiGiuseppe, 1991). Practitioners from therapeutic orientations which are far less directive than REBT consider disputing irrational beliefs to involve the therapist arguing (in the sense of fighting) with the client or worse, brainwashing the client. As we shall see, while the REBT therapist does argue with her client, it is in the sense of having a healthy debate with him rather than fighting with him. With regard to the accusation of brainwashing, nothing could be further from the truth in that when the therapist is engaged in disputing he is involved either in asking the client questions or providing him with short explanations which put the rational perspective, but without foisting this onto the client. I will discuss this issue further later in the chapter.

The Four Tasks to Accomplish before Beginning Disputing

After you have assessed your client's specific example of her target problem, you have four tasks to accomplish before you begin to dispute her irrational beliefs. These tasks are: (i) reviewing the ABC; (ii) helping your client to understand the connection between her irrational beliefs and her emotional and/or behavioural response at C (this is known in REBT circles as helping your client to understand the iB-C connection); (iii) helping your client to see that changing her irrational beliefs will help her to achieve her goal; and (iv) preparing your client for disputing by explaining what you will be doing in the disputing process.

Task 1: Reviewing the ABC

Although you have already ensured the accuracy of the ABC assessment that you have carried out on the specific example of your client's target problem, it is useful to check this again just before you begin to dispute her irrational beliefs. This is particularly the case when there has been any kind of interval between assessment and disputing. Thus, this review should certainly be done if you have completed the assessment at the end of one session and plan to begin disputing at the beginning of the following session. However, there is no harm in instituting this review if the interval between assessment and disputing is short and even when there is no interval at all between the two activities.

The purpose of this review is for you to double check the accuracy of your ABC assessment. When an interval of time has elapsed between assessment and disputing, your client may have had second thoughts on the accuracy of the original ABC and you need to be aware of her *CURRENT* thoughts on the ABC. Even if there is no such interval, double checking the accuracy of the ABC not only shows your client that you are keen to understand her problem, but also demonstrates the care you are taking in helping her to deal with her problems.

Task 2: Ensuring that your Client Understands the iB-C Connection

In addition to reviewing the accuracy of the ABC that you have identified, it is important that you ensure that your client understands the connection between her emotional and/or behavioural C and the irrational beliefs that underpin this C. Helping your client to understand the iB-C connection builds an important bridge between assessment and disputing and gives disputing a direction. Thus, if your client understands that her problem at C is determined by her irrational beliefs, it is easier for her to see the sense of disputing these beliefs as a primary way of overcoming her problem than if she lacks understanding of the iB-C connection. I will demonstrate this point when I present the disputing work that I did with Carol later in this chapter.

Task 3: Demonstrating that Changing Irrational Beliefs Will Help Goal Achievement

Having helped your client to understand the iB-C connection, your next task is to help him to see that if he wants to achieve his goal he needs to change his belief. You only need to do this in a general sense at this point. For example, once your client has understood the iB-C connection, asking him what he needs to change in order to achieve his goals usually elicits the desired goal: 'my beliefs'.

Task 4: Preparing your Client for your Disputing Interventions

The final task you need to accomplish before getting down to disputing your client's irrational beliefs is to tell him, again in general terms, what you will be doing during the disputing process. As I will discuss in greater detail later in this chapter, disputing involves you asking your client questions about his irrational beliefs (as in Socratic disputing) and giving short explanations (as in didactic disputing).

The Aims of Disputing

The aims of disputing are to help your client to evaluate the rationality both of her irrational beliefs and of their rational alternatives. As with the assessment of your client's problems, disputing is theory-driven. You know on theoretical grounds that your client's irrational beliefs are, in fact, irrational and the rational alternatives to these beliefs are, by definition, rational and your goal is to encourage your client to see this for herself. Thus the major aim of disputing is to help your client to UNDER-STAND the rational solution to her problems. It is not designed to help her to integrate this solution into her belief system. There are a variety of other methods designed to facilitate such integration, as I will show you in the following three chapters.

The Four Irrational Belief Targets

As discussed in Chapters 2 and 4, there are four irrational beliefs that you need to dispute in brief REBT. As noted in Chapter 4, do not assume that, in a specific emotional episode, your client has all four irrational beliefs. Rather, proceed on the basis that your client has a primary demanding belief and at least one irrational derivative from that must. If your client's target problem is an example of ego disturbance then at least one of those derivatives will be a self-downing belief, while if it is an example of a discomfort disturbance belief then he will not have a self-downing belief. Before I consider the types of argument you will employ when you dispute your client's irrational beliefs, the following will serve as a reminder concerning the nature of the irrational belief targets for your disputing strategies:

- Musts (expressed as absolute should, have to, got to, etc.).
- Awfulizing (expressed as 'It's terrible that . . .', 'It's the end of the world that . . .', etc.).
- Low frustration tolerance (expressed as 'I can't stand it', 'I can't bear it', etc.).
- Self/other-downing (expressed as 'I am . . . or you are . . . no good/ worthless/inadequate/bad', etc.).

The Four Major Arguments

When you dispute your client's irrational beliefs, you can use four major types of arguments: the first concerns whether the belief is flexible or dogmatic and the others concern the empirical, logical and pragmatic status of these beliefs. I will deal with each in turn.

Arguments Concerning Flexibility/Dogmatism

These arguments are designed to help your client to consider whether her irrational beliefs are dogmatic or flexible. If you use REBT theory to inform your interventions on this point, you are on safe ground since the theory states that irrational beliefs are inflexible. For example if a client believes 'I must do well in my exams', this is rigid since it does not allow for the person not to do well.

Empirical Arguments

When you employ empirical arguments while disputing your client's irrational beliefs, you are basically asking her to provide evidence that her irrational beliefs are consistent with reality. If you use REBT theory to inform your interventions on this point, you are on safe ground since according to this theory there is no empirical evidence in support of any of the four irrational beliefs. For example if a client says 'I am worthless', then for this to be empirically true everything that the client has ever thought, felt and done in the past has to have been worthless and everything that she will think, feel and do in the future will also have to be worthless since 'I am worthless' means that my being or essence is worthless, and therefore everything that emanates from me is bound to be worthless. This is empirically unsustainable, although your client may well say that she has a strong 'FEELING' that she is worthless, but all this proves is that she has a strong 'FEELING' which in fact is a strongly held belief which can be subject to empirical scrutiny.

Logical Arguments

When you employ logical arguments while disputing your client's irrational beliefs, you need to refer to her rational beliefs and ask her whether or not her irrational beliefs follow logically from them. Again, if you use REBT theory to inform your interventions on this point, you are on safe ground since according to this theory an irrational belief does not follow logically from a rational belief. For example if a client says 'I am worthless for failing to get into university', then you need to ask him whether or not it is good logic for him to conclude that his being (i.e. the whole of him) is worthless because he failed in one aspect of his life at a given point of time. Obviously, this conclusion is quite illogical and remains so no matter how strongly your client 'FEELS' (i.e. believes) that it is logical.

Pragmatic Arguments

When you employ pragmatic arguments while disputing your client's irrational beliefs, you are basically asking him to consider the effects of holding these beliefs and to compare these effects with those that he would get if he held rational beliefs. Once again using REBT theory is helpful here because it spells out the emotional, behavioural and cognitive consequences of holding irrational beliefs and their rational counterparts. On this point, I suggest that you review Table 2.2 and refer to it while using pragmatic arguments in a disputing sequence.

It is worth noting that your clients may have their idiosyncratic ideas about the benefits of certain unhealthy negative emotions and thus of the irrational beliefs that underpin them. For example, some clients believe that anger is a productive emotion and will therefore consider that an irrational belief such as 'You absolutely should not block me' will have positive effects. This is, of course, far from the case, but you have to explain this to your client in different ways before he is able to see what you mean.

The Two Major Disputing Styles

As noted earlier, there are two major disputing styles – Socratic disputing and didactic disputing – and I will deal with each in turn. Please note, though, that in the reality of clinical practice you will often need to use a combination of both styles with the majority of your clients.

Socratic Disputing

Socratic disputing involves your asking your client questions which are designed to have him consider the empirical, logical and pragmatic status of his irrational beliefs and whether they are rigid or flexible. Here are examples of such questions:

(i)   'Is your belief that your tutor must like you rigid or flexible?' (dispute concerning the nature of the belief – rigid or flexible).
(ii)   'Where is the law of the universe that says your tutor must like you?' (empirical dispute).
(iii)   'Does it logically follow that because you want your tutor to like you therefore he has to do so?' (logical dispute).
(iv)   'Is believing that your tutor must like you going to help you or hinder you?' (pragmatic dispute).

If your client provides the correct answer to your question it is important to ask him why it is the correct answer. For example:

THERAPIST: Where is the law of the universe that says your tutor must like you?

CLIENT: There is no such law.

THERAPIST: That's the right answer. Now why is it the right answer . . .?

The goal of disputing is not just to help your client to know *THAT* his irrational beliefs are irrational, but also to understand *WHY* they are irrational. Similarly, the goal of disputing is not just to help your client to know *THAT* his rational beliefs are rational, but also to understand *WHY* they are rational.

If your client provides the wrong answer to your question, briefly explain to him why his answer is incorrect and then ask the question again in the same or similar form. For example:

THERAPIST: Where is it written that your tutor must like you?

CLIENT: Well, my life will be easier if he does.

[Here the client provides evidence why it is desirable for his tutor to like him, but not evidence why his tutor MUST like him.]

THERAPIST: Well, let's suppose that. That is only evidence why it would be desirable for him to like you, but does he have to do what is desirable?

CLIENT: No, he doesn't.

THERAPIST: That's correct. Now why is it correct?

Didactic Disputing

Didactic disputing involves your explaining to your client why his irrational beliefs are irrational and why his rational beliefs are rational, using the same four arguments as previously discussed. When doing this it is important to bear in mind the following points:

(i)   Keep your explanations as short and to the point as possible. It is important to avoid longwinded, rambling expositions.

(ii)   Explain one major point at a time. It is important to avoid covering several major points in one lengthy explanation.

(iii)   Once you have finished giving your explanation, check whether or not your client has understood the point that you have been making.

Don't forget that the goal of didactic disputing is to facilitate your client's understanding of the rational solution. It is not to demonstrate your knowledge. Given this, in order to determine whether or not your client has understood the point that you have just explained, say something like:

'I'm not sure that I have made myself clear. Could you put into your own words the point that I have just made.'

Note that this intervention makes it quite clear that it is your primary responsibility to put the rational point as clearly as you can and if your client doesn't understand you, then the onus is on you to make it clearer. Thus, if your client indicates that she has not understood your rational point, correct her misunderstanding by giving another, brief, didactic explanation and then check her understanding. Proceed in this way until your client has understood the point.

Helping Clients to Construct Rational Beliefs and Understand Why they are Rational

Let's suppose that you have just moved into a new house where the garden is overgrown with weeds, and you want to have a nice garden with flowers in it. What do you have to do in order to achieve your goal? First, you need to cut down the weeds and uproot them. Then you need to plant your flowers and water them to ensure that they grow and flourish. This sequence also holds true in the disputing. Helping your client to see that her irrational beliefs are irrational is akin to cutting down the weeds and keeping them under control, and helping her to see what her rational beliefs are and why these are rational is akin to planting and tending the flowers.

Having then disputed your client's irrational beliefs you need to do two things. First, you need to point out what are the rational beliefs. Then, you need to help your client to understand why these rational beliefs are, in fact, rational. As you will see when I show how I disputed Carol's irrational beliefs, this involves subjecting these beliefs to the four criteria for rationality: (i) are they flexible? (ii) are they consistent with reality? (iii) are they logical? and (iv) are they helpful?

Disputing Carol's Irrational Beliefs

I will now illustrate some of the points that I have made with respect to disputing irrational beliefs by referring to my work with Carol. In doing so I will provide a running commentary so that you can understand as fully as possible the disputing work that I am doing with her.

WINDY: Now, Carol, let me write up on this whiteboard the ABC that we have just done so that I can check its accuracy.

[I proceed to write the following on the board which I routinely use in therapy. I do so because I have found it very useful to use the visual channel of communication with clients as well as the verbal channel.]

A = It's 11 o'clock. I've promised myself that I will go to bed, but I haven't finished the knitting section that I am working on.

B = I must finish the knitting section. I couldn't bear leaving the knitting section unfinished.

C = Continue to knit until I've finished the section.

Is that accurate?

CAROL: Yes, it is.

[Here I am reviewing Carol's ABC as a final check on its accuracy before beginning to dispute her irrational beliefs – see pp. 100–101.]

WINDY: Now, can you see the link between your beliefs and your behaviour in this situation?

[Here I am endeavouring to ensure that Carol understands the iB-C connection – see p. 101 above.]

CAROL: Yes, I think so.

WINDY: Can you put this understanding into your own words?

CAROL: I continued to knit beyond the time that I had promised myself that I would go to bed, because of the beliefs that I had about not finishing the knitting section that I was working on.

WINDY: That's exactly right. It was your belief that you had to finish the unfinished section and not the **unfinished work itself** that led you to continue to knit into the early hours. Now, let me ask you a very important question . . .

[Whenever you want your client to pay particular attention to what you are about to say, it is worth emphasizing this by a phrase like the one I used above, i.e. 'let me ask you a very important question'.]

. . . If you want to go to bed on time or more generally leave something unfinished when it is in your interests to do so, what do you need to change first before being able to do that?

CAROL: My beliefs that I have to finish things and that I can't stand leaving things unfinished.

[I am now satisfied that Carol understands the iB-C connection and that she needs to change her beliefs if she is to achieve her goal. My next step is to let her know what I will be doing to help her change her irrational beliefs.]

WINDY: Right and I will help you to change your irrational beliefs. What I'll do is ask you certain questions designed to help you to think about how flexible, realistic, logical and helpful your irrational beliefs are and if you find that these beliefs are rigid, inconsistent with reality, illogical and unhelpful, I'll help you to develop rational beliefs that will be more flexible, consistent with reality, logical and helpful. During this process if any points aren't clear I'll explain them to you. Does that make sense to you?

CAROL: Yes, it does. You're going to help me question my irrational beliefs and help me to change them if need be.

[I have now accomplished all four of the preparatory tasks that need to be done before the process of disputing can properly begin (see pp. 100–101 for a review of these tasks). In the following dialogue with Carol, I want you to note that I target for change one irrational belief at a time. This is an important guideline to follow.]

WINDY: Right. Now let's take your demand that you must finish the knitting section that you were working on. Let's see if if this is flexible or rigid.

CAROL: It's rigid.

WINDY: Why?

CAROL: Well, musts are rigid. By saying that I must finish the knitting, I'm not even allowing for the possibility that I may leave it unfinished and there is always this possibility. By saying that I must finish it, I am treating myself as a robot who has no free choice and that's ridiculous.

WINDY: Good answer. Now, let's first see how realistic that belief is. Now is there any law of the universe that decrees that you must finish the knitting section before going to bed?

CAROL: Well, if I don't I'll feel edgy and uncomfortable.

[Here, Carol explains why it is undesirable not to finish the knitting section before going to bed, but does not provide any evidence in support of her belief that she must do so. I will now point this out.]

WINDY: That's why it might be desirable to finish it. But where is it written that you have to do the desirable thing in the short term when it stops you from getting what you want in the longer term, i.e. it interferes with your getting to work on time?

CAROL: Well, I guess I don't have to do it.

[Carol's correct answer here is put very tentatively. I will now encourage her to state why that is the right answer.]

WINDY: Now that's the right answer, but why is it the right answer?

CAROL: Because if there was such a law, I would have no control over my behaviour in this respect. I would have to complete the knitting section no matter what. But I do have control over my behaviour. Stopping at 11 o'clock with the knitting section unfinished is difficult but it is possible. If there was a law that stated that I had to finish it before going to bed, it would be impossible for me to go against that law. It is possible for me to stop, therefore such a law does not exist.

[This is an excellent response and indicates that she has understood the point. I now state this and proceed with the logical dispute.]

WINDY: That's an excellent answer, Carol, you really seem to have grasped that to demand that you have to finish something just because you have started it is unrealistic.

[Note that I have used this opportunity to go from the specific (Carol does not have to finish the knitting section) to the general (Carol does not have to finish anything that she has started). As I discussed earlier, in brief REBT it is important to use opportunities to help your client to generalize her learning.]

Now let's consider the logic of your demand. We know that you would like to finish the knitting section, but does it logically follow therefore that you must do so?

CAROL: I'm not sure I understand.

WINDY: Well, would you like £1 million to fall in your lap now?

CAROL: That's silly because it won't.

WINDY: But would you like it to?

CAROL: Of course.

WINDY: So does it follow that because you want it to therefore it must?

CAROL: No, of course not.

WINDY: Why not?

[Here again having established that Carol has given me the right answer, I encourage her to provide reasons why the answer she has given is correct. Doing so, as I have stated before, helps the client to think for herself. What you want to guard against is your client giving you the correct answer because you have either stated or intimated that it is the correct response and for no other reason.]

CAROL: Well, they are not connected.

WINDY: Correct, Your desires and your demands are not connected in any logical way. So you want to finish whatever you have started, but it isn't logical for you to conclude that you must do so.

[Again note that I have used an opportunity to state the rational point in a general form so that Carol can generalize her learning on this issue.]

Finally, let's consider how helpful your demand is. When you insist that you must, literally must, finish your knitting is this belief helpful to you or not?

CAROL: It's basically unhelpful.

WINDY: Why?

[You should now understand why I asked this question. If not, re-read the above sections where I asked Carol to explain to me why her correct answers to my questions were, in fact, correct.]

CAROL: Well, for a start, it keeps me up into the early hours of the morning so that I go to bed exhausted and wake up late and tired to boot. Second, if I actually leave the knitting unfinished when I believe that I have to finish it, then I will feel intolerably uncomfortable.

WINDY: But at least it helps you finish it.

CAROL: But I would still finish it later if I stopped at 11 o'clock that night.

WINDY: So what you're saying is that on balance your demand that you must finish what you've started, such as your knitting, is not helpful to you.

CAROL: Correct.

[I will now help Carol to construct her rational belief and help her to understand why this belief is rational.]

WINDY: So you can now see that your belief 'I must finish what I've started', in this case your knitting, is rigid, inconsistent with reality, illogical and unhelpful. Now what would the rational alternative to this belief be?

CAROL: I would like to finish what I've started.

[Here Carol has provided a partial version of her rational belief. Note how I help her to develop the full version of this rational belief.]

WINDY: That's half of it, but a full rational belief asserts what you would like, but also negates the demand, which in this case would be what?

CAROL: But I don't have to finish it.

WINDY: Right, so the full version of your rational belief is: 'I would like to finish what I've started, but I don't have to do so'. Now let's see whether or not this belief is in fact rational. We'll do this by seeing if it meets the four criteria for rationality: (i) is it flexible? (ii) is it consistent with reality? (iii) is it logical? and (iv) is it helpful?

Let's start with flexibility. Is your rational belief 'I would like to finish what I've started, but I don't have to do so' flexible or rigid?

[Note once again that I am working with the general rational belief rather than with the specific version. As you will see throughout this sequence, I will start with the general rational belief and then encourage Carol to apply her learning to her specific rational belief in the knitting example. Thus, at times I move from the specific to the general and at other times I move from the general to the specific. I do this with Carol because she is able to handle this 'two-way traffic'. With other clients who are not able to handle this, I might only move from the specific to the general, for example. With yet other clients who are not able to follow my moving from the specific to the general, I will work just at the specific level. However, this group of clients will benefit the least from brief REBT because they are unable to generalize their learning.]

CAROL: It's flexible.

WINDY: Why?

CAROL: Because it allows for the possibility of not finishing what I've started.

WINDY: Right. Now is your rational belief 'I would like to finish what I've started, but I don't have to do so' consistent with reality or not?

CAROL: It is consistent with reality.

WINDY: Why?

CAROL: Because it states what I want, but it also points out that there is no law of the universe which decrees that I must get what I want.

WINDY: Very good. Now is that same belief logical or illogical?

CAROL: It makes perfect sense to me so it must be logical.

WINDY: How so?

CAROL: Well . . . I'm not sure how to explain it.

WINDY: You're right. Explaining why a rational belief is logical is difficult. I usually explain it like this. Your rational belief 'I would like to
finish what I've started, but I don't have to do so' follows logically
from your more general belief that you would prefer to get what you
want, but you don't have to get it.

CAROL: Oh right. I see.

WINDY: Finally, is your belief 'I would like to finish what I've started,
but I don't have to do so' helpful or unhelpful?

CAROL: It's helpful because it increases my chances of getting to work
on time. I also won't feel as uncomfortable leaving the work unfinished
as I would if I believed that I must finish it.

WINDY: That's very good. Now let's apply all these arguments to the
knitting example. First, what is your specific rational belief in this
situation?

CAROL: I would like to finish my knitting before I go to bed, but I don't
have to do so.

WINDY: Right, and is this belief flexible or rigid?

CAROL: It's flexible because it allows me to choose to stay up and finish
the knitting or to go to bed with it unfinished.

WINDY: Is it consistent with reality or not?

CAROL: It's realistic because it acknowledges that I'd rather finish my
knitting, but it also acknowledges that there is no law that stipulates
that I have to do so.

WINDY: Third, is this belief logical or illogical?

CAROL: Definitely logical because, as you said earlier, it follows from
my more general belief that I want what I want, but I don't have to get
it.

WINDY: Finally, is your specific rational belief 'I'd like to finish my
knitting before going to bed, but I don't have to do so' helpful or not?

CAROL: It's helpful because it increases my chances of getting to work
on time and it means that I can go to bed with some discomfort, but not
too much pain.

WINDY: That's really good. Do you think that it might be useful if you listened a few times to the tape of this disputing sequence so you can go over the arguments for yourself?

CAROL: That's a really good idea.

[It is often helpful to encourage your client to listen to clear disputing sequences because it helps them to review the kinds of questions you have asked and their responses to these questions. This acts as an aid to your client beginning to internalize the disputing process for herself. However, if, in your opinion, the disputing sequence has not been clear then it is best to wait until you and your client have produced a clearer example before you suggest that she listen to a recording of it. At this stage you want to promote clarity and minimize confusion for your client.]

Now I will show you how I disputed Carol's LFT belief. Due to space constraints I will only include the part of the process where I helped her to dispute her general LFT belief, i.e. 'I can't bear leaving things unfinished'.

WINDY: Now, let's dispute your other irrational belief in the same way that I did your demand. Let's look at it in its general form: 'I couldn't stand it were I to leave things unfinished'. Is that accurate?

CAROL: Yes.

WINDY: Let's start with the question of flexibility or rigidity. Is your belief 'I couldn't stand it were I to leave things unfinished' flexible or rigid?

CAROL: It's rigid.

WINDY: Because?

CAROL: Because it is extreme. There's no allowance being made for the fact that I may be able to tolerate it, albeit with difficulty.

WINDY: Right, let's now use the empirical argument. Is it true that you couldn't stand it were you to leave something that you really wanted to finish, like a knitting section?

CAROL: No, it's not true.

WINDY: Why not?

CAROL: Well, it's not going to kill me to leave it.

WINDY: And could you have future happiness if you did leave whatever it is unfinished?

CAROL: (*laughs*) Of course I could.

WINDY: But I can't stand it means either disintegrating on the spot or forfeiting the chance of any future happiness.

CAROL: That's obviously not true.

WINDY: Now let's go on to see whether your belief 'I couldn't stand it were I to leave things unfinished' is logical or not. Now we know that leaving things unfinished is difficult for you to tolerate, but does it logically follow that therefore it is intolerable to leave things unfinished?

CAROL: No, it's not.

WINDY: Why not?

CAROL: Because if you are tolerating something with difficulty, you are still tolerating it and it is nonsense to conclude therefore that you can't tolerate it.

WINDY: Good point. Now let's consider whether or not your belief 'I couldn't stand it were I to leave things unfinished' is helpful to you.

CAROL: Obviously not.

WINDY: Why obviously?

CAROL: Well, if I tell myself that I can't stand leaving things unfinished that will lead me to stay up all hours until I finish it.

WINDY: Anything else?

CAROL: Well, telling myself that I can't stand leaving things unfinished will increase the intensity of my frustrated feelings if I ever manage to leave it unfinished.

WINDY: OK, good. So you can now see that your irrational belief 'I couldn't stand it were I to leave things unfinished' is rigid or extreme as you put it, inconsistent with reality, illogical and unhelpful. Now, what do you think the rational alternative to this irrational belief is?

CAROL: I can stand it if I were to leave things unfinished?

WINDY: That is part of the belief. The full belief is: 'I can stand it if I were to leave things unfinished, although it is difficult to tolerate'. Now is this belief rigid or flexible?

CAROL: It's flexible because it indicates that I am tolerating it albeit with difficulty.

WINDY: Right, now is that belief consistent with reality?

CAROL: Yes, it is. I am standing it so to say that I can stand it is realistic.

WINDY: Indeed, even when you are telling yourself that you can't stand leaving things unfinished you still can stand it. Let's move on to logic. Does your belief 'I can stand it if I were to leave things unfinished, although it is difficult to tolerate' logically follow from your general belief that you can tolerate frustrating situations, albeit with difficulty?

CAROL: Yes it does, the specific instance follows the general rule.

WINDY: Good. Now, finally, is your belief 'I can stand it if I were to leave things unfinished, although it is difficult to tolerate' helpful or unhelpful?

CAROL: It's helpful because it will help me to stop doing things when it is in my interests to do so, even though they remain unfinished.

WINDY: Right, so you can now see that your irrational belief 'I couldn't stand it if I were to leave things unfinished' is rigid, inconsistent with reality, illogical and unhelpful and that your rational belief 'I could stand it were I to leave things unfinished' is flexible, realistic, logical and helpful.

Eliciting a Commitment to her Goals from your Client

Having disputed your client's irrational beliefs that underpin her target problem, and having helped her to understand why her irrational beliefs are irrational and why her rational beliefs are rational, you are now ready to ask your client to commit herself to her goals with respect to her target problem.

In doing so, you take both her goal with respect to her problem as defined and her goal with respect to her problem as assessed. Then you ask her whether she is ready to commit herself to work towards these goals, based on the work you have done with her so far on her target problem. It is unlikely that she will say 'no' to this invitation, but if she does or if she displays ambivalence then it is important that you understand these responses and problem-solve accordingly.

Eliciting a Commitment to her Goals from Carol

WINDY: Carol, I've now helped you to see why your irrational beliefs about leaving tasks unfinished are, in fact, irrational and why your rational beliefs about the same issue are rational. Let me remind you of what your goals are on this issue. First, you said that you wanted to get to work on time. Then, as we looked more closely at what was involved in stopping you from doing this we found that you had difficulty in stopping doing things that you had already started. With respect to this problem, you said the following: 'Whenever it is in my longer term interests to do so, I will stop doing a task even though I might be in the middle of it and I will put up with the discomfort of so doing'. Do you recall these goals?

CAROL: Yes, I do.

WINDY: Are they still relevant to you?

CAROL: Very much so.

WINDY: Then, let me ask you an important question. Are you ready to commit yourself to work towards achieving these goals?

CAROL: Yes I am.

WINDY: Good, then let's take the next step.

Carol now understands why her irrational beliefs are irrational and why the rational alternatives to these beliefs are rational. As I said to her, she is now ready to take the next step and to do the work that she needs to do in order to integrate this understanding into her belief system so that her rational beliefs make a difference to the way that she thinks, feels and acts on this issue. Doing so will help her to reach the goals that she has just committed herself to achieving. This will be the subject of the next chapter. But, first, I want to show you how to teach your client to use a written self-help form that will help her to consolidate her understanding of the rational solution to her target problem, and that she can use with her other problems.

TEACHING YOUR CLIENT HOW TO USE A
WRITTEN SELF-HELP FORM

One of the most frequently used methods of helping clients to understand the rational solution to their problems is through the use of written self-help forms. There are many such forms in use and often REBT therapists construct their own. However, what these forms do share in common is that they are based on the ABCDE framework that is the hallmark of REBT. In this section of the chapter, I will introduce you to the written self-help form that I constructed with an ex-student, Jane Walker (see ABC of Emotional and Behavioural Problems, pp. 117–120) and I will outline the steps that you need to take in using it with your client.

ABC
OF
EMOTIONAL AND BEHAVIOURAL PROBLEMS

A   **C**

Major unhealthy negative
emotion:

Major self-defeating
behaviour:

A = ACTIVATING EVENT

- Describe the aspect of the situation you were most disturbed about

- Assume temporarily that A is true

- An A can be *internal* or *external*

- An A can refer to an event in the *past, present or future*

- An A can be an *inference*

C = CONSEQUENCE

Unhealthy Negative Emotions:

- Anxiety

- Depression

- Anger

- Guilt

- Shame & Embarrassment

- Hurt

- Jealousy

iBs   D

DOGMATIC DEMAND:	Is it true? Is it logical? Is it helpful?
AWFULIZING:	Is it true? Is it logical? Is it helpful?
LOW FRUSTRATION TOLERANCE:	Is it true? Is it logical? Is it helpful?
SELF/OTHER DOWNING:	Is it true? Is it logical? Is it helpful?

iBs = IRRATIONAL BELIEFS

Look for:

- DOGMATIC DEMANDS
  (musts, absolute shoulds,
  oughts)

- AWFULIZING
  (It's awful, terrible, horrible)

- LOW FRUSTRATION
  TOLERANCE
  (I can't stand it, I can't bear it)

- SELF/OTHER-DOWNING
  (bad, worthless, less worthy)

D = DISPUTING

- Where is the evidence to
  support the existence of my
  irrational belief? Is it *consistent
  with reality?*

- Is my belief *logical?* Does it
  logically follow from my
  rational belief?

- Where is holding this belief
  getting me? Is it *helpful?*

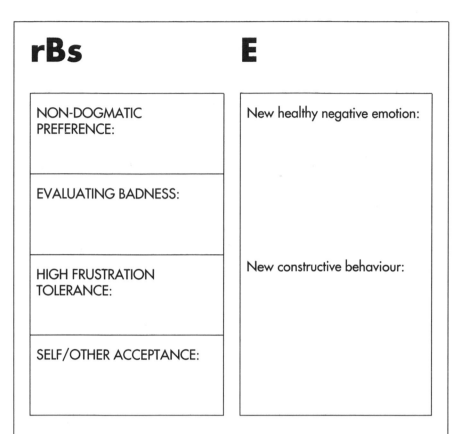

rBs

| NON-DOGMATIC PREFERENCE: |
| EVALUATING BADNESS: |
| HIGH FRUSTRATION TOLERANCE: |
| SELF/OTHER ACCEPTANCE: |

E

New healthy negative emotion:

New constructive behaviour:

rBs = RATIONAL BELIEFS

Strive for:

- NON-DOGMATIC PREFERENCES
  (wishes, wants, desires)

- EVALUATING BADNESS
  (It's bad, unfortunate)

- HIGH FRUSTRATION TOLERANCE
  (I can stand it, I can bear it)

- SELF/OTHER ACCEPTANCE
  ('Fallible human being' concept)

E = NEW EFFECT

Healthy Negative Emotions:

- Concern

- Sadness

- Annoyance

- Remorse

- Disappointment

- Regret

- Concern about my relationship

HOMEWORK:

Step 1. Explain the form to your client

The first step in using the form with your client is to explain it to her. This involves taking her through the form point by point in the order in which you want her to complete it. To help her in this respect it is useful to provide an explanatory sheet along the lines of the example on pp. 122–123.

When using the form it is worth noting that your client will probably find identifying the critical A the most difficult part of the form. To help her do this, you will probably have to use inference chaining, a skill which only a minority of clients will be able to use for themselves (see Chapter 4). However, as therapy proceeds, and with your help, your client will learn to identify for herself the activating events which trigger her irrational beliefs.

Step 2. Take your client through a model form

Once you have explained the form to your client it is useful to take her through it again using a model example as a guide. This might be taken from a completed form that one of your other clients has completed (in which case you need to get permission from that client to use the form for such a purpose), or you might construct an example yourself. In either case, the example needs to demonstrate the accurate use of the form.

Step 3. Take your client through the form using a specific example of her target problem

Your client should now be ready to use the form on a specific example of one of her own problems, preferably one that she has experienced recently, so that the relevant information is fresh in her mind. Again you should take the lead as you take the client through the form.

Step 4. Encourage your client to take the lead on completing the form using another example of her target problem

Here, you should prompt the client as she goes through the form, correcting her when she makes errors and briefly explaining why she needs to put the information in the right places.

Step 5. Ask your client to complete the form on her own in the therapy session

As she does this you can leave your office so that she is not tempted to ask you for help. Give her 10-15 minutes to do this. When you return, go over the completed form, give your client feedback on her responses, praise her effort and achievement and correct any errors that she has made.

Step 6. Ask your client to use the form on one of her problems as a homework assignment

When you suggest to your client that she completes the form as a homework assignment, stress that you do not expect her to master it quickly as it is a difficult skill to acquire.

Sheet Explaining the Use of Dryden & Walker's (1992) Written Self-Help Form

When using this form it is very important that you select a specific example of your problem. The more specific you can be, the better. Then complete the form in the following order.

First, Complete 'C'

(i) Choose one unhealthy negative emotion from those listed (which could be the main one) and write down the self-defeating behaviour associated with it.

(ii) Use one form for each emotion if you experienced more than one unhealthy negative emotion in the episode under consideration.

(iii) If your problem is associated only with self-defeating behaviour leave the 'emotion' section blank.

Second, Complete 'A'

(i) Here, it is very important that you focus on the aspect about which you were most disturbed.

(ii) As it says on the form, it is most important that you assume temporarily that 'A' is true. You will have an opportunity later to check on its accuracy.

Third, Write Down your 'iBs' about 'A'

(i) Work from the top of the form to the bottom and complete the relevant sections.

(ii) Leave blank any section that does not apply.

Fourth, Complete the 'D' Section

(i) Answer each of the three questions.

(ii) Don't give a 'parrot' answer. Think through each of your responses and prove to yourself why the correct answer is 'no'.

Fifth, Complete the 'rB' Section

(i)   Again, work from the top of the form to the bottom and complete the relevant sections.

(ii) Make sure that you assert the rational belief and negate the irrational belief in each completed section.

Sixth, Complete the 'E' Section

(i)   Provide a healthy negative emotion from those listed, making sure that it is a constructive alternative to the unhealthy negative emotion listed under 'C'.

(ii) Write down your constructive negative behaviour associated with the new emotion.

(iii) If your problem was associated only with self-defeating behaviour, just complete the 'new constructive behaviour' part of the form, leaving the 'emotion' section blank.

Seventh, Reconsider 'A'

(i)   While holding the new rational beliefs go back to 'A' and correct any distorted inferences that you find there.

Finally, Homework

(i)   DIscuss a suitable homework assignment with your therapist to strengthen your conviction in your rational beliefs.

Step 7. Review the form that your client did for homework at the beginning of the next session

As I will stress in Chapter 9, reviewing your client's homework at the beginning of the next session communicates to her that completing the form is an important part of brief REBT and that you are interested in her progress. You are now ready to help your client to begin to integrate the rational solution into her belief system so that she can overcome her problems. In the next chapter, I will show you how to explain to your client what this integration process involves.

6

EXPLAINING WHAT INTEGRATION INVOLVES

INTRODUCTION

In this and the following two chapters, I deal with the issue of how to help clients to integrate the rational solution to their problems into their belief system so that it affects their thoughts, feelings and behaviour. In this chapter, I concentrate on how to explain what is involved in the integration process and will illustrate my points with dialogue from my work with Carol. In Chapter 7, I will discuss and illustrate ways of promoting such integration within therapy sessions, while in Chapter 8, I will discuss what you need to do to encourage your client to facilitate this process between therapy sessions.

In the previous chapter, I explained the major differences between your client understanding the rational solution to her problems on the one hand, and on the other hand being able to integrate that solution into her belief system so that it makes a positive difference to her thoughts, feelings and behaviour, with the result that she does not experience the target problem. I suggest that you review this material so that you understand it fully since such understanding is necessary if you are to explain the integration process to your client.

As with other rational principles, it is important that your client under stands this integration process before she embarks on it. Having such understanding will help her to persist with the therapeutic change process even when she isn't making progress or when she actually falls back into old problem-related habits. Here is a list of points regarding the integration process that you need to help your client to understand if she is to make full use of it. These points relate to what your client needs to do both within and between therapy sessions if she is to integrate the rational solution into her belief system. I will deal with each point in turn and, as I said earlier, illustrate this with reference to my work with Carol.

1. The basic difference between understanding the rational solution and integrating it into one's belief system.
2. When to help your client understand this difference.
3. The importance of developing a large number of persuasive arguments against irrational beliefs and a similarly large number in support of rational beliefs.
4. The importance of taking action.
5. The importance of using force and energy in the integration process.
6. The importance of vividness in the integration process.
7. The importance of repetition, persistence and regularity in the integration process (even when nothing is happening).
8. The importance of doing things uncomfortably and unconfidently and with putting up with feeling unnatural during the integration process.
9. The importance of understanding and dealing with obstacles to integration.
10. Your client's and your respective roles in the integration process.

THE BASIC DIFFERENCE BETWEEN UNDERSTANDING AND INTEGRATION

As I discussed in the previous chapter, when your client just understands the rational solution to her problems, she can see why her irrational beliefs are irrational and why her rational beliefs are rational, but she believes this lightly and only occasionally, usually at times when she is not facing relevant, critical As. Furthermore, mere understanding of this rational solution has minimal impact on her thoughts, feelings and behaviour, with the result that she will still respond to relevant, critical As with the same unhealthy negative emotions and self-defeating behaviours which were her responses before she understood the rational solution. It is thus possible to say that while she has integrated this understanding into her knowledge system, she has not integrated it into her belief system.

However, when she has been able to integrate the rational solution into her belief system, she not only sees why her irrational beliefs are irrational and why her rational beliefs are rational, but she believes this strongly and frequently even when she is facing relevant, critical As. Furthermore, integrating this rational solution has a decided beneficial impact on her thoughts, feelings and behaviour, with the result that she is able to respond to relevant, negative critical As with healthy negative emotions and self-enhancing behaviours. Here is how I helped Carol to understand this basic difference.

WINDY: You now understand why your irrational beliefs are irrational and why your rational beliefs are rational. However, do you think that this knowledge alone will make a difference to the way you think, feel and act, the next time you face a situation where you really want to finish something that you have started, even though it will be counter-productive for you to do so?

CAROL: I'm not sure, it might.

WINDY: Possibly, but I want you to have a realistic picture of what to expect from therapy, so let me explain why knowledge alone, while important, is not sufficient for you to overcome your problems. Is that OK?

CAROL: Fine.

WINDY: Please bear with me while I use an analogy that will help you to understand what I'm talking about. You may think that I'm going off at half cock, but trust me, I'm not. OK?

CAROL: OK.

[In REBT, it is often helpful to explain what you are about to do and ask for permission to do it, particularly when your client may think that you are going off at a tangent.]

WINDY: Let's suppose that you want to improve your body tone and develop your muscle tone, what would you need to do to achieve this?

CAROL: I would need to work out two or three times a week and pump some iron. Stuff like that.

WINDY: But what good will just knowing what you need to do be if you don't do it?

CAROL: It will have no effect whatever on my body and muscle tone.

WINDY: Humour me for a moment; why not?

CAROL: Because muscle tone doesn't respond to knowledge, it responds to the muscles being exercised.

WINDY: That's exactly the same in therapy. Just knowing why your irrational beliefs are irrational and your rational beliefs are rational will have little effect on your thoughts, feelings and behaviour in the same way that knowledge about how to improve your muscle tone has little or no effect on that tone. Do you see the point that I'm making?

CAROL: Yes, it seems that knowing why my rational beliefs are rational gives me an understanding of what I need to do to overcome my problems, but unless I put this understanding into practice, then I won't actually overcome these problems.

WINDY: Exactly. You've understood my point very well. What do you think about this point?

[Notice the distinction I've drawn between my client's understanding of the point that I've made and her views on it. She could, for example, understand the point, but not agree with it. Given this possibility, it is often useful to ask both questions.]

CAROL: I agree with it. It makes perfect sense to me.

WINDY: That's good. What this means is that together we need to work out ways of helping you to really believe that you don't have to finish things when it is not in your interests to do so, and to integrate this with your thoughts, feelings and behaviour. But before we do that, let me mention one important effect of the difference between understanding and integration. OK?

CAROL: Fine.

WINDY: When people only understand why their irrational beliefs are irrational and their rational beliefs are rational, but have not yet integrated this understanding into their belief system, they say things like, 'I can accept what you say intellectually, but not emotionally', or 'I see it up here' (*pointing to my head*) 'but I don't feel it down here' (*pointing to my gut*) . . .

CAROL: It's funny that you should mention that, but I was just thinking something similar myself. I had such a reaction when we'd finished disputing my beliefs about not leaving something until I had finished it.

WINDY: That's a very, very common reaction. I mention it because I don't want you to be put off by it. A number of clients think quite unrealistically that they will have that gut feeling straight away. But that will come once they have integrated their understanding of the rational solution into their belief system and, as we'll soon see, that only happens after a lot of practice.

CAROL: So, that sense of seeing it up here (*points to her head*), but not feeling it down here (*points to her gut*) is quite typical and natural and I'll feel it down here (*points to her gut*) after a while?

WINDY: Correct, although only it's not the passage of time, but what you do in the passage of time that counts.

CAROL: Yes, that's what I meant. I'll only improve my muscle tone if I actually pump iron.

WINDY: Exactly. That's what I call the 'head–gut' issue. You won't feel down here (*points to gut*) what you know up here (*points to head*) until you pump a lot of therapeutic iron.

WHEN TO HELP YOUR CLIENT UNDERSTAND THE BASIC DIFFERENCE

The most obvious time to help your client to see the basic difference between understanding and integration is after she has reached the stage of understanding why her irrational beliefs are irrational and her rational beliefs are rational, but before she has begun the process of integration. It is at this time that she is likely to note that she understands the rational solution, but that she doesn't believe it yet. Consequently, addressing this issue when your client is likely to be concerned with it is the best time to do it. We saw this with Carol above when she said, 'It's funny that you should mention that, but I was just thinking something similar myself. I had such a reaction when we'd finished disputing my beliefs about not leaving something until I had finished it' after I had explained the 'head–gut issue' to her.

While helping your client to see the basic difference between understanding and integration is most frequently done once she has reached the stage of understanding without integration, there are two other times when you might profitably address this issue with your clients. First, you might do so before you begin to dispute your client's irrational beliefs. This is particularly useful for clients who wish to know what is coming next in the therapeutic process. Second, you might help your client appreciate the basic difference between understanding and integration before therapy has begun when the person is still an applicant (see Chapter 3). There are some people who will not commit themselves to brief REBT until they have understood the entire therapeutic process before they start. These are people who like to see the big picture before they commit themselves to anything important. In my experience, it is best to go along with their request and offer them an outline of a typical course of brief REBT while stressing that you cannot guarantee that this will apply exactly to the course of their own therapy.

The following points can be covered with your client either before you initiate the integration process or before you introduce a technique related to the point during this process. However, it is important to distinguish between helping the client to understand a principle and implementing a technique based on that principle. Consistent with this distinction, in this chapter, I will discuss how you might help your client to understand the principle itself and in the following two chapters I will discuss and demonstrate the techniques based on these principles.

THE NEED TO DEVELOP PERSUASIVE ARGUMENTS

Clients often think that because they can give one or two reasons why an irrational belief is irrational and the rational alternative is rational then this will suffice. While such little evidence may suffice for the purposes of understanding the rational solution, it will not aid integration. For integration to be achieved, one of the things that your client needs to do is to develop numerous arguments to undermine his irrational belief and an equally large number to support his rational belief. As discussed above, you need to help your client to understand this before employing such a technique with him. Thus below, I will show how I helped Carol to understand this important point and in the following chapter I will demonstrate how I used the technique with her.

WINDY: I want you to learn about some of the important ways in which you can go from understanding the rational solution to being able to integrate it into your belief system so that you can overcome your problem and really believe your rational beliefs. Would you be interested in doing that?

CAROL: Yes, that would be useful.

WINDY: The first way concerns the volume of arguments you need to marshal in order to undermine your irrational beliefs and to strengthen your rational beliefs. I'd like to deal with this point by using an analogy. Is that OK with you?

CAROL: That's fine. In general, I find analogies useful.

WINDY: Good. Now, imagine that you are accused of murder and you employ a top lawyer to defend you. Let's suppose that every time he is called upon to cross-examine a prosecution witness he declines the opportunity to dismantle their evidence. Also, when he has an opportunity to present evidence for the defence, all he does is stand up and say, 'Your honour, ladies and gentlemen of the jury, this person is innocent'. How persuasive would he be to the jury, do you think?

CAROL: That's all he does?

WINDY: Yes.

CAROL: Then, I'm going to be found guilty, no question.

WINDY: Why's that?

CAROL: Because, as you said, he isn't dismantling the evidence of the prosecution witnesses and he isn't presenting any evidence to prove my innocence.

WINDY: So what would you want him to do?

CAROL: I'd want him to rip to shreds the evidence provided by the prosecution witnesses, using as many persuasive arguments as possible, and I'd want him to present as many persuasive arguments as he could find to show that I was innocent.

WINDY: Quite. Now exactly the same process applies in the integration process. If you can develop as many persuasive arguments as you can to prove to yourself why your irrational beliefs are irrational, and as many persuasive arguments as you can to prove to yourself why your rational beliefs are rational, then you have more chance of integrating your rational beliefs into your belief system than if you only use a few weak arguments on either side.

CAROL: That's a very good point and makes good sense.

WINDY: Now, this is not the only way of integrating your rational beliefs, but it is a powerful cognitive technique that I'll help you use a little later.

ACTING AGAINST IRRATIONAL BELIEFS, AND IN A WAY THAT IS CONSISTENT WITH RATIONAL BELIEFS

Taking action in a way that is against your client's irrational beliefs and consistent with her rational beliefs is perhaps the most powerful way of integrating her rational beliefs into her belief system. Indeed, if your client never took action that was based on her new rational belief and continued to take action that was based on her old irrational belief, she would probably not give up the latter or acquire the former. Unless you help your client to acquire and act on this insight then her gains from brief REBT will be severely limited. This is how I got this point over to Carol.

WINDY: Now what do you think is one of the most powerful ways of integrating your new rational belief into your belief system?

CAROL: Other than generating numerous persuasive arguments in favour of your rational belief and against your irrational belief?

WINDY: In some ways more powerful than that.

CAROL: I'm not sure.

WINDY: Well, let me put it this way. Let's suppose that you generated numerous persuasive arguments against your irrational belief and an equal number of such arguments in favour of your rational belief. However, what would happen if you kept on working on something until you finished it when it was not in your best interests to do so?

CAROL: Well, you wouldn't really change your belief.

WINDY: Why not?

CAROL: Because you would be undoing with your behaviour all the hard work you have done generating your persuasive arguments.

WINDY: That's right. That's why taking action that is against your irrational beliefs and consistent with your rational beliefs is such an important part of the integration process. So what implications do you think this has for our work together?

CAROL: It obviously means that on this problem, I am going to have to keep to my agreements with myself about stopping doing things even though I'm in the middle of doing them.

WINDY: Correct, because every time you work to finish something at a time that is against your other interests to do so, you are unfortunately weakening your rational belief and strengthening your irrational belief.

CAROL: I can now understand why your publishers describe your approach as no-nonsense!

THE IMPORTANCE OF USING FORCE AND ENERGY

Albert Ellis (1979) has written an important paper on the use of force and energy in behavioural change. In this paper he argues that your client is more likely to integrate her rational beliefs into her belief system so that they make a difference to the way she thinks, feels and acts if she challenges her irrational beliefs forcefully and energetically than if she challenges them weakly and without force. This is how I helped Carol to understand this concept.

WINDY: There are two ways in which you can challenge your irrational beliefs. I'll describe them both to you and you tell me which method you think will help you most to integrate your rational beliefs into your belief system. OK?

CAROL: OK.

WINDY: Let's imagine that I believe that I must have the approval of my boss and if I don't get his approval it means that I am worthless. Now my therapist helps me to understand that I don't need my boss's approval and if, in fact, he does disapprove of me I can accept myself as a fallible human being. Now I can challenge my irrational belief weakly like this: 'I don't need my boss's approval, although I'd prefer him to approve of me. I'm fallible whether or not he approves of me' (*said in a weak and quiet manner*). Or I can challenge my irrational belief more forcefully like this: 'I DAMNED WELL DON'T NEED MY BOSS'S APPROVAL, ALTHOUGH I'D PREFER HIM TO APPROVE OF ME. I DEFINITELY CAN ACCEPT MYSELF AS A FALLIBLE HUMAN BEING EVEN IF HE HATES MY GUTS!!' (*said in forceful strong manner*). Which of these approaches will help me integrate my rational belief?

CAROL: The second way.

WINDY: Why?

CAROL: Because it arouses your emotions.

WINDY: That's right. If I dispute it weakly, I keep it a distance from myself and it tends to be something of an intellectual exercise. However, if I dispute it forcefully I make my rational belief more immediate and it is, as you say, more of an emotional experience. What implication does this have for you?

CAROL: It means that I will have to dispute my own irrational beliefs forcefully if I wish to integrate my rational belief into my belief system.

WINDY: And I will help you to do this by playing devil's advocate and taking a forceful irrational position. This will help you to defend your rational belief in a forceful, energetic manner.

THE IMPORTANCE OF VIVIDNESS

The process whereby your client integrates the rational solution into her belief system so that the new rational beliefs make a difference to the way she thinks, feels and acts with respect to relevant, negative As depends in part on the extent to which she remembers the rational solution and the vividness with which she remembers it. In the early 1980s, I published a series of papers (collated in Dryden, 1986) on what would now be called vivid REBT in which I outlined a series of techniques the purpose of which was to increase the likelihood that clients would remember and thus apply rational concepts. Since many of these techniques tend to be out of the ordinary it is very important that you explain the rationale for the use of vivid techniques before implementing them. The following excerpt demonstrates how I did so with Carol.

WINDY: In order for you to be able to integrate the rational solution to your problems into your belief system and hence really believe, feel and act on it, you need to be able to call the relevant rational principle to mind. Would you agree?

CAROL: Right. Unless I remember my rational beliefs, I'm hardly likely to practise strengthening them.

WINDY: So it follows that one of the things that we need to consider is how to make your rational belief memorable. Right?

CAROL: Right.

WINDY: What I will do then is to help you to do this by putting rational concepts in a vivid manner so that you might easily remember them. Would that be helpful?

CAROL: That's difficult to say.

WINDY: Agreed, but what if I try a few vivid interventions and see how you respond?

CAROL: Fair enough.

WINDY: Now they may seem a bit strange at first, but you may find that they will help you to remember the relevant concept and will thus serve as an aid to integration.

PERSISTENCE, HOMEWORK AND REPETITION

While the issues of force and energy on the one hand, and vividness on the other can be seen to represent the exciting side of furthering the integration process, there is also a far less exciting side. Albert Ellis sums up this latter side when he says that change involves: 'Work and practice! Work and practice! Work and practice!' If we break down this unexciting side of the integration process, we may see that it comprises three related issues. First, your client needs to be persistent in the change process; second, she needs to work on herself at regular intervals; and third, she needs to go over things repetitively if she is to integrate the rational solution into her belief system. Here is how I presented these ideas to Carol.

WINDY: Now do you think that you need to work on yourself outside therapy sessions or do you think that the work we will do in these sessions will suffice?

CAROL: Well, when we spoke about the importance of taking action against my irrational beliefs, it seemed to me quite clear that I needed to put into practice outside what I learned inside therapy sessions.

WINDY: Right. Now in order to integrate the rational solution into your belief system, do you think you need to do such assignments regularly or once in a while?

CAROL: Regularly.

WINDY: Why?

CAROL: Well if I do them once in a while, I won't be getting enough practice at strengthening my rational beliefs to integrate them, but if I do them regularly, I will get the practice that I need.

WINDY: Right, now let's consider a single homework assignment, do you think that you will need to do that once or repeatedly?

CAROL: Unfortunately, repeatedly.

WINDY: Why unfortunately?

CAROL: Doing something repeatedly sounds like a drag.

WINDY: Well, you could experiment by doing it a different way each time, but let's suppose that it is a drag. If it helps you to overcome your problem is it worth putting up with the 'dragginess'?

CAROL: Put like that, yes.

WINDY: So if it gets to be a drag, you need to remind yourself of the purpose of putting up with the 'draggy' aspects of the integration process. Right?

CAROL: Right.

WINDY: Now from what I've said so far, do you think that you need to be persistent in the integration process or not?

CAROL: I'll need to be persistent.

WINDY: Another rare delight, eh?

CAROL: Yeah, thrilling.

WINDY: Here's another thrill. The nature of change is such that there will be times when you'll be working away and not getting any obvious benefit from it. Do you think it's best to stop altogether, or to persist until you start deriving benefit from the work again, which I can assure you will happen?

CAROL: If I know that, I'll persist and it won't seem so bad. But I'm glad you warned me of that.

WINDY: So to recap, if you want to integrate the rational solution into your belief system so that it makes a real difference to your life, you need to be persistent, do homework assignments regularly and repeatedly. How do you honestly feel about that, dare I ask?

CAROL: I think you know how I feel about that!

WINDY: I know. I'd be surprised if you felt like jumping up and down with joy. But I'd be lying to you if I promised you an easy ride.

CAROL: I know and I appreciate your honesty. It reminds me of the old adage: 'No gain without pain'.

WINDY: Right, and if you take it a day at a time, which is another old adage, it won't seem *THAT* bad.

CAROL: Good point.

DOING THINGS UNCOMFORTABLY AND UNCONFIDENTLY AND PUTTING UP WITH FEELING UNNATURAL

If your client is to integrate the rational solution into her belief system then she will not only experience a fair measure of tedium as shown above, but she will also experience a good deal of discomfort which she needs to tolerate if she is to integrate her rational beliefs into her belief system. For example, she will frequently not feel comfortable about doing something, but she needs to do it anyway; she will often not feel confident about doing something, but if she does it unconfidently and keeps doing it unconfidently, then the confidence and the integration will come.

Also, it is in the nature of change that there will be a period where your client, if she is in the process of integrating the rational solution, will feel unnatural or as if she is 'not herself'. Again if she understands and is willing to tolerate this state of 'feeling all wrong' while continuing to work towards integration, then this state will pass and she will begin to feel natural with her newly integrated rational beliefs. Here is how I dealt with this issue with Carol.

WINDY: Let's consider a different, but related issue. As I've just shown you, there is an aspect of the integration process that involves tolerating tedium. There is unfortunately another aspect that involves tolerating discomfort . . . (*seeing Carol cringe*), I thought you'd like that.

CAROL: You really are the bearer of glad tidings.

WINDY: I know. But this is what I mean. If you needed to do something that would help you to integrate the rational solution, but which was difficult for you, what would happen if you waited to feel comfortable when you did it before you actually did it?

CAROL: I wouldn't do it.

WINDY: Why not?

CAROL: Because no matter how long I wait, I'm not going to feel comfortable until I've done it many times.

WINDY: That's exactly right. Now let's suppose you lacked the confidence to do it; what would happen if you told yourself that you would only do it when you felt confident about doing it?

CAROL: I wouldn't do it for the same reasons. Confidence comes after you do things, not before.

WINDY: That's why I said that you will need to put up with and go through discomfort and you will need to do things unconfidently if you are to integrate the rational solution into your belief system. Now there's one more issue that is relevant to this point.

CAROL: I thought you might say that!

WINDY: You know me, good news is my middle name! Anyway, let's suppose that you do begin to integrate the rational solution, do you think that this will be a comfortable process?

CAROL: I'm not sure.

WINDY: Well, if you're used to operating according to your irrational beliefs so that it is a habit, will beginning to operate on your rational beliefs be natural to you?

CAROL: Oh, I see what you mean. No, it won't. It'll seem strange to me.

WINDY: That's right. It'll seem strange because you're not used to it. You might even feel 'phoney' as some people say, because the 'real' you, if we can call it that for the moment, is used to thinking and acting irrationally in this area.

CAROL: Right.

WINDY: Now, is it best to stop at that point or to keep going even though you feel strange?

CAROL: It's best to keep going.

WINDY: Why?

CAROL: Because by doing so you will become natural later when the rational beliefs become more habitual.

WINDY: (*humorously*) Now, that's not so bad is it?

CAROL: (*humorously*) No, doctor!

UNDERSTANDING AND DEALING WITH OBSTACLES

No matter how well you prepare your client for the exigencies of the integration process, and no matter how skilful you are as a brief REBT therapist, there will still be obstacles to integration during this phase of brief therapy. As Albert Ellis (1985) has noted, obstacles to integration can be due mainly to client variables, to therapist variables, to the interaction between client and therapist variables, or to other factors, and the interested reader should consult Ellis's text for a thorough discussion of this important clinical issue. As far as we are concerned here, it is important to bear in mind that obstacles to integration will probably occur with all your clients and that you should strive to identify and deal with such obstacles in an accepting manner. Here is how I introduced this issue with Carol.

WINDY: Now, Carol, do you think that the integration process will go smoothly, without any hiccups, and that you will always do your homework assignments?

CAROL: I hope so.

WINDY: But do you think that it will be like that?

CAROL: I doubt it.

WINDY: Why do you doubt it?

CAROL: Well, because it sounds as if this integration, like the course of true love, never runs smoothly.

WINDY: Right, and that's because we are human and we bring our problems to therapy and the integration process. So, if we are realistic, at some point we will confront some obstacle to your integrating the rational solution. When that happens it is important that we should investigate together the source of the obstacle and plan a way over or around it. What do you think of that?

CAROL: Once again it makes sense to me. I like it.

OUTLINING YOUR RESPECTIVE ROLES

Your client is now ready to hear what your respective tasks are in this part of the brief therapy process. Simply, your tasks are as listed in Table 6.1.

As you will see in Table 6.2, your client's tasks in the integration process are complementary to your own in this process.

Since you have already discussed these points with your client, I suggest that you give her a list of her tasks and a list of your tasks as they appear in Tables 6.1 and 6.2 as a stimulus for discussion. (You will, of course, wish to use your own words.) This is what I did with Carol, as shown below.

WINDY: Would you like a summary of the points we have covered about the integration process?

Table 6.1: The Therapist's Tasks in the Integration Process

1. To ensure that you cover the basic differences between your client understanding the rational solution and her integrating it into her belief system until she grasps this point.
2. To encourage your client to develop a large number of persuasive arguments against her irrational beliefs and a similarly large number in support of her rational beliefs.
3. To ensure that you present rational ideas in such a way that your client will remember them when she needs to use them.
4. To encourage your client to dispute her irrational ideas in a forceful and energetic manner.
5. To encourage your client to act on her rational beliefs again in a forceful and energetic manner.
6. To encourage your client to undertake the repetitive use of homework assignments on a regular basis and to persist with this even when she is receiving no immediate benefit from doing so.
7. To encourage your client to do things uncomfortably and unconfidently until she becomes comfortable and confident in doing so and to put up with feeling unnatural during the integration process.
8. To help your client to identify and deal with obstacles to integration.

Table 6.2: The Client's Tasks in the Integration Process

1. To see that there is a basic difference between understanding the rational solution and integrating it into her belief system.
2. To develop a large number of persuasive arguments against her irrational beliefs and a similarly large number in support of her rational beliefs.
3. To commit herself to remember her rational beliefs and to remind herself of them when she needs to practise them.
4. To dispute her irrational ideas in a forceful and energetic manner.
5. To act on her rational beliefs again in a forceful and energetic manner.
6. To undertake the repetitive use of homework assignments on a regular basis and to persist with this even when she is receiving no immediate benefit from doing so.
7. To do things uncomfortably and unconfidently until she becomes comfortable and confident in doing so and to put up with feeling unnatural during the integration process.
8. To help the therapist identify obstacles to integration and to deal with them.

CAROL: That would be very helpful.

WINDY: I've written them in the form of tasks. On this form (*hands Carol the list of therapist's tasks*) is a list of my tasks as I see them and on this sheet (*hands Carol the list of the client's tasks*) is a list of your tasks as I see them. Why not read them over and then we can discuss them.

CAROL: This is a good summary of what we discussed together.

WINDY: Good. Are there any of the tasks that I have in this phase of therapy that you don't understand?

CAROL: No, they seem quite clear and to use that overworked phrase, they make sense.

WINDY: Do your tasks make sense to you as well?

CAROL: Yes, they do.

WINDY: Good. Now, I'm prepared to commit myself to carrying out my tasks, are you prepared to commit yourself to carrying out yours?

CAROL: Yes, I am.

WINDY: Good, now let's make a start with helping you to integrate the rational solution into your belief system so that it helps you to leave things unfinished when it is in your interests to do so.

In this chapter, I have focused on the important issue of preparing your client for the integration process by helping her to understand what is involved for both of you in this process. In the next chapter, I will discuss ways that you can facilitate the integration process inside therapy sessions.

7

HELPING CLIENTS TO INTEGRATE THE RATIONAL SOLUTION: I. INSIDE THERAPY SESSIONS

In this chapter, I will describe and illustrate several techniques that you can use with your client in therapy sessions to help her to integrate the rational solution into her belief system. I should point out at the outset that these techniques can all be employed by your client outside therapy sessions, but they are first used inside these sessions. There are many techniques that you can choose to employ in therapy sessions with your client which will facilitate the integration process. However, to describe and illustrate them all is beyond the scope of this present volume. (The interested reader is advised to consult McMullin (1986) and Bernard and Wolfe (1993) for a description of a large variety of such techniques.) What I will do in this chapter is to describe and illustrate the methods that I use most frequently in brief REBT to facilitate the in-session integration process. To this end, I will discuss and demonstrate how to use the following techniques: (i) the rational portfolio; (ii) rational-irrational dialogues; (iii) rational-emotive imagery.

THE RATIONAL PORTFOLIO

As I mentioned in the previous chapter, it is important to help your client to develop a large number of persuasive arguments against her irrational belief and a similar number in favour of her rational belief. I normally initiate the integration process by using this technique (which I call the rational portfolio) because I have found it to be important to have my client lay down a solid foundation of arguments to support the internalization of her rational belief. I have already discussed the rationale for this technique in Chapter 6, so I will demonstrate how to use it by giving examples from my work with Carol.

You will recall that Carol's irrational beliefs about finishing a task that she had started contained a primary must (i.e. 'I must finish a task once I've started it') and a secondary LFT belief (i.e. 'I can't stand leaving a task unfinished'). To illustrate the rational portfolio technique I will present and comment on the work that I did with Carol in helping her to develop persuasive arguments against her must and a similar number of persuasive arguments in support of her preference. Separately, I did help her to do a similar job on her secondary LFT and HFT beliefs, but I will not report this work here. Although I helped Carol to develop a separate rational portfolio of arguments for her primary musts/preferences and her secondary LFT/HFT beliefs, it is possible to use this technique with the primary and secondary (irrational and rational) beliefs taken together.

Helping Clients to Develop Arguments Against Irrational Beliefs

In this section, I demonstrate how I worked with Carol to elicit her persuasive arguments against her irrational belief, while in the next section, I will show how I helped her to develop persuasive arguments in support of her rational belief. It is important to keep these tasks separate at first and the reason I begin with weakening the hold of the client's irrational belief before moving on to strengthen her rational belief is that this mirrors the order in which integration of the rational solution normally occurs, at least in my experience. It is also the order which makes most sense to the majority of clients. However, if some of your clients are, in your opinion, likely to derive more benefit from beginning with addressing the rational belief, by all means begin this way. As with other therapeutic issues in brief REBT, it is valuable first to check out your hunch with the client concerned. Here is how I helped Carol to develop arguments against her primary irrational belief.

WINDY: I'd like to help you to take the first step in integrating the rational solution into your belief system so that you can reach your goals. OK?

CAROL: Fine. What did you have in mind?

WINDY: Well do you remember that I stressed the importance of developing a large number of arguments against your irrational beliefs and an equally large number in support of your rational beliefs?

CAROL: Yes, I do.

WINDY: Well, in my experience this is a good place to start in helping you to integrate your rational beliefs. So are you ready?

CAROL: As ready as I'll ever be.

WINDY: Good. Now, I suggest that you take a piece of paper because it's helpful to keep a written note of the points that you'll be making as you develop what I call a rational portfolio of arguments to underpin your rational belief.

Now let's start with your irrational belief about finishing a task, which I'll write up on this whiteboard. Can you phrase it in your own words?

CAROL: Once I've started a task, I must finish it before I do anything else.

[Note that Carol decided to put this irrational belief in a fairly general form. Because I think she is able to work at this general level and will derive benefit from doing so, I decide to proceed at this level. If I had my doubts on this point, I would suggest that she state her irrational belief in a specific form related to the knitting scenario that she identified at the outset of her work on her target problem.]

WINDY: OK. Now just write that at the top of your paper. Now, I want you to develop as many arguments as you can against that belief.

CAROL: Can I draw on the arguments that I used on the ABC form?

WINDY: Yes, of course.

[If your client experiences difficulty generating arguments against her irrational belief at this point, you can take Carol's suggestion and refer her to her rational responses on one of her ABC forms to start her off.]

CAROL: OK. Well, there's no law which states that I have to finish what I've started because if there was, I would have no choice but to finish it. But I do have a choice. So I don't have to finish it.

WINDY: That's a good empirical argument and one to write down . . .

[You will note here and below that when Carol makes an argument, I categorize it as either empirical, logical or pragmatic and one that classifies the belief as either flexible or rigid. However, I make no attempt to encourage Carol to develop arguments within a given category before moving onto another category. If I thought that she needed the additional structure of developing argument within rather than between categories, I would have encouraged her to do this.

Also you will note that I suggest that Carol writes down each of her responses. I will omit these suggestions from the remainder of the dialogue.]

. . . Let's move on to the next argument.

CAROL: As long as I believe that I must finish whatever I've started I won't have the flexibility to respond to issues that become more important, particularly in the longer term like getting to work on time.

WINDY: That's a good pragmatic argument.

CAROL: It's illogical for me to conclude that because I might prefer to finish a task once I've started it, I have to do it. As you've said, there's no logical connection between what I want and what I believe I must get.

WINDY: That's a good logical argument against your demand.

CAROL: Believing that I must finish what I've started will mean that I am constantly trying to catch up with myself and that I will always be vulnerable to arriving late at work. If this continues I will very likely be dismissed from my job and I really don't want such a thing to happen.

WINDY: That's another good pragmatic dispute.

I will end the dialogue at this point because I think that I have shown what is involved in encouraging your client to develop arguments against her irrational belief, and Carol's responses illustrate the kind of arguments that you are looking for from your client. Before I demonstrate the complementary activity of encouraging your client to develop a list of persuasive arguments in support of her rational belief, let me address a number of important points which relate to the generation of both types of arguments.

Prompt your Client

It is important to prompt your client if she is struggling without reward with developing salient arguments. Actually, it is no bad thing if your client does struggle with this assignment because it probably means that she is thinking for herself. However, if her honest endeavours do not bear fruit help her out. You will, however, have clients who are not used to thinking for themselves and who will give up very quickly at this task. Tacitly, these clients want you to do the work for them and it is crucial that you resist the temptation of doing so. First, you need to point out to such a client that he has given up too soon, then ask him to spend about five minutes thinking about it on his own. You might leave the room at this point since your presence may be an inhibiting factor as your client may be anxious about you seeing him struggle. After five minutes, offer suitable prompts to encourage your client to think for himself. Throughout this exercise, guard against doing too much of the work for the client.

Correct your Client's Errors

It is important to correct your client's arguments either when they are clearly wrong or when they do not address the point. For example, this is how I would have responded if Carol came up with the following incorrect arguments against her must about finishing tasks.

CAROL: If I believe that I must finish a task once I've started it, then my anxiety will help me to stop halfway.

WINDY: Let's see if that's correct. Can you remember that time when you stayed up quite late until you finished your knitting? Let's suppose you had decided to stop at 11; do you think that the anxiety that you would have felt would have helped you to stop or encouraged you to stay up until you finished it?

CAROL: I see what you mean. I guess I would have stayed up to finish it.

WINDY: So that isn't a good argument against your must.

CAROL: Yes I can see that.

Now this is how I would have responded if Carol had come up with the following irrelevant argument.

CAROL: As long as I believe that I must finish a task that I've started, then my bad luck will change.

WINDY: Tell me how believing that you must finish a task means that your luck will change?

CAROL: I guess it doesn't.

WINDY: Why not?

CAROL: Because there's no logical connection between the two.

Ask your Client to Complete the Task as a Homework Assignment

The final point that I want to make concerning this in-session task is that it is useful to leave the task uncompleted in the session and to encourage your client to complete the task as a homework assignment. Don't forget that one of your major goals in brief REBT is to encourage your client to put into practice outside therapy sessions what she has learned inside these sessions. Encouraging your client to complete the rational portfolio task as a homework assignment is one way of achieving this goal. Asking your client to develop a list with a minimum of ten arguments including the ones she developed in the session is a realistic goal. Here, you can tell your client that the arguments don't have to be completely separate, but if possible they do need to have a distinct meaning in the client's mind.

Helping Clients to Develop Persuasive Arguments in Support of Rational Beliefs

Having helped your client to get started on the task of developing arguments against her irrational belief and suggested that she complete this task as a homework assignment, you are now ready to help her to develop a list of arguments in support of her rational beliefs. As you will discover, this task does overlap to some degree with the previous task, but it also involves the development of new arguments. Even if there is a high degree of overlap between the two tasks, it is still worth keeping the tasks separate for the following reason. Developing arguments against an irrational belief helps the client to weaken the impact of that belief, whereas developing arguments in support of the alternative rational belief helps your client to strengthen her conviction in this belief. At different points in brief REBT, your client will need to call upon these different, albeit overlapping, skills. Let me now show how I helped Carol to develop arguments in support of her rational belief.

WINDY: Now, I'd like to help you to take the next step in integrating the rational solution into your belief system and this involves developing persuasive arguments in support of your rational belief. OK?

CAROL: OK.

WINDY: Good. Now, again I suggest that you take a piece of paper and make a note of the points that you develop in support of your rational belief. So, let me write your rational belief about finishing a task on the whiteboard. Can you phrase this in your own words?

CAROL: Once I've started a task, I would like to finish it before I do anything else, but I don't have to do so.

[Again note that Carol decided to put her rational belief in a fairly general form. This again guides the ensuing work for reasons that I have previously discussed.]

WINDY: OK. Now just write that at the top of your paper. Now, I want you to develop as many arguments as you can in support of this rational belief and again you can draw on the arguments that you used on your ABC form.

CAROL: OK. Now, let's see. This belief is flexible and it thus provides me with a choice of what to do at the time. So, if I consider that it is in my interests to stop with the task unfinished, this belief allows me to do so, although I'll still feel uncomfortable about doing so. However, if I'm not going to suffer later by finishing the task there and then, this belief also allows me to finish it.

WINDY: That's a very good argument. It states that the belief is flexible and it also shows that it is consistent with reality or empirical. Next argument.

[Again, I classify the kind of argument that Carol is making concerning why her rational belief is, in fact, rational. As before, I do this after every argument that she comes up with.]

CAROL: Well, it would be nice if I could finish every task that I start without stopping and get away with it, but believing that I don't have to do so is much more sensible than believing that I have to. The connection between I'd like to finish it, but I don't have to finish it is not an illogical one, whereas the connection between I want to finish it and therefore I have to is clearly illogical.

WINDY: Right, that's a good logical argument. What's your next one?

CAROL: Well, if I believe that I'd like to finish a task, but I don't have to do so, then I'll be able to go to bed at 11 o'clock and increase my chances of turning up to work on time. This will allow me to pursue my career plan. So this belief is clearly in my best interests.

WINDY: That's a good pragmatic argument. Next.

CAROL: Well, this belief will lead me to have a greater sense of being in control of my life. At the moment my must leads me to finish things at times when it would be far better if I was in bed or doing something more productive. So at present I feel that my compulsion rules me. But believing that I don't need to finish a task in one sitting, although it might be nice if I did, means that I can pick and choose which task to leave and which task to finish. So the rational belief will help me to be more in control of my life than I feel now.

WINDY: That's another good pragmatic argument. Now as with your arguments against your irrational beliefs, I'd like to suggest that you finish this list as a homework assignment and we'll consider it next time. Again aim to develop a list with a minimum of ten arguments that may overlap with one another, but are distinct in your mind. Does that make sense?

CAROL: Fine.

As I mentioned earlier when I was discussing helping your client to develop arguments against her irrational belief, it is important to prompt your client when she becomes stuck at trying to develop persuasive arguments in support of her rational belief. Also, it is important to correct the errors that she makes in the session or in the arguments that she develops as part of her homework assignment.

Reviewing the Two Completed Lists of Arguments

At the beginning of the next session with your client it is important to review her two completed lists of arguments (one against her irrational belief and the other in support of her rational belief). As I will discuss in the following chapter, if you do not review your client's homework, then you communicate to her that you do not think that the assignment is important and it is likely that she will be quite influenced by this view. So make it a point to review the work that she has done on the two lists. As mentioned earlier, it is important that you correct any errors that your client has made in her arguments. It is worthwhile re-reading the material on p. 145 for an example of how to do this.

A second task that you have in reviewing your client's arguments is to help her to make these arguments more persuasive. This involves asking her if she can see ways of doing so for herself, drawing her attention to areas where more powerful points might be made and then asking her to make these points for herself, or making direct suggestions yourself concerning ways in which her arguments might become more influential.

Third, it is also important for you to elicit and deal with any doubts, objections or reservations that your client has about any of the arguments that she has generated. If you do not do this, then your client's doubt, objection or reservation will remain and this will prove to be an obstacle to her being able to integrate the rational solution into her belief system. I have found that it is best to elicit and deal with any doubts, objections or reservations clients have about any of their arguments after you have identified and corrected any errors in these arguments.

Here is an example of how to do this from my work with Carol.

WINDY: OK. Now, let me focus on an important issue. Do you have any doubts, objections or reservations about any of the arguments that you have developed?

CAROL: I'm not sure.

WINDY: Well, look down both lists and see if you want to answer back to any of the arguments as if you object to them for some reason. Am I making myself clear?

CAROL: Yes, I see now . . . (*looks down both lists*). Yes there are two here that I just found myself objecting to in some way.

WINDY: OK. Let's take them one at a time. First, tell which list the first argument is on.

CAROL: They're both on the against the irrational belief list.

WINDY: What's the first one?

CAROL: It's one that I developed here with you. I'll read it out to you: 'It's illogical for me to conclude that because I might prefer to finish a task once I've started it, I have to do it. As you've said, there's no logical connection between what I want and what I believe I must get.'

WINDY: What's your doubt, reservation or objection to that argument?

CAROL: Well, I don't find it very persuasive.

WINDY: Can you say why?

CAROL: Well, I can understand that there's no logical connection between wanting to finish something and believing that I have to do it, but it doesn't mean that much to me I guess.

[This is a common reaction to logical arguments. Your client can see the logic of a rational belief or the illogic of an irrational belief, but does not find such logical arguments very persuasive. However, there are clients who do find such arguments very persuasive. Thus, you should appreciate that there are individual differences concerning which type of argument your client will find most persuasive. That is why it is important to cover the different types of arguments until you discover which arguments your client will best be persuaded by. Then you may wish to highlight variations of such arguments in your work with your client. However, don't neglect any argument even if your client does not find it that persuasive. It still may add a little to the value of the rational portfolio even it does not add a great deal. In my experience, clients find pragmatic arguments the most persuasive and logical arguments the least persuasive.]

WINDY: You're not alone in that. Many people can understand the logical arguments, but don't find them that persuasive. However, it's still worth keeping them as a part of your rational portfolio because it adds a little to the overall value of the portfolio even though on its own it does not count for much in your mind.

CAROL: OK.

WINDY: Now let's go over the second item on your 'against' list that you had a reservation about.

CAROL: Well, I've written down here: 'As long as I believe that I must finish any important task that I've started, I'll be less effective in the future than I would be if I didn't believe this must.'

WINDY: OK. What's your reservation about that argument?

CAROL: I'm not sure that it's true.

WINDY: Well, let's see. What you could do is the following experiment. For a couple of weeks you can act on the belief that you must finish everything important that you've started, and then for the two weeks after that you could operate according to the rational alternative and see which belief leads you to be more effective. However, it's important that you keep a note of other outcomes as well, such as how tired and stressed you get, how early or late you get to work and things like that. And then as a result of that experiment, you need to judge what might happen over the long haul as a result of holding those two beliefs.

CAROL: Oh, I see. So, if I believe that I must finish what I've started, I might be more effective in the short term than if I believe and act on the rational alternative, but in the longer term I might become less effective because the other negative consequences might catch up with me.

WINDY: That's right. And even if you are more effective in the longer term by believing that you must finish what you've started, it still might not be worth it because, on the whole, the disadvantages from holding the irrational belief might outweigh the advantages.

CAROL: I'd never thought of that.

WINDY: So, might I suggest that you consider the advantages and disadvantages of both beliefs from both a short- and long-term perspective before you conclude which belief is healthier for you, all things taken into consideration.

[This is a useful technique to use when your client has doubts about the negative consequences of her irrational belief and the positive consequences of her rational belief.]

CAROL: I'm pretty sure how it will turn out . . .

WINDY: How?

CAROL: The rational belief will be better for me.

WINDY: Why not do the task anyway so that you can be sure.

CAROL: OK, I'll do that for next week.

Now that I have explained how to help your client to develop a rational portfolio, I will describe a second in-session technique which facilitates your client's integration of the rational solution into her belief system.

RATIONAL-IRRATIONAL DIALOGUES

In this section, I will show you how to use a series of techniques based on the idea that your client needs to engage in an ongoing dialogue between his rational and irrational beliefs, the purpose of which is to strengthen his conviction in his rational belief and weaken his conviction in his irrational belief. The rationale behind this technique is that one gains strength in struggling against adversity and just as in judo where you improve your skills by fighting increasingly more challenging opponents, your client can strengthen his conviction in his rational belief by learning to defend this belief against increasingly more difficult irrational challenges. It is hypothesized that engaging in dialogues based on this principle will help your client to integrate the rational solution into his belief system. I will demonstrate the dialogue techniques in this section in the order that I suggest that you introduce them into brief REBT.

The Zig-Zag Dialogue Form

Figure 7.1 outlines what I call the 'zig-zag' dialogue form. I call it this because the oblong boxes are positioned in the form of a zig-zag. This is how you use the form with your client.

First, you need to provide a rationale for its use. Here, it is important to stress that the form will allow your client to gain practice at strengthening her rational belief by attacking it with irrational arguments and responding to these irrational arguments with rational rebuttals until she cannot think of any more irrational arguments.

Having obtained your client's agreement to participate, you then instruct her in its use. These are the instructions you need to give her.

1. Write down your rational belief in the top left-hand oblong.

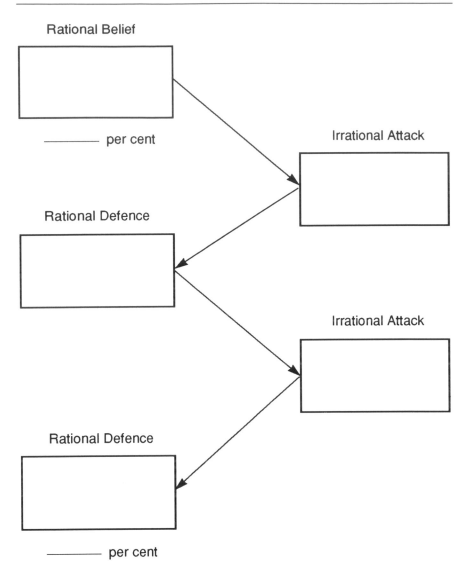

Figure 7.1: The Zig-Zag Dialogue Form

2. Rate your present level of conviction in this belief on a 100-point scale with 0 = no conviction and 100 = total conviction and write this rating down in the space provided on the form.
3. Respond to this rational belief with an irrational statement that is directed at the rational belief. This may take the form of a doubt, reservation or objection to the rational belief. Make this irrational

statement as genuinely as you can. The more it reflects what you actually believe the better. Write this irrational 'attack' down in the first oblong on the right.

4. Answer the irrational attack as fully as you can. Make sure that you respond to each element of the attack. Do so as persuasively as possible and write this rational defence in the second oblong on the right.

5. Continue in this vein until you have answered all your irrational attacks and cannot make any more. As you do this exercise, make your irrational attacks gently at first. Then when you find that you can respond to these attacks quite easily with rational defences, begin to make the irrational attacks more biting. Work in this way until you are really throwing yourself into making very strong irrational attacks. When you make an irrational attack, do so as if you want yourself to believe it. And when you mount a rational attack again throw yourself into it and again do so with the intention of demolishing the irrational attack and raising your level of conviction in the rational belief. Don't forget that the purpose of this exercise is to strengthen your rational belief so it is important that you stop when you have answered all your irrational attacks. Use as many forms as you need. However, if you make an irrational attack that you cannot respond to, stop the exercise and we will discuss how you can best respond to it.

6. Finally re-rate your level of conviction in the rational belief as before. If you have been successful at responding to your irrational attacks, then this rating will have gone up. If it has not increased or has done so only a little, we'll discuss the reasons for this.

Having given your client these instructions, encourage her to begin the exercise by writing her rational belief in the top left-hand oblong and by rating her level of conviction in this belief. Ask her to make two attacks and two defences on paper and then show these to you. Your role at this point and throughout this exercise is to encourage your client to keep to the point in her attacks and defences and to correct any errors that she makes during the exercise. Thus, if one of her attacks is, in fact, not an attack, bring this to her attention, discuss why she thought it was an attack, explain why it is not and help her to formulate an 'on-target' attack.

It is again helpful to leave the task uncompleted in the session so that your client might complete it as a homework assignment. If you do this, make sure that you check the assignment at the beginning of the following session.

The Two-Chair Rational-Irrational Dialogue

The two-chair rational-irrational dialogue is based on the same principle as the zig-zag dialogue form, i.e. it engages your client in a dialogue between her rational and irrational beliefs. However, where the zig-zag technique requires your client to put her dialogue in written form, the two-chair technique requires her to carry out the dialogue in verbal form.

As with the zig-zag technique, your first step is to provide your client with a rationale for the use of the two-chair rational-irrational technique. Again you need to stress that this technique will allow your client to gain practice at strengthening her rational belief by attacking it with irrational arguments and responding to these irrational arguments with rational rebuttals until she cannot think of any more irrational arguments. However, you need to tell her that this time she will be doing the task verbally. Furthermore, you need to explain that you will ask her to occupy one chair from which she is to defend her rational belief and then switch to another chair from which she is to attack her rational belief with irrational arguments.

Having obtained your client's agreement to participate, you then instruct her in its use. These are the instructions that you need to give her.

1. First, stay in the chair that you usually sit in during the therapy sessions and imagine that you are talking directly to another part of you seated in the second chair. This other part of you will be adhering to the irrational belief. Tell that other part of you what your rational belief is. Henceforth when you are sitting in the chair that you are seated in now, you will be defending your rational belief.

[I consider that it is important to ask your client to occupy her normal chair when she is defending her rational belief. Doing so allows her to associate that chair with rational thinking. Alternatively, if you ask your client to sit in her normal chair while taking the irrational part of herself, then there is the danger that she will associate that chair with irrational thinking. If this happens, then you will find it more difficult to encourage her to think rationally then you would if she defended her rational belief in her normal chair.]

2. Rate your present level of conviction in this belief on a 100-point scale with 0 = no conviction and 100 = total conviction and let me know what this rating is.
3. Once you have done this, move to the second chair and respond to this rational belief with an irrational statement that is directed at the rational belief. Talk directly to the you that is sitting in the rational chair.

As with the zig-zag technique, this may take the form of a doubt, reservation or objection to the rational belief. Make this irrational statement as genuinely as you can. The more it reflects what you actually believe the better.

4. Next, move back to the other chair and answer the irrational attack as fully as you can. Make sure that you respond to each element of the attack. Do so as forcefully and persuasively as you can.

5. Continue in this vein until you have answered all your irrational attacks and cannot make any more. As with the zig-zag technique, make your irrational attacks gently at first. Then when you find that you can respond to these attacks quite easily with rational defences, begin to make the irrational attacks more biting. Work in this way until you are really throwing yourself into making very strong irrational attacks. When you make an irrational attack, do so as if you want yourself to believe it. And when you mount a rational attack again throw yourself into it and again do so with the intention of demolishing the irrational attack and raising your level of conviction in the rational belief. Again realize that the purpose of this exercise is to strengthen your rational belief so it is important that you stop when you have answered all your irrational attacks. Swap chairs as many times as necessary. However, if you make an irrational attack that you cannot respond to, stop the exercise and we will discuss how best to respond to this attack.

6. Finally re-rate your level of conviction in the rational belief as before and let me know what this is. If you have been successful at responding to your irrational attacks, then this rating will have gone up. If it has not increased or has done so only a little, we'll discuss the reasons for this.

Having given your client these instructions, encourage her to begin the exercise by stating from her present chair her rational belief and by rating her level of conviction in this belief. Ask her then to move to the other chair to make an irrational attack on the stated rational belief and then to respond rationally to this attack from her original chair. Your role throughout this exercise is to encourage your client to keep to the point in her attacks and defences and to correct any errors that she makes during the exercise. Thus, if one of her rational defences does not address the irrational attack, bring this to her attention, discuss why she thought it was an adequate defence, explain why it is not and help her to formulate an 'on-target' response. You also need to encourage your client to be more forceful in making her rational defences than when making her irrational attacks. This is difficult for most clients since they are used to being forceful when irrational and tend to be mild in their rational responses. Consequently, clients need much encouragement, help and practice on this point.

The following interchanges show Carol using the two-chair rational-irrational dialogue technique. I have already provided Carol with a rationale for the use of this technique and have explained to her how to use it as described above.

WINDY: OK, Carol, will you state your rational belief.

CAROL: It would be nice if I finished a task that I have started, but I don't have to do this. I can choose not to finish a task when it is in my interests to leave it.

[It's a good idea to make a written verbatim note of this rational belief so that you can read it to your client at the end of the dialogue and have her re-rate her level of conviction in it.]

WINDY: Good. Now on a scale from 1 to 100 how much do you believe that now?

CAROL: About 50 per cent.

WINDY: Right, now move over to this chair and try to rip up that rational belief and get that rational side of you to think irrationally.

CAROL: (*changing chairs*) . . . That's pathetic; you have to finish what you've started, otherwise you'll never get anything done.

WINDY: OK. Change chairs and respond rationally to that idea.

CAROL: That's preposterous. I'll probably get more done in the long term if I consider my long-term interests and stop a task when it is time to go to bed for instance. Believing that I have to finish all important tasks that I've started is not good for me.

WINDY: Change chairs again.

CAROL: But if you set your store at finishing something then you have to finish it.

CAROL: (*changing chairs of her own accord*) . . . That's nonsense. You're saying that I have to get what I want, but I don't have to get what I want . . .

[Noticing that Carol's tone is quite mild here, I interject by saying the following:]

WINDY: Try getting that point over more forcefully. Raise your voice a little more.

CAROL: You're saying that I have to get what I want. But THAT'S DAMNED RIDICULOUS. THERE'S NO LAW OF THIS OR ANY

UNIVERSE THAT SAYS THAT I HAVE TO GET WHAT I WANT. I DON'T HAVE TO AND I'D BE WISE TO ACCEPT THAT.

WINDY: That was very good. Did the altered tone make a difference to how you felt?

CAROL: Yes, I did feel that I was getting through to myself.

WINDY: Good, now change chairs and continue . . .

Carol continued in this vein until she had run out of irrational attacks. At which point I said:

WINDY: Now rate your belief in your original rational belief which was: 'It would be nice if I finished a task that I have started, but I don't have to do this. I can choose not to finish a task when it is in my interests to leave it.'

CAROL: 85 per cent.

[At this point it is important to determine whether or not your client has any remaining doubt, reservation or objection about her rational belief that is interfering with her full acceptance of this belief. As a rough guide any rating below 75 per cent probably indicates the existence of such a doubt, etc. However, even if your client rates her level of conviction in her rational belief above 75 per cent, it is worth checking for the existence of a lingering doubt, reservation or objection.]

WINDY: Do you have any lingering doubts, reservations or objections to your rational belief?

CAROL: No, I don't believe I do. But I think that I need to do this exercise more so that I can get more practice defending my rational belief.

[Carol's response shows quite succinctly the major reason why she has not accepted her rational belief 100 per cent. She needs more practice integrating it into her belief system. Her response also indicates the importance of negotiating a between-session assignment to provide her with that practice. A useful technique which fulfils this requirement is known as 'tape-recorded disputing'. I will describe this technique by showing how I explained it to Carol.]

Tape-recorded Disputing

WINDY: I agree with you. I suggest that you use a technique called tape-recorded disputing. Do you have a tape recorder?

CAROL: I do.

WINDY: Good. Now what you do is this. First, you find a time and space when you won't be interrupted. Put your answer machine on or take the phone off the hook. You'll need about 20 or 30 minutes for this exercise. Take your tape recorder and record a similar dialogue to the one that you've just done. Start by stating your rational belief and make a note of your level of conviction in it. Then, try to get yourself to think irrationally by attacking your rational belief. Then, defend your rational belief by responding to the irrational attack. Proceed in this way until again you can think of no more irrational attacks. Then re-rate your level of conviction in your rational belief. You might find it useful to use two chairs as you did today, although this is up to you. Is that clear?

CAROL: Perfectly.

WINDY: Try to keep to the point and make your rational defences more forcefully than your irrational attacks. Listen to the tape afterwards and make a note of other more persuasive ways of defending your rational belief and use these arguments the next time that you practise tape-recorded disputing. I suggest that you do this three times between now and next week. Will you agree to do this?

CAROL: Yes, I will. I think that's a great idea.

WINDY: Bring one of the tapes next time and I'll give you feedback on it. Agreed?

CAROL: Agreed.

When you give your client feedback on her tape-recorded dialogue, it is important to correct her errors and listen, in particular, for times when her irrational attacks were more forceful than her rational defences. If you discover such episodes, explore with your client the reason for this. If it is just a matter of differential force, urge her, in future, to be more forceful when defending her rational belief. However, if this can be explained by an implicit doubt, reservation or objection to her rational belief, deal with this until you have helped her to dispel the doubt, etc.

Devil's Advocate Disputing

Devil's advocate disputing is similar to the other dialogue techniques described thus far in that your client's role is to defend her rational belief against attack. However, it differs in that you adopt the role of devil's advocate, putting arguments to your client based on her irrational belief. This technique should be introduced when your client has already developed some expertise at defending her rational belief against her own irrational attacks that she launched in one of the other rational-irrational dialogue methods already described.

Once again it is important to begin by providing your client with a rationale for the use of devil's advocate disputing. Remember to stress again that this technique will allow your client to gain practice at strengthening her rational belief by making rational rebuttals to your irrational arguments until she has answered all of them.

Having obtained your client's agreement to participate, you then instruct her in its use. These are the instructions you need to give her.

1. State your rational belief.
2. Rate your present level of conviction in this belief on a 100-point scale with 0 = no conviction and 100 = total conviction and tell me what this is.
3. I'll then respond to this rational belief with an irrational statement that is directed at the rational belief. This may take the form of a doubt, reservation or objection to the rational belief. My goal throughout this exercise is to try and make you think irrationally. Your goal is to rebut my attacks until they have all been adequately answered.
4. Answer each irrational attack as fully as you can. Make sure that you respond to each element of the attack and do so as persuasively as possible.
5. We will continue in this vein until you have answered all of my irrational attacks and I cannot make any more. I'll make my irrational attacks gently at first. Then I will make the irrational attacks increasingly more biting. We will work in this way until you can respond very forcefully to my very strong irrational attacks. When you make a rational defence, really throw yourself into it and again do so with the intention of demolishing my irrational attack and raising your level of conviction in the rational belief. Again, the purpose of this exercise is to strengthen your rational belief so it is important that we stop when you have answered all of my irrational attacks. If I make an irrational attack that you cannot respond to, we'll stop the exercise and we will discuss how you can best respond to it.
6. Finally re-rate your level of conviction in the rational belief as before and tell me what this is. If you have been successful at responding to my irrational attacks, then this rating will have gone up. If it has not increased or has done so only a little, we'll discuss the reasons for this.

Having given your client these instructions, encourage her to begin the exercise by stating her rational belief and by telling you her conviction rating. Then attack her belief and see how she responds. In addition to attacking her rational belief, your role at this point and throughout this exercise is to encourage your client to keep to the point when she makes her rational defences and to correct any errors that she makes during the exercise. Thus, if one of her defences is, in fact, not a defence, bring this to her attention, discuss why she thought it was an adequate defence, explain why it is not and help her to formulate an 'on-target' defence.

The following is how I employed devil's advocate disputing with Carol. I have already explained its rationale to her and described how we will proceed.

WINDY: OK, Carol, state your rational belief and give it a conviction rating.

CAROL: It would be preferable if I finished a task that I have started, but I don't have to finish it. I can choose to leave a task unfinished when it is in my interests to leave it. The rating is 80 per cent.

WINDY: Right, now I'm going to attack it. It's not just preferable to finish a task. It's absolutely necessary to do so.

CAROL: No, it's not. It only reflects what I would ideally like. And what I'd ideally like is hardly necessary. If it was I'd have to do it and there's no law of the universe to say that.

WINDY: That's all very well in theory, but in the real world you have to finish what you've started.

CAROL: That's not true. Because in the real world, as you call it, there's still no law which states that I have to finish what I've started. If there was, then I'd have no choice. I'd be a puppet and that's clearly not the case. So there's only evidence of what I would like to happen, not what has to happen.

WINDY: But leaving a task unfinished is lazy and you absolutely must not be lazy.

CAROL: It's not lazy to leave a task unfinished. It's good sense to do it sometimes.

WINDY: (*stepping out of role*) . . . Let's pause there for a moment, Carol. While you were right to challenge the inference that leaving a task is lazy, it's still important to dispute the idea that you must not be lazy. Otherwise, you will still be vulnerable to completing an unfinished task when it's not good for you to do so if you were to think that you were, in fact, being lazy by leaving it. Let me show you how to deal with that attack. You attack me with that statement and I'll respond to it.

[It's often very useful to swap roles with your client at certain points in the devil's advocate dialogue when you want to show your client how to deal with an irrational attack that she either cannot respond to or responds to incompletely.]

CAROL: But leaving a task unfinished is lazy and you absolutely must not be lazy.

WINDY: First of all, leaving a task unfinished is not necessarily lazy. Stopping my knitting at 11 o'clock to go to bed so that I can get to work on time the next morning is not laziness, but good sense. However, even if leaving a task unfinished is being lazy, there's no law of the universe which states that I must never be lazy. I'm a fallible human being who can make the error of laziness. It may be wrong to act lazily, but there's no reason why I must never make mistakes . . . (*coming out of role again*) . . . So, Carol, do you see what I've done here?

CAROL: Yes, you first challenged the idea that leaving a task unfinished is laziness. Then, you assumed that it might mean this and you disputed the demand that you must never be lazy.

WINDY: Good. Let me use that same attack and you defend it.

[After switching roles with your client to demonstrate how to respond to a particular irrational attack, it is useful to assume the devil's advocate role again and have your client resume the rational role so that she can practise the response that you modelled for her.]

WINDY: But leaving a task unfinished is lazy and you absolutely must not be lazy.

CAROL: Not finishing a task is not always being lazy. Sometimes it's a very good idea to do so. However, even if not finishing a task is being lazy, there's no reason why I must never be lazy. I'm an ordinary mortal who makes mistakes at times. If there was a law of the universe which states that I must never make mistakes then I would never make mistakes. But being fallible means making errors at times which disproves my must.

WINDY: Excellent. Here's my next attack . . .

Carol and I proceeded in this way until she had answered all my attacks and any further attacks would have been repetitions of the ones that I had already made. I then asked her to re-rate the level of conviction in her original rational belief which in this case went up to 90 per cent.

Having described and demonstrated the use of a variety of rational-irrational dialogue techniques, I will now consider the use of two versions of an imagery method known as rational-emotive imagery.

RATIONAL-EMOTIVE IMAGERY (REI)

In this section I will deal with two versions of rational-emotive imagery (REI) and illustrate their use with my work with Carol.

As with the other techniques described in this section, REI is used primarily to help your client to integrate the rational solution into her belief system. It is best seen as an emotive-imagery technique in that it asks clients to use their imagery modality in a powerful, emotive way as we shall see.

My own practice is to employ rational-emotive imagery after using the various dialogue techniques that I described in the previous section. I prefer this order because the dialogue techniques help your client to gain proficiency at developing rational responses to irrational arguments. Such proficiency will help your client to get the most out of REI.

Since the rationale for both versions of REI is the same let me outline this before describing each version, in turn. When stating the rationale for REI, it is once again important to stress that this technique is designed to help your client integrate her rational beliefs into her belief system. Explain that it draws on the capacity of humans to use their imagination for better or for worse. Thus, you can explain that frequently we use our imagination to disturb ourselves. Thus, we may imagine a negative activating happening and bring our irrational beliefs at B to this imagined A, thus creating our emotional disturbance at C. In this way, you can stress to your client, we practise disturbing ourselves. However, if we use our capacity for imagery for worse, we can also use it for better. Thus, while imagining the same negative event at A, we can practise thinking rationally about it at B and thus create a more healthy emotional and behavioural response at C.

Having outlined the rationale for REI, let me now describe the version of rational-emotive imagery recommended by Albert Ellis (Maultsby & Ellis, 1974).

Rational-Emotive Imagery: Ellis's version

I will illustrate how to use Ellis's version of REI by showing you how I used it in my work with Carol. In doing so I will outline the steps that you need to take when using this version of REI. In my experience, REI is more effective when your client is asked to imagine a very specific A rather than one that is more general. This explains why I select Carol's original A in the following dialogue.

WINDY: Close your eyes and vividly imagine that it is 11 o'clock and you are only half way through your knitting and let me know when you have done this.

[Step 1: Ask your client to imagine a specific A.]

CAROL: OK.

WINDY: Now see yourself continuing to knit past the 11 o'clock deadline that you have given yourself. Let me know when you can see this.

[Step 2: Ask your client to feel her unhealthy negative emotional C or see herself act according to her self-defeating behavioural C, while still imagining the same A.]

CAROL: OK, I've got that.

WINDY: Now while still vividly imagining that it's 11 o'clock and the knitting is still unfinished, see yourself stopping the knitting and going to bed. Again, let me know when you've changed that in your mind's eye.

[Step 3: Ask your client to change C to something relevant, but more healthy, while still imagining A.]

CAROL: Fine.

WINDY: Now, how did you change your reaction from continuing to knit to stopping knitting and going to bed?

[Step 4: Ask your client how she changed her C.]

CAROL: I told myself that I didn't have to finish the knitting and that since it was in my interests to go to bed, I would.

[Step 5: Ensure that your client has changed her C by changing her irrational belief to a relevant rational belief. If not, correct her error and explain the importance of changing C by changing B. If you had to do this go back to step 1.]

WINDY: Now, do you think it would be useful to practise this technique between now and next week?

CAROL: Yes, that would be good.

WINDY: It's a good idea to practise it three times a day for five or ten minutes each time. Would you agree to do that?

CAROL: OK.

[Step 6: Suggest that your client does REI for homework and negotiate accordingly.]

In the Ellis version of REI, your client gains practice at changing C by changing B indirectly. In the version of REI developed by Maxie Maultsby (Maultsby & Ellis, 1974), as you will very soon see, your client gains practice at changing C by changing B much more directly.

Rational-Emotive Imagery: Maultsby's Version

I will illustrate how I employ Maultsby's version of REI by showing you how I would have used it in my work with Carol had she not been able use the Ellis version. In doing so I will outline the steps that you need to take using this version of REI. As with the Ellis version, it is best to use the Maultsby version of REI with a very specific A.

WINDY: Close your eyes and vividly imagine that it is 11 o'clock and you are only half way through your knitting and let me know when you have done this.

[Step 1: Ask your client to imagine a specific A.]

CAROL: OK.

WINDY: Now see yourself continuing to knit past the 11 o'clock deadline that you have given yourself because you are telling yourself that you absolutely have to finish it. Let me know when you can see this.

[Step 2: Ask your client to keep imagining the same A and to feel her unhealthy negative emotional C or to see herself act according to her self-defeating behavioural C because she is rehearsing her irrational belief.]

CAROL: OK, I've got that.

WINDY: Now while still vividly imagining that it's 11 o'clock and the knitting is still unfinished, tell yourself that you don't have to finish it and that since it is in your longer term interests to do so, you are going to bed. Then see yourself stopping the task and going to bed. Let me know when you have done this.

[Step 3: Ask your client to continue to imagine A and to practise her rational belief so that she can see herself changing her emotional or behavioural C.]

CAROL: Fine.

WINDY: Now, do you think it would be useful to practise this technique between now and next week?

CAROL: Yes, that would be good.

WINDY: It's a good idea to practise it three times a day for five or ten minutes each time. Would you agree to do that?

CAROL: OK.

[Step 4: Suggest that your client does REI for homework and negotiate accordingly.]

The reason I like to use Ellis's version in preference to Maultsby's version is that it puts a greater onus on the client to change her emotions and/or behaviour by changing her belief. However, the Maultsby version is a good technique for those who, for one reason or another, cannot use the Ellis version or do not benefit from it.

I have mentioned that your client can use several of these in-session techniques as homework assignments. In the following chapter, I will discuss the use of between-session techniques more fully.

8

HELPING CLIENTS TO INTEGRATE THE RATIONAL SOLUTION: II. OUTSIDE THERAPY SESSIONS

In this chapter, I will consider how to encourage your client to integrate the rational solution into her belief system. First, I will consider the place of behavioural techniques in the integration process and, in particular, the importance of using behavioural and cognitive techniques together. Second, I will discuss the use of emotive techniques in this part of the therapeutic process. Finally, I will discuss the major issues that you need to cover when negotiating and checking your client's homework assignments.

Although you can do much to help your client to internalize her rational beliefs within therapy sessions (as discussed in the previous chapter), what really determines the extent to which she will integrate the rational solution into her belief system is the amount and quality of the work that she does on herself between these sessions. As such it is important to take care when considering how to encourage your client to put her therapy-derived learning into practice in her everyday life. I will first discuss the use of behavioural techniques in brief REBT.

CONJOINT USE OF BEHAVIOURAL AND COGNITIVE TECHNIQUES

Stated quite baldly, unless your client acts in a way that is consistent with her rational belief and against her irrational belief, she will not integrate the rational solution into her belief system, although she will still understand why her rational belief is rational and why her irrational belief is irrational.

Thus, unless Carol actually stops working at tasks and leaves them un-finished when it is in her interests to do so, then she will not truly believe her rational belief. Indeed, it is important to guard against your client saying one thing (e.g. proclaiming a rational belief) and doing another (i.e. acting accord-ing her to irrational belief). For example, Carol could SAY that she doesn't have to complete a task once she has started it, while contradicting this by going beyond her personally set deadline to finish such a task.

Alternatively, a client might act according to her rational belief, but in some way undermine her conviction in this belief cognitively. For ex-ample, Carol might leave her knitting unfinished to go to bed on schedule at 11 o'clock, while telling herself that she is only doing this to please me and next time she will finish it without telling me.

It is for these reasons that REBT therapists encourage their clients to act according to their rational beliefs and to rehearse these beliefs at the same time. In addition, when reviewing activity-based homework assignments, REBT therapists take care to ask their clients what they were telling themselves at the time to determine whether or not they undermined their rational belief in some subtle way.

Encourage your Client to Act Rationally Repeatedly

As discussed in Chapter 7, repetition is an important ingredient in the integration process. The more your client acts in a way that is consistent with her rational belief and simultaneously rehearses that belief cog-nitively, the more she will facilitate the integration process. Thus, Carol will integrate the rational solution more quickly, for example, if she acts in a way that is consistent with her rational belief four times a week than if she does so once a week. Consequently, it is important for me to discuss the value of therapeutic repetition when negotiating homework assign-ments with her (see pp. 134–136).

Behavioural Assignments and the Hierarchy of Difficulty

REBT theory states that your client will benefit most if she fully exposes herself to situations about which she is most disturbed and practises thinking rationally in these situations. Indeed, if your client will agree to do this and is able to do so frequently, then she will get the most from REBT. However, in my experience most clients will not go to the top of their hierarchy of difficulty. If this is the case, I suggest that you ask her to do something that is 'challenging, but not overwhelming' for her. This means that she will do something in the mid-range of her hierarchy of difficulty. Try to avoid having her do something that is low on her hierarchy of difficulty since doing such tasks may reinforce her philosophy of low frustration tolerance (Ellis, 1985).

Carol initially refused to practise acting in accord with her rational belief about leaving tasks unfinished when it came to exercising at her local gym because doing so proved to be very high on her hierarchy of difficulty. Thus, I encouraged her to work in the middle of her hierarchy by doing such things as stopping her knitting half way through a pattern, leaving her tax return half completed, and stopping reading part way through a chapter. These were all tasks that, at the time of asking, she found 'challenging, but not overwhelming'. After she had completed these tasks, she was able to deal successfully with items at the top of her hierarchy of difficulty, including leaving half way through her gym exercise programme. I want to stress that all these tasks involved Carol acting in a way that was consistent with her rational belief about leaving tasks unfinished AND rehearsing her rational belief cognitively.

THE USE OF EMOTIVE TECHNIQUES

In REBT, emotive techniques are methods which your client carries out which fully involve her emotions. There are basically two types of emotive techniques: (a) those which are intrinsically emotive and (b) those which become emotive when additional force and energy are used in their application.

Intrinsically Emotive Techniques

Certain REBT techniques are intrinsically emotive for most clients. This means that when clients carry out these techniques they experience powerful (usually disturbed) negative emotions in doing so. Their task, then, is to use the skills that they have learned in therapy to make themselves undisturbed. For example, later in therapy, Carol agreed to undertake a 'courting discomfort' exercise with respect to her problem about being in debt. This problem stemmed from her compulsion to buy clothes. Thus, Carol agreed to go into her favourite clothes store and try on clothes that she really liked and refrain from buying them while tolerating the great discomfort that she would feel.

One of the most frequently used intrinsically emotive techniques in REBT is known as the 'shame-attacking' exercise. The purpose of this exercise is to encourage your client to do something 'shameful' in public while (a) accepting herself as a fallible human being for acting foolishly and (b) tolerating the discomfort of acting 'shamefully'. This technique is particularly useful for clients who are socially anxious or who are governed by the perceived views of others.

When suggesting a shame-attacking exercise to a client it is important to give a proper rationale for its use. However, this explanation can be adapted according the client you are working with. Thus, with one client who wanted to act more spontaneously in public, but was scared about the reactions of others, I stressed that it is an exercise that would help her to accept herself in the face of social disapproval and to break free of the constraining influence of others.

Having explained the rationale of this technique, it is important to stress the following to your client: (i) she should not do anything illegal; (ii) she should not do anything to alarm or be unfair to other people; (iii) she should not do anything which threatens her job or career prospects.

Late in therapy, Carol agreed to do the following shame-attacking exercise which related to her problem of responding to men whom she found attractive. Thus she agreed to tell a man whom she knew socially that she found him attractive while accepting herself for doing something 'shameful' and in the event that he spurned her advance. She also did so while tolerating the discomfort that she felt while telling the man about her feelings towards him.

Adding Force and Energy to the Conjoint Use of Behavioural and Cognitive Techniques

In the previous chapter, I discussed how your client can use force and energy in the rational-irrational dialogue methods that I described there. Your client can also add force and energy to the conjoint use of behavioural and cognitive techniques. An example of this is when your client rehearses her rational belief in a forceful and energetic manner while acting in a way that is consistent with this rational belief.

For example, Carol used force and energy in tackling her problem with snacking between meals which caused her to be overweight. Thus, she monitored her urge to eat chocolate when she was not really hungry while holding and smelling the chocolate (behavioural component) at the same time telling herself forcefully and with energy, 'I would like to eat this chocolate bar, BUT I DON'T DAMN WELL HAVE TO HAVE WHAT I WANT. If I want comfort, I can get it in a more healthy way.'

Having discussed how your client can use behavioural, cognitive and emotive techniques between sessions, I will now turn my attention to the issues that you need to consider when you negotiate and check homework assignments.

NEGOTIATING AND CHECKING HOMEWORK ASSIGNMENTS

Research has shown that clients who complete homework assignments between therapy sessions gain more from cognitive-behaviour therapy than clients who do not (Burns & Nolen-Hoeksema, 1991). Thus, encouraging your clients to carry out such assignments and reviewing what they actually did at the following session are important therapist skills in brief REBT.

Let me first discuss a few general issues concerning negotiating and checking homework assignments, before taking you through a homework form that I have devised.

General Issues

The first point to discuss with the person seeking help concerning homework assignments is a rationale for their use. This needs to be done very early in brief REBT so that the person understands that she is expected to do things to help herself outside as well as inside therapy sessions. This is best done in the first session when you are outlining the tasks that you and the applicant need to accomplish if brief REBT is to be effective (see Chapter 3, pp. 62–65).

However, if the person seems puzzled when you first try to negotiate a homework assignment with her, this probably means that she did not grasp this point when you first raised it. In this event, it is important that you reiterate the rationale for the use of homework assignments and discuss any doubts, reservations and objections that she may have about the place of these assignments in brief REBT. If the applicant refuses to do such assignments and thinks that they have no place in therapy, then she is not a good candidate for brief REBT and should be referred to a practitioner of a therapeutic approach that is more consistent with her preferences for therapy.

Second, it is important that you give yourself and your client plenty of time to negotiate homework assignments. If you negotiate these assignments with your client at the end of the therapy session then it is useful to allocate about ten minutes to doing so. It is easy to lose track of time in a therapy session with the result that you may find yourself with only one or two minutes remaining in which to negotiate suitable tasks that your client can do for homework. This is to be avoided, if at all possible. Thus, it is good practice to train yourself to pace the session in such a way that you begin to discuss homework assignments ten minutes before the end of a session. To do this you will need to keep one eye on the clock, which should be placed in such a position that you can do this.

Later on in therapy, you will probably negotiate certain assignments during the course of the session. If you do this, it is a good idea to go over what these assignments are at the end of the session and thus, you will still need to allocate an adequate period of time to carrying this out.

Thirdly, one of your tasks during the latter stages of therapy is to encourage your client to become her own therapist. One way of doing this is to hand over responsibility to your client for setting her own homework assignments. I will discuss this issue more fully in the next chapter and illustrate it in my work with Carol in the final chapter.

The final general issue that I wish to discuss with respect to homework assignments concerns the importance of reviewing them with your client. I suggest that you do so routinely at the beginning of the following session. This communicates to your client that you regard the completion of homework assignments as a central component of brief REBT and it indicates that you are interested in her progress. Conversely, failure to review these assignments routinely communicates that you regard them as having only peripheral importance in the therapeutic process and that you are not keenly interested in what your client is doing to help herself between sessions.

Using the 'Client's Homework Assignment Form'

The 'Client's Homework Assignment Form' which I use with my clients (one form per homework assignment) to increase the chances that they will do their homework assignments is shown on p. 172. In this section of the chapter, I will take you through the form and discuss the issues that arise at each point. Please note that items 1–7 are completed by your client after she has agreed to do the assignment (normally at the end of a therapy session) and items 8–10 are completed by her after she has completed the assignment. These three items are normally discussed with your client at the beginning of the following session.

CLIENT'S HOMEWORK ASSIGNMENT FORM

(Complete 1–7 with your therapist after you have agreed to do the assignment. Complete 8–10 after you have carried out the assignment)

1. THE ASSIGNMENT I HAVE AGREED TO DO:

2. THE PURPOSE OF THE ASSIGNMENT:

3. HOW OFTEN I WILL CARRY OUT THE ASSIGNMENT:

4. WHERE I WILL CARRY OUT THE ASSIGNMENT:

5. WHEN I WILL CARRY OUT THE ASSIGNMENT:

6. POSSIBLE OBSTACLES TO CARRYING OUT THE ASSIGNMENT:

7. HOW CAN I OVERCOME THESE OBSTACLES:

8. WHAT I ACTUALLY DID:

9. HOW I STOPPED MYSELF FROM CARRYING OUT THE
   ASSIGNMENT AS AGREED
   (If relevant):

10. WHAT I LEARNED FROM CARRYING OUT THE ASSIGNMENT:

1. Have your client make a written note of the assignment that she has agreed to do for homework.

When you agree a homework assignment with your client it is important that she writes down the nature of the assignment on the form. Otherwise, she may forget what the assignment is or she may change it in some way. Since even a small change in the nature of a homework assignment may dilute its therapeutic value, anything that your client can do to carry out the task as agreed is useful.

2. Have your client make a written note of the purpose of the assignment.

It is generally accepted that if your client understands the purpose of the homework assignment, she is more likely to do it than if she doesn't understand its purpose. Given this, it is important that you and your client keep her therapeutic goals very much in mind while negotiating the assignment. When she sees how carrying out the assignment will help her to achieve a particular goal (or goals), have her write this down on the homework form.

3. Have your client make a written note of the frequency with which she has agreed to do the task.

Within reason, the more frequently your client does a homework assignment, the more benefit she will derive from doing the task. So agree with her how often she will do the negotiated homework assignment and have her write this down on the form.

4. Have your client make a written note of where she will do the task.

The more specific your client can be in delineating the places where she will carry out the task, the more likely it will be that she will remember to do the task in the first instance and actually do it in the second instance. So agree with her where she will do the task and have her write these places down on the homework form.

5. Have your client make a written note of when she will do the task.

Following on from the above, the more specific your client can be in delineating the times when she will carry out the task, the more likely it will be that she will both remember the task and do it. So agree with her when she will do the task and have her write these times down on the homework form.

6. Have your client identify and make a written note of potential obstacles to carrying out the homework assignment.

It would be nice if your clients always carried out their homework assignments as negotiated, but sadly, this is not the case. Here, you need to encourage your client to identify possible obstacles to carrying out the agreed homework task and write these down.

7. Help your client to plan ways of overcoming the potential obstacles to carrying out the task and have her make a written note of these plans.

After helping your client to identify potential obstacles to carrying out the agreed homework assignment, you need to help her to discover effective ways of overcoming these obstacles. This may involve a period of brainstorming possible solutions followed by a careful assessment of each potential solution. Once you have helped your client to choose ways of overcoming the obstacles identified above which she can see herself using, have her write these down.

8. Ask your client to make a written note of what she actually did for homework.

Just because your client has made a written note of the agreed homework assignment including how often, where and when she will do it, it does not follow that she will do the task exactly as agreed. Consequently, it is important that you ask her to write down exactly what she did. If she does this, you can then explore with her any changes she made to the assignment and why she made these changes (see below).

9. Ask your client to make a written note of any ways in which she stopped herself from carrying out the homework assignment as agreed.

If your client did not attempt the assignment at all, it is important that you both understand the reasons for this. Your client should be encouraged to take the lead here by writing down the reasons why she did not attempt the task. If she is unsure about the nature of these reasons, you can have her complete the form shown on pp. 176–177.

Second, if your client attempted the task, but did not complete it, you need to explore the reasons why she stopped the task when she did. Third, as noted above, your client may have made slight modifications to the task as agreed. In all these circumstances, you need to help your client to identify, challenge and change any irrational beliefs that explained why she did not carry out the assignment exactly as agreed. Then, suggest that she carry out the task if it is still important that she do it as originally agreed.

10. Have your client make a written note of what she learned from carrying out the assignment.

While it is obviously important that your client should complete homework assignments as agreed, it is even more important that what she learned from doing these tasks is consistent with the rational solution to her problems. Asking her to write down what she learned from doing a particular task is a good way of monitoring her learning. If what your client has learned is inconsistent with the rational solution, then you need to discuss this with her and correct any misconceptions she may have about the task and the reason why she did it in the first place. Having done this, you might suggest that she re-do the assignment, while keeping the rational solution firmly in mind.

On the other hand, if the client has learned what you hoped she would, then you can suggest that she carries out another task to extend her learning and promote change on the target problem or core irrational belief (see Chapter 9) under discussion.

I have now described all the individual elements that comprise brief REBT. We are now ready to see how these elements are put together in the unfolding process of this approach to brief work. The remaining two chapters address this important issue.

Possible Reasons for not Completing Self-help Assignments

(To be Completed by Client)

The following is a list of reasons that various clients have given for not doing their self-help assignments during the course of therapy. Because the speed of improvements depends primarily on the amount of self-help assignments that your are willing to do, it is of great importance to pinpoint any reasons that you may have for not doing this work. It is important to look for these reasons at the time that you feel a reluctance to do your assignment or a desire to put off doing it. Hence, it is best to fill out this questionnaire at that time. If you have any difficulty filling out this form and returning it to your therapist, it might be best to do it together during a therapy session. (Rate each statement by ringing 'T' (True) 'F' (False). 'T' indicates that you agree with it; 'F' means the statement does not apply at this time).

1. It seems that nothing can help me so there is no point in trying. T/F

2. It wasn't clear, I didn't understand what I had to do. T/F

3. I though that the particular method my therapist had suggested would not be helpful. I didn't really see the value of it. T/F

4. It seemed too hard. T/F

5. I am willing to do self-help assignments, but I keep forgetting. T/F

6. I did not have enough time. I was too busy. T/F

7. If I do something my therapist suggests I do, it's not as good as if I come up with my own ideas. T/F

8. I don't really believe I can do anything to help myself. T/F

9. I have the impression my therapist is trying to boss me around or control me. T/F

10. I worry about my therapist's disapproval. I believe that what I do just won't be good enough for him/her. T/F

11. I felt too bad, sad, nervous, upset (underline the appropriate word(s)) to do it.   T/F

12. It would have upset me to do the homework.   T/F

13. It was too much to do.   T/F

14. It's too much like going back to school again.   T/F

15. It seemed to be mainly for my therapist's benefit.   T/F

16. Self-help assignments have no place in therapy.   T/F

17. Because of the progress I've made these assignments are likely to be of no further benefit to me.   T/F

18. Because these assignments have not been helpful in the past, I couldn't see the point of doing this one.   T/F

19. I don't agree with this particular approach to therapy.   T/F

20. OTHER REASONS (please write them).

9

DEVELOPING AND ENDING THE THERAPEUTIC PROCESS

So far in this book, I have focused on how to help your client with a single problem. The information I have given you applies whatever target problem your client is currently focusing on. However, your client is likely to have several problems for which she is seeking help and I have not yet addressed this and other issues that are usually considered under the rubric, 'case management'. In this chapter, then, I will consider the following 'case management' issues: (i) deciding when to move from one target problem to another; (ii) linking problems together so that one can identify and work with core irrational beliefs; (iii) dealing with obstacles to client progress; (iv) encouraging your client to be her own therapist; (v) dealing with relapse prevention; and (vi) ending the therapeutic process.

MOVING FROM ONE TARGET PROBLEM TO ANOTHER

As I mentioned above, it is very unlikely that your client will have only a single problem for which she is seeking help. Rather, it is more common that she will have several emotional and/or behavioural problems, as was the case with Carol (see Chapter 3). As I showed in Chapter 3, it is important to define all the problems that your client puts on her problem list and elicit her goals for each one. However, since it is unlikely that you will be able to help your client with all these problems in the brief time you have with her, it is important to encourage her to prioritize these problems. I stated in the earlier chapter that in the 11 sessions that you have with your client, you will only have time to focus in depth on two of her problems. However, as I will discuss later in this chapter, you will also have the time to help your client to see the link between her problems and to generalize her learning from the two target problems to her other problems.

Since your time is limited in brief REBT, it is important to use it wisely in dealing with the two target problems that your client has prioritized. What I tend to do is ask my client to select which of the two prioritized problems she wishes to concentrate on first. In doing so I emphasize that it is important that we stay with this problem until my client has made sufficient progress to allow us to concentrate our therapeutic efforts on the second problem. This does not mean that we have exhausted all our therapeutic efforts on the first target problem. As you will presently see from my work with Carol, this is certainly not the case. However, it does mean that we have probably 'broken the back' of the first problem. In a practical sense, I tend to move on to my client's second target problem when she has done some integration work on her first problem. For example, with Carol, I began to assess her second problem in session 5, after she had completed her rational portfolio on her first problem and after I had taught her how to apply the zig-zag technique to this problem.

It is very important that you explain to your client the rationale for remaining with the first target problem until she has initiated the integration process on this issue. While there are important exceptions to this rule, it is a major principle to which you both need to adhere if your client is to get the most out of brief REBT. The alternative, where you both deal with whichever problem is salient for your client for that particular week, is in my experience far less effective. If you take this latter stance, you will have the frustrating experience of assessing your client's problem at the end of one session and changing tack to address a new problem in the following session. If this develops into a pattern, which it easily can do as the client thinks this is how she is expected to proceed in therapy, then you will develop the sense that you are like the man in the circus who is trying to keep a number of plates spinning on their respective poles: everything is in play, but much activity is spent keeping everything that way with the inevitable result that all the plates eventually come crashing to the ground (i.e. no one target problem ever gets fully dealt with).

If you and your client agree to focus on a problem until you both have 'broken the back of it', then you will need to steer your client away from another problem that she is currently preoccupied with until she has done sufficient work on the first problem to justify moving on to the second. Unless your client fully understands the reason for your refusal to work on the new problem, adopting this stance could seriously threaten the therapeutic alliance.

While this principle helps to ensure that your client will develop sufficient skills to integrate the rational solution into her belief system on her
target problems, there are exceptions to this rule. Let me now deal with
them.

Changing Tack

As discussed above, the best and most obvious time to change tack and
focus your therapeutic efforts on a second target problem is when you
and your client have 'broken the back' of the first target problem.
However, there are other reasons to change tack and deal with a second
problem before your client has made much progress on the first problem.
The first reason to change tack is to preserve the working alliance. Here,
your client wishes to discuss a second problem before she has made
sufficient progress on her first target problem and will not accept your
rationale for remaining with the initial problem. If you press your client
on this issue when she clearly wishes to change tack then you may win
the argument, but lose the alliance. My advice under these conditions is to
change tack to preserve the working alliance.

When you change tack under these conditions, then it is important that
you and your client remain with the second target problem until you have
both 'broken the back' of it. If your client wishes to change back to the
original problem or to start discussing a third problem before she has
made sufficient progress on the second problem to warrant changing
tack, you should be aware that this may mean that your client is using
changing tack in this manner as an avoidance strategy, and you should
certainly be prepared to discuss this possibility with her. If you are correct
and your client concurs then you need to help her to identify and deal
with the irrational belief which underpins such avoidance behaviour. If
this is not the case, then you need to consider the possibility that your
client may not benefit from brief REBT and that you need to negotiate a
different type of therapeutic contract with her.

A second reason to change tack prematurely and move from your client's
first target problem to a second problem is that she is facing a crisis in the
second problem area. Thus, you may be working purposefully and with
some success with your client's anxiety about committing herself to her
relationship with a man, when she has just learned that she has been
reprimanded at work. Since work-related issues were on her original
problem list and the client is facing a crisis situation, then it makes good
clinical and common sense to change tack and deal with her second
problem.

The same is also true when your client experiences a crisis in an area which was not on her problem list. Thus, if your client arrived in a tearful state and related that her mother had just died, I hope that you wouldn't say something like: 'I'm very sorry to hear that, but we need to focus on your anxiety about your relationship with your boyfriend!' You would, of course, attend to her experiences relating to the sudden loss of her mother.

When your client experiences a crisis during therapy, sometimes you can deal with it quite quickly and return to the original focus of brief REBT. However, at other times you will need to abandon your original brief contract and negotiate a contract for longer work. For example, one of my clients was doing very well in brief REBT when she suddenly learned that she was diagnosed as having cancer. I immediately suggested that we changed the nature of her contract and I saw her regularly over a two-year period until she sadly died. It would have been heartless and cruel to have done anything else.

Here, as elsewhere, it is important that you be flexible and respond to the unique circumstances of your client. Remember that brief REBT is a means to an end, not an end in itself.

Changing Tack Later in Therapy

As I will discuss presently, as brief REBT progresses you will move away from a focus on problems to one which places greater emphasis on core irrational beliefs and client self-therapy skills. Thus, when your client has made significant inroads into dealing with her two prioritized problems and you have identified core irrational beliefs linking these problems with the other problems on her list, it is likely that your client can apply her newly acquired self-therapy skills to these other problems. If this is the case, then later in therapy you may change tack from one problem to the next, encouraging your client to apply her self-therapy skills to the problems as required. However, with other clients you will not get further than dealing with their two prioritized problems so that this does not become an issue.

LINKING PROBLEMS AND IDENTIFYING CORE IRRATIONAL BELIEFS

After you have helped your client to make progress on her two prioritized target problems, you can encourage her to look at other listed problems and look for links between them. A useful point to bear in mind

as you do this is the distinction made in REBT theory between ego disturbance and discomfort disturbance (see Chapter 1). These two concepts
may help you and your client to identify what are known in REBT theory
as her core irrational beliefs, if you cannot identify these from considering
her problem list and the irrational beliefs that account for the existence of
her two prioritized target problems. A core irrational belief is an irrational
belief that accounts for a number of your client's problems. As such it
tends to be general in nature.

Here is a guide to how you can assist your client to make links between
her problems and thence to help her discover her core irrational beliefs.

1. First, take the two prioritized target problems that you and your client
   have worked on so far in therapy and write these up on your
   whiteboard.
2. Second, write down on the whiteboard the irrational beliefs that account for the existence of these problems. Use the general form of these
   irrational beliefs (see Chapter 4 for an example of how to discover a
   general irrational belief from working on a specific example of your
   client's target problem).
3. Third, write down on the board a list of the remaining problems on
   your client's problem list.
4. Fourth, ask your client if she can see any link between her two prioritized target problems and her remaining problems. In particular,
   ask her to focus on the irrational beliefs that underpin her two target
   problems and to think whether or not they might be responsible for the
   existence of any of the remaining problems on her list. Use the distinction between ego and discomfort disturbance if your client experiences
   difficulty in identifying such beliefs.
5. Encourage your client to refine the wording of any beliefs that do
   account for the existence of two or more problems on her list. These are
   her core irrational beliefs.
6. Focus on your client's core irrational beliefs for the remainder of
   therapy if you can.
7. Take the problems that are not explained by the core irrational beliefs
   and, if you have time, help your client to assess and dispute the irrational beliefs that underpin these problems. However, it is likely that
   you may not have the time to accomplish this task. Remember that in
   brief REBT, you will frequently not have the time to cover all of your
   client's problems in depth and you will not have time to deal with
   some problems at all. However, if your client has learned the skills that
   she will need to become her own therapist, you can encourage her to
   use these skills with those problems which you have not dealt with

during brief REBT. Indeed, if you have helped your client (i) to make progress on her two prioritized problems; (ii) to identify and begin to change her core irrational beliefs; and (iii) to use her REBT skills to deal with her remaining problems after therapy has finished, you have, in my opinion, achieved your goals as a brief REBT therapist. Anything else you achieve, you can regard as a bonus. I will discuss how I helped Carol to find links between her problems and identify her core irrational beliefs in Chapter 10.

DEALING WITH OBSTACLES TO CLIENT PROGRESS

The course of brief REBT, like the course of true love, rarely runs smoothly. Consequently, it is important that you and your client work together to identify and overcome obstacles to her progress. A full consideration of this topic would necessitate a volume in its own right and indeed, Albert Ellis (1985) has written a book on this subject which interested readers should consult for a comprehensive discussion of the many factors that can block client progress.

What I will do here is to list some of the major obstacles to client progress (in Table 9.1) and argue that you can encourage your client to take the lead in identifying these obstacles so that you can both work together to overcome them.

When your client isn't making progress, then it is important that you both address this as openly as you can. Referring this issue to the reflection process (see Chapter 3) is perhaps the best approach to the problem. When you do so, you need to stress to your client, both verbally and, more importantly, by your therapeutic attitude that you are genuinely interested in her opinion about the reasons for her lack of progress. In particular, you need to encourage your client to criticize your work as a therapist, if she genuinely believes that the major source of her lack of progress resides in one or more therapist factors. In doing so you will need to be non-defensive and model self-acceptance. Hearing that your client experiences you as sarcastic or unhelpful, for example, is perhaps one of the most stressful aspects of being a therapist and to deal with this productively, you first need to work on developing your own self-accepting attitude; otherwise your client will spot your defensiveness and back away from being honest with you.

Having indicated that you are open to hearing such feedback, then you can give your client a copy of Table 9.1 and ask her to take the lead in identifying possible reasons for her lack of progress. You may well have

Table 9.1: Major Obstacles to Client Progress

Relationship Factors

- My therapist and I do not have a good working relationship
- My therapist and I are working at a different pace
- My therapist and I are talking at a different level of abstraction
- My therapist and I are working towards different goals
- My therapist and I seem to be at cross-purposes concerning what to do in therapy

Therapist Factors

- My therapist is unhelpful
- My therapist does not execute her tasks skilfully
- My therapist is demanding too much change in me
- My therapist is seeking my approval rather than attending to the work of therapy
- My therapist does not suggest that I put my therapy-derived learning into practice
- My therapist does not teach me the skills of self-therapy
- My therapist seems too inexperienced to help me
- My therapist is sarcastic
- My therapist doesn't understand me
- My therapist does not accept me
- My therapist is not genuine
- My therapist doesn't seem interested in my welfare
- My therapist is impatient with me
- My therapist doesn't explain what she is doing in therapy and/or why she is doing it
- My therapist does not explain what I am supposed to do in therapy and/or why I am supposed to do it
- My therapist is too easy on me in therapy

Client Factors

- I don't listen to what my therapist says to me
- I don't agree with this approach to therapy
- I don't bother to do any homework assignments
- This therapy is too hard for me
- I don't like/respect my therapist
- I am waiting for my therapist to cure me
- I enjoy talking about myself, but I don't want to do anything else that my therapist suggests
- I really want to be in long-term therapy, so if I don't improve quickly my therapist will have to see me for a longer period of time
- I don't believe that I can change, so there's no point in doing anything to help myself
- If I can get my therapist to accept me for long-term therapy, then I can continue to avoid my responsibilities in life
- I resent being in therapy
- I resent my therapist
- I just can't do the things that my therapist asks me to do

- My problems are too complicated to be dealt with in brief therapy
- I'm too disturbed to be helped in brief therapy
- I'm too lazy to help myself
- I'm ashamed to be in therapy
- Change should be easier than my therapist says that is
- There's nothing wrong with me, other people in my life should change
- It is my life situation that is the problem, not my beliefs about them

Environmental and Other External Factors

- People in my life are deliberately sabotaging my efforts to help myself
- People in my life are sabotaging my efforts to help myself, although they don't mean to
- If I achieve my therapeutic goals, then I will be worse off (at home, at work, etc.)
- I am only coming to therapy because someone in my life is making me come (e.g. spouse, boss, court). I wouldn't come if it was up to me

---

your own ideas about the source of the obstacle to your client's progress, but in brief REBT, it is best to wait to hear what your client has to say before sharing them. Doing so indicates to your client that you value her views and indicates that she can take the lead in identifying such blocks to change.

Dealing with the Identified Obstacles

Having identified an obstacle to client progress, the next step is to deal with it productively so that your client may move forward. How you and your client will deal with an obstacle depends, in part, on the source of that obstacle. As Table 9.1 shows there are four major sources of such obstacles: (i) relationship factors; (ii) therapist factors; (iii) client factors; and (iv) environmental and other external factors. However, before I consider how to deal with these different types of obstacles, let me make the following suggestions concerning how to deal with such obstacles in general.

1. Invite your client to identify the obstacle(s) to progress as she sees it/ them.
2. Ask her to give you one or two examples which illustrate the obstacle(s).
3. Ask her to suggest what needs to be done to overcome the obstacle(s).
4. Suggest possible ways of overcoming the obstacle(s) yourself.
5. Discuss with your client your respective suggestions and decide on a course of action which may involve a change in behaviour and/or attitude.

6. Implement the chosen course of action. This may mean that your client does something different, you do something different or a joint course of action is called for.
7. Evaluate the outcome of the course of action. If the action is successful your client should begin to make progress. If she does not, go back to step 1.

Let me now outline briefly the points you need to consider when attempting to deal with the four different types of obstacles to client progress.

Dealing with Relationship Obstacles to Progress

If your client identifies the major source of her obstacle to making progress as residing in the relationship that you have with her, strive to understand as clearly as you can where she thinks the trouble lies. Once you have identified the root of the difficulty, ask yourself what you can do to improve the working alliance between the two of you. It is important to bear in mind here that I am not suggesting that you adhere to a naïve principle of consumerism (as criticized by Ellis [1989]). Thus if your client thinks that her relationship with you will improve if you meet outside sessions, this is not a good enough reason to do so. However, if your client thinks that you are working at a pace which is too fast for her, this is useful feedback and something that you can implement without compromising therapeutic effectiveness and efficiency (Ellis, 1980). Thus, when your client gives you feedback about your relationship, consider the likely long-term impact of altering your contribution to the relationship. If you do not think that the change that your client is suggesting is in her long-term interests, explain why. You may help to correct a misconception about the therapeutic relationship. However, since your client may want a type of therapeutic relationship that you are not willing to offer, it may be best for you to refer your client to a therapist who will offer a therapeutic relationship that is consistent with what your client is looking for.

Since problems in a dyadic relationship involve two people, it is also important that you ask your client what she can do to improve the working alliance between you. Again it is important to encourage your client to be as specific as she can about her suggestions. This will enable you to give her constructive feedback on them and it will help her to put her own suggestions into practice.

In Chapter 3, I mentioned the importance of developing the reflection process whereby you and your client stand back from your interaction so that you can reflect on what has just transpired between you. When you and your client have identified threats to the working alliance and have developed ways of dealing with these threats, you can refer future threats to the reflection process so that you can implement your new strategies and reflect on their outcome.

Finally, you and your client can monitor the threats to your working alliance and your strategies for dealing with these threats at the end of each session as well as at the formal progress review if this is relevant.

Dealing with Therapist Obstacles to Progress

Many of the points outlined above with respect to dealing with relationship obstacles to client progress are relevant to dealing with therapist obstacles when they are identified by your client. Thus, when your client points to an aspect of your behaviour that she considers may be responsible for her lack of progress, you need to receive this information non-defensively and give serious consideration to its validity. If you think that your client's opinion does have merit, discuss this issue with her and modify your behaviour accordingly. Also, ask your client to give you ongoing feedback if she detects the same problematic behaviour in you so that you are aware of it as it happens and can modify it there and then.

However, you may consider that your client's view of your behaviour is more a reflection of one of her problems than it is of your actual behaviour. Don't forget that your client is likely to bring her problems to therapy and these may well colour the inferences she makes from your behaviour. If you consider that this might be the case, then you need to put it to her as a hypothesis to be considered. If she thinks that this hypothesis does have merit, then you can help her to identify, challenge and change the irrational belief that has given rise to her inferential distortion.

Finally, you might consider that an aspect of your behaviour and/or attitude that your client has not mentioned might be an obstacle to her progress. In which case, check this out with your client and modify this behaviour and/or attitude if she agrees with your hypothesis.

Dealing with Client Obstacles to Progress

If your client identifies an obstacle to her progress that resides within herself, then it is important that you check to see whether or not this obstacle is explained by an irrational belief. If it is, it is important that you help her to identify, challenge and change it. Assessing whether the obstacle is explained by the existence of an irrational belief isn't always an easy task. For example, let's suppose that your client states that the reason that she isn't making progress is due to the fact that she doesn't respect you; how can you judge whether or not this is based on an irrational belief? Here is one way of approaching this question.

THERAPIST: So, you are saying that the reason that you haven't been making progress is due to the fact that you don't respect me. How has that opinion affected your progress?

CLIENT: It has meant that I don't take on board what you've been saying to me.

THERAPIST: If you did respect me, do you think that you would take it on board more?

CLIENT: Yes, I think I would.

THERAPIST: OK, Let's look more closely at your opinion of me, which I guess can't have been easy for you to tell me about.

CLIENT: That's right. I had to pluck up courage to let you know how I felt.

THERAPIST: I'm pleased that you did. When did you start feeling this way about me?

CLIENT: About the fourth session.

THERAPIST: Was there anything that I did or said that contributed to your view or was it more to do with what I did not say or do?

CLIENT: Well, I got the feeling that you were more interested in practising therapy by the book than you were about helping me with my problems.

THERAPIST: Can you be more specific?

CLIENT: Well, you kept asking me what seemed to be the same type of questions over and over.

THERAPIST: How did you feel about my doing that?

CLIENT: Angry.

THERAPIST: What stopped you from telling me how you felt about my style of questioning?

CLIENT: I was afraid to.

THERAPIST: So am I right in assuming that you have been feeling angry and frightened for about three sessions?

CLIENT: Yes, that's right.

THERAPIST: Are these feelings related to your opinion of me?

CLIENT: Yes, I suppose they are.

THERAPIST: Well, let's see. Would you still not respect me (a) if you felt annoyed with my behaviour but not angry about it, and (b) if you were able to talk to me about how you felt about my behaviour?

CLIENT: I see what you mean. I still wouldn't like your behaviour, but I guess I wouldn't disrespect you.

THERAPIST: So how about if we consider the irrational beliefs that underpin your anger and anxiety?

CLIENT: OK.

Other client-based obstacles to client progress do not necessarily reflect the presence of irrational beliefs, but rather examples of A-C thinking. Thus, when your client says things like: 'There's nothing wrong with me, other people in my life should change' or 'It is my life situation that is the problem, not my beliefs about them', such statements indicate that your client is not taking responsibility for her own feelings. However, you should be aware that such statements may be defensive in nature and overlay a self-downing philosophy. For example, when your client says that there is nothing wrong with her and that other people in her life should change, to test the existence of an implicit self-downing belief, you might ask a question like: 'But, if there was something wrong with you how would you feel about that?' If your client's answer indicates the presence of an unhealthy negative emotion, then her original statement may well be ego-defensive in nature and you need to address yourself to any underlying irrational beliefs that she may have. However, if there is no unhealthy negative emotion present, then the original statement is simply an example of A-C thinking and should be dealt with as such.

Finally, a client obstacle to progress might indicate that your client may not be finding REBT helpful and this requires close investigation. If her view of REBT is based on a misconception of this approach to therapy, then you should correct this. However, another possibility might be that your client could benefit from a different approach to therapy. If this proves to be the case, then I suggest that you effect a suitable referral.

Dealing with Environmental and Other External Obstacles to Progress

In dealing with environmental and other external obstacles to client progress, you have three basic options. The first option is to involve the other people who are wittingly or unwittingly sabotaging your client's progress. If you have evidence that other people are unwittingly sabotaging your client's progress it is worthwhile considering inviting them to attend a therapy session so that you can help them to respond to your client in more constructive ways. Devoting one of your client's sessions to this issue can be, in my experience, time very well spent as the client's significant others realize the impact of their behaviour on the client and resolve to act in a more constructive manner.

I am much more hesitant to suggest that you involve significant others who are wittingly attempting to sabotage your client's gains in the context of your client's brief therapy. It is very unlikely that much productive work can come out of such an attempt in the course of one or two sessions and to devote more than two sessions to this kind of 'family' work is not appropriate in the course of individual, brief, 11-session REBT. So, if your client's significant others are wittingly sabotaging her progress, then you would be wise to consider making a referral to a skilled family therapist at the end of brief REBT.

Your second basic option in helping your client to deal with environmental and other external obstacles involves helping her to change what she can change and not to disturb herself about what she can't change. The first step in this process is to help your client to think rationally about the external obstacle as it exists at the moment. Then you can help her to develop a list of possible ways of changing the external obstacle. As part of this process, and particularly if the external obstacle is erected by another person or group of people, you might role play such change attempts and help to shape up influential strategies designed to neutralize the sabotaging attempts of others. If these attempts do not overcome the obstacle, the final attempt in this process is to help your client to think rationally about the continued existence of this external obstacle and to choose to remain in the situation in which the obstacle exists or to leave it if it is in her best interests to do so.

The third basic option you have in helping your client to deal with an environmental or external obstacle is to encourage her to leave or avoid the problematic situation. While this is not a preferred approach in REBT, it is something to consider when your client is not able to think rationally about the obstacle, and when it is not in your client's interests to remain in the situation in which the obstacle exists.

ENCOURAGING YOUR CLIENT TO BE HER OWN THERAPIST

I agree with Maxie Maultsby (1984) who has said that ultimately the effectiveness of REBT depends, in large part, on the ability of the client to develop and use rational self-help skills. This is something of a contentious issue in brief REBT. Since the time that you spend with your client is limited, you need to ask yourself, how you can help your client deal effectively with her prioritized problems AND teach her to become her own therapist. Maultsby's (1984) solution is to teach clients to master the skills of what he calls 'rational self-counselling' right from the outset. Thus, he is more concerned to help his clients learn these skills than he is with helping them overcome their prioritized problems. He will, certainly, deal with these problems, but is not as concerned as I am with keeping the therapeutic focus on these prioritized problems. Maultsby's work is important and I encourage interested readers to familiarize themselves with it.

My focus is different from Maultsby's in the sense that I am particularly concerned to help my clients be problem-oriented from the outset. I believe that doing so helps them to learn useful self-help skills more effectively than if we switched from problem to problem. The question concerning which approach is more effective in the long term is an empirical one and this question is well worth researching. Let me now outline how to help your client to become her own REBT therapist.

Encouraging Responsibility for Assessing and Dealing with Problems

When you first address your client's prioritized target problem, you will take her through a process with which she is unfamiliar. Therefore you will need to assume the lead in guiding her through the following steps:

1. Select a specific example of your client's target problem.
2. Identify C. This will be her most prevalent unhealthy negative emotion and/or self-defeating behaviour.
3. Identify your client's critical A.
4. Assess her irrational beliefs at A.
5. Help her to see the iB-C connection and realize that in order to change C she needs to change B.
6. Help her to dispute her irrational beliefs.
7. Help her to see that her rational beliefs are more likely to lead to her goals than her irrational beliefs.

8. Encourage your client to practise weakening her irrational beliefs and strengthening her rational beliefs.

After you have taken your client through this sequence two or three times, she should be familiar enough with the process to begin to take the lead herself in assessing and dealing with a specific example of her target problem. However, you will need to prompt her. For example, instead of asking her the same assessment questions as you asked the first few times you took her through the above sequence, you might say instead:

- 'What do you identify first in the ABC format?'
- 'What questions can you ask yourself to identify C?'
- 'How can you best identify the aspect of the situation about which you were most disturbed?'
- 'What irrational beliefs might you have held that accounted for your anxiety?'
- 'What questions can you ask to dispute your irrational belief?'

If your client claims that she does not know the answer to any of these questions, help her by offering her choices. Try not to answer the questions for your client since you will doing the work for her at a time when she is able, with help from you, to do more of the work for herself. Here is an example of what I mean:

THERAPIST: What irrational beliefs might you have held that accounted for your anxiety?

CLIENT: I don't know.

THERAPIST: Well, do you think you were telling yourself: 'It would be bad if Mary criticizes, but it certainly wouldn't be terrible' or do you think you could have been telling yourself: 'It would be terrible if Mary criticized me?'

CLIENT: Put like that, I was telling myself that it would be terrible if she criticized me.

After your client has responded to this first level of prompting, you might move to a second level of minimal prompting which is designed to encourage your client to take even more responsibility for the work that she needs to do. Examples of minimal prompts include the following:

- 'What was your C?'
- 'What was your A?'

- 'What were your irrational beliefs?'
- 'Dispute that belief.'
- 'How can you strengthen that rational belief?'

Remember that your goal is to help your client to do the work for herself. So again, when she cannot immediately use your minimal prompts, give her a little more help, but don't do the work for her.

You can also use minimal prompts as an aid to your client when you ask her to take the lead in assessing and dealing with a specific example of her target problem. When you judge that your client is ready to do so, you can explain that you want her to take the lead in assessing and dealing with the problem and you will be on hand to help her if she gets stuck or goes off track, but that she should not otherwise look to you for help. If your client does this successfully a number of times, she is showing that she has internalized the REBT self-help sequence.

You will recall that this sequence is similar to the sequence that I described when I discussed teaching your client how to use my self-help form. There I included the printed instructions that I give my clients to help them to use the form between sessions. Following on from this you might consider giving your client a written summary of the self-help sequence along the lines of the points I listed on pp. 191–192.

Giving Clients Responsibility for Self-change Methods

In Chapters 5, 7 and 8, I described the use of a number of techniques to help your client to understand the rational solution to her problems and to integrate this solution into her belief system so that she can overcome these problems. After you have taught your client how to use these techniques, it is important that you suggest that she practises the use of them between sessions. As I mentioned in Chapter 8, it is very important that you check on your client's use of these techniques as homework assignments so that you can give her feedback on any errors that she has made in carrying these out. The main reason for doing so is to help your client to become competent in using these self-change methods as part of a general strategy of encouraging her to become her own therapist.

When your client has proved that she can use these techniques competently, the next step in encouraging her development as her own therapist is to suggest that she should implement the techniques on her own. Here, you take responsibility for suggesting the use of a particular technique for a specific problem. Thus, you might suggest that she employs as a homework assignment the Ellis version of rational-emotive imagery (REI) to deepen her conviction of a particular rational belief. As before, it is important to check her assignment and give feedback to enhance her skilled practice of this method.

The final step in encouraging your client to become her own therapist with respect to using the self-change techniques that I have described in this book, is to suggest that she takes the lead in choosing which methods to use in addressing her problems. The main point to emphasize to her is that she should select a technique consistent with the stage of change she is in with respect to the problem under consideration. For example, you can ask her to choose from a range of techniques to promote integration of the rational solution into her belief system. Here, it is a good idea to outline for her an ideal order for the use of integration-promoting techniques. I suggest that clients use such techniques in the following order between therapy sessions:

- Rational portfolio
- The zig-zag method
- Tape-recorded disputing
- Rational-emotive imagery
- The conjoint use of behavioural and cognitive techniques
- Emotive techniques (such as shame-attacking exercises)

However, I do wish to point out that this order is only suggestive and should not be used dogmatically by clients. Clients differ in the therapeutic value they derive from different techniques and their preferences in this regard should be respected. Also, clients may well differ concerning the order in which they use techniques. Thus, one client may find using techniques in the suggested order most useful, while another may find it helpful to use REI before the rational portfolio, for example. Unless there is a good reason for doing otherwise, I suggest that you should respect your client's wishes in this matter. Finally, as before, it is important that you check on your client's use of her self-selected techniques and give feedback where applicable.

I will discuss how I helped Carol to become her own therapist in Chapter 10.

DEALING WITH RELAPSE PREVENTION

In this section, I will consider the question of helping your client to prevent relapse. This work, known as relapse prevention, originated in the treatment of substance abuse (Marlatt & Gordon, 1989), but latterly has been applied to psychotherapy generally. The principle behind re-lapse prevention is that it is important to help your client to identify situations that she might encounter which could provide the context for a relapse. Once you have identified such situations, you then help your client to draw upon the skills that she has learned in therapy and to develop plans to deal with these situations based on those skills. Having dealt with this issue in therapy, you would then help your client to seek out the identified situations and gain practice at using her self-therapy skills in these situations so that she can experience using the skills in difficult circumstances. This is usually done in a graduated way in order to help your client develop a sense of self-efficacy in dealing with these difficult circumstances.

You may find it useful to help your client to see that there is a distinction between a relapse and a lapse. A lapse is a minor occurrence of your client's problem and is a very common, and some would say an inevit-able, part of psychological change. On the other hand a relapse is a significant return to the state for which the client originally sought therapy. A relapse tends to occur when smaller lapses are not dealt with effectively. Some clients are very afraid that they might experience a relapse. In my experience, such clients overestimate the chances of re-lapse because they hold irrational beliefs about experiencing lapses. Effectively they believe that they must not experience any lapses and that it would be awful if they did. Helping such clients to identify, challenge and change demanding beliefs about lapses, means that they become concerned but not frightened about lapsing briefly into their problem state and thus are able to make more realistic inferences about their prospects of experiencing a full-blown relapse. Consequently they are more able to participate effectively in relapse-prevention procedures than if they held irrational beliefs about experiencing a lapse.

Having described the nature of relapse prevention, let me stress that due to the lack of time at your disposal, you may not be able to deal with this topic as thoroughly as you might ideally like. Nevertheless, it is important to put this on the agenda towards the end of brief REBT so that you can introduce the concept and help your client to do some planning in this area. I will show how I used relapse prevention with Carol in Chapter 10.

ENDING THE THERAPEUTIC PROCESS

While brief REBT lasts for 11 sessions, you are free to schedule these sessions over whatever period is suited to your client's therapeutic and practical needs. Thus, while you might decide to see one client once a week over an 11-week period, you might see another client once every two weeks over a 22-week period. Having said this, I find that with most clients I schedule weekly sessions for the first six to seven meetings and then increase the interval between the final four to five sessions to enable my clients to practise the skills that they have learned in therapy and thus begin to get used to becoming their own therapist.

The second question to consider concerns when to raise the issue of ending brief therapy with your client. My practice is to do this when I first discuss increasing the frequency of time between sessions with my client. I then remind her how many sessions we have left at the beginning of every session.

You may, however, need to deal with the issue of ending therapy earlier with some clients who are particularly anxious about the brevity of a brief therapy contract, even though they have agreed to the terms of this contract. In my experience, clients who demonstrate anxiety about the ending of brief therapy early in the process are those who have dependency-related irrational beliefs. They are typically clients who doubt their ability to cope on their own and believe that they need to rely on someone stronger than themselves. As such it is likely that these clients will reveal their dependency-related irrational beliefs in the target problems that they choose to focus on in brief therapy. When this happens it is useful to point out to your client the link between her anxiety about the end of therapy and her other target problems and to enable her to see that if you help her to deal successfully with her target problems she will be able to apply this learning to the issue of the end of therapy. Alternatively, you might target your client's anxiety about the end of therapy for direct intervention. Encouraging her to overcome this anxiety will help her to concentrate on her target problems more effectively than if her anxiety about the end of therapy was present throughout the brief therapy process.

Your clients may also reveal anxieties about the end of therapy in the later stages of brief REBT. These anxieties are less likely to reflect core irrational beliefs than those disclosed earlier on in the therapeutic process, and they are more likely to express common concerns concerning coping on one's own without the active help of a therapist. The way to deal with your client's anxiety about independent coping after therapy has ended is to target the inference 'I may not be able to cope without the active help of my therapist' and to encourage your client to test this out in the remainder of the therapy sessions. This normally is sufficient to help your client to see that she can cope on her own post-therapy. If this approach fails to dispel her anxiety then you need to identify, challenge and change the irrational belief that is sustaining her anxiety (e.g. 'I must know now that I will be able to cope on my own after therapy and I can't stand the uncertainty of not knowing').

Evaluation

At the final session, it is important to discuss with your client how much progress she has made on her problems since the start of brief REBT. You can do this both qualitatively and quantitatively. A qualitative assessment of progress involves your client telling you what difference therapy has made to that part of her life in which her problems feature. This is done in an open-ended way where your role is to encourage your client to be as explicit as possible about how she is managing situations to which she once responded with unhealthy negative emotions and/or self-defeating behaviour. While much of your discussion will focus on those of your client's problems to which you devoted most time in therapy, you will also wish to discover what progress she has made compared to her original problem list. Throughout this process, you need to help your client to specify the factors that accounted for the progress she has shown in managing previously 'problematic' situations.

Taking a slightly different stance, you can explore with your client the progress she has made in reaching her goals by asking her to give examples of such progress. Again, your role is to help your client to be as specific as possible in relating examples of the progress she has made towards goal achievement and to tease out the factors that accounted for the changes that she has made.

A quantitative assessment of your client's progress involves your collecting numerical data at the beginning and end of brief REBT with respect to the prevalence of your client's problems and the extent to which she has reached her goals. Thus, on the problem prevalence scale '0' represents the absence of the problem, while '10' represents the prevalence of the problem to its fullest extent. On this scale, then, the steeper the descent of the client's ratings the more progress the client has made during brief REBT. However, on the goal attainment scale, '0' represents no progress being made towards the client's goal, while '10' represents the goal being achieved. Here, the steeper the ascent of the client's ratings, the more progress she has made towards achieving her goals over the course of brief REBT. For more information on qualitative and quantitative approaches to doing research on your psychotherapy practice, consult Barker, Pistrang and Elliott (1994) and McLeod (1994).

When your client has not made progress from brief REBT, you need to arrange further help for her; to do otherwise is, in my opinion, irresponsible. You have two major choices here. First, you might suggest that your client receive a longer term course of REBT with yourself or with another REBT therapist, if she finds this therapeutic approach helpful, but insufficient in the limited time available in a brief-term contract. Second, if your client has not found REBT helpful, then you might refer her to a therapist from a different therapeutic persuasion, one which more closely meets your client's treatment preferences.

Follow-up Sessions

Follow-up sessions form an important part of an evaluative approach to psychotherapy. However, holding such sessions not only gives you an opportunity to monitor the longer term effects of brief REBT, it also communicates to your client that you are interested in her continued welfare. My practice is to hold one or two follow-up sessions. These should be scheduled in such a way that the first session does not take place until a period of time has elapsed not less than the time the client has spent in therapy. Thus, if your client was in therapy with you for 11 weeks, the first follow-up session should occur no less than 11 weeks after her final therapy session. It should be made clear to your client that follow-up sessions are not therapy sessions. They are an opportunity to monitor progress and fine-tune her self-help skills.

In my brief REBT practice, the first follow-up session takes place about five to six months after therapy has ended. At the end of the first follow-up session I ask my client if she wants another similar session and if she does, I schedule one between six to nine months after the first. If your client has deteriorated since brief REBT has finished, you need to assess the reasons for this and if it is the case that she needs another brief period of therapy you should offer her this, but the number of sessions should preferably be kept to a minimum. Here, the emphasis should be on providing your client with a brief top-up or revision period of therapy and not another full course of brief REBT. Of course, if your client has deteriorated markedly since the end of brief therapy, you need to consider a referral to longer term therapy either with yourself or with another therapist. In the latter case, whether or not this other person should be an REBT therapist will depend on your assessment at follow-up. However, if you and your client have fulfilled your respective tasks during brief REBT, this latter situation should be rare and if it does occur, it is either the case that your client was more disturbed than she appeared to be during brief therapy or that she has faced stress well beyond her ability to cope with between the end of therapy and the follow-up session.

This brings us to the end of the penultimate chapter. You will recall that I have used my work with Carol to illustrate many of the points that I have considered in this volume. In the final chapter of this book, I will summarize this work and give an account of the course of brief REBT with Carol. This will demonstrate how brief REBT unfolds over time with a client who has used the techniques on offer and has made progress as a result.

10

THE PROCESS OF BRIEF REBT: THE CASE OF CAROL

Drawing on the previous chapters, I will now present a brief session-by-session account of my work with Carol so that I can illustrate the process of brief therapy. Please note that in all sessions, I set an agenda at the beginning of the session and elicited feedback from Carol at the end of the session. I will begin by reintroducing Carol and will present a summary of the relevant session (and pre-therapy contact) with an accompanying commentary when I wish to highlight a point. Since I am illustrating points previously discussed in the text, I will refer you to the relevant section of the book where appropriate.

THE CLIENT

At the time she first contacted me, Carol was a 28-year-old woman who had consulted her GP for 'stress problems'. The GP, who had known Carol for several years, considered that she had a healthy 'pre-morbid' personality and could benefit from a brief period of focused therapy. Her referral letter mentioned difficulties at work and in her relationships with men. Carol had not received any counselling or psychotherapy before the referral.

THE INITIAL PHONE-CALL

'Keen to Get Started'

Carol telephoned to inform me that her GP had referred her to my brief therapy practice. I suggested that we meet to discuss her problems and see whether or not brief REBT was the most helpful therapy for her at the present time. By her tone and manner, it struck me that Carol was keen to get started, which seemed to me a good sign.

The Fee

Therapists have different views on whether or not it is a good idea to discuss one's fee over the telephone before one has met the client face to face. To some therapists doing this seems too mercenary and conveys to the person seeking help that you are primarily interested in money. On the other hand, not to inform the person what your fee is before you meet may mean that she is shocked when she does learn what you charge. My own practice is reflected in how I raised the issue with Carol:

WINDY: I would like to ask you whether you would like to know what my fee is now or whether you'd prefer to wait until we meet to discuss it. Some people like to know about such matters before they come, while others prefer to wait. Do you have any questions about my fee, right now?

CAROL: Yes, I'd like to know what you charge.

I then told Carol my fee which she accepted. If she had balked at the fee, I would have referred her to a colleague whose fee matched what Carol could afford.

A Thumbnail Sketch of REBT

As I mentioned in Chapter 3, it is useful to give your client a brief thumbnail sketch of REBT over the telephone, if she is interested. Here is how I dealt with Carol's enquiry about REBT on the telephone.

WINDY: REBT is an approach to therapy which helps you to understand and change the self-defeating attitudes that lie at the bottom of your problems. You and I will work together in an active way to help you do this so you can overcome your problems and live a more satisfying life.

Carol then asked me to elaborate, but I declined since I did not want to get drawn into a lengthy discussion which would not be appropriate over the telephone.

CAROL: That sounds interesting. Can you tell me more?

WINDY: I will be pleased to do so at our first meeting if you wish to make an appointment.

Carol replied that she would like to make an appointment and we agreed on a date.

THE FIRST SESSION

In Chapter 3, I outlined the major tasks that you need to accomplish at the first session. I stressed that at this point the person seeking help is best viewed as an applicant rather than a client. In the first session, I did the following.

1. I invited Carol to tell me what her problems were. While she did this I showed her that I understood her from her frame of reference and helped her to summarize her problems. This led naturally to the second task.
2. I helped Carol to develop a problem list and elicited her goals in line with these defined problems (see pp. 53–54).
3. I then asked her to select the two problems that she wanted particular help with. These became her prioritized target problems (see pp. 56–58).
4. Next, I explained to Carol the ABCDEs of REBT with particular emphasis on musts and awfulizing and their healthy alternatives, using the money example (see pp. 58–61).
5. Following on from this, I outlined the tasks that Carol and I needed to accomplish if brief REBT was to be successful, and answered the questions that she had about these tasks (pp. 61–65).
6. At this point, I decided that Carol was a good candidate for brief REBT, using the criteria that I outlined in Chapter 1.
7. Having determined that Carol was a good candidate for brief REBT, I explained to her what this approach to therapy entailed and offered her a brief therapy contract which she accepted. The contract stipulated that Carol would receive 11 sessions of brief REBT (including the current session). Once Carol accepted the offer of help, she moved from being an applicant to becoming a client.
8. Then, by following the points that I discussed in Chapter 3 (pp. 45–48), I determined the bond that I needed to develop with Carol if she were to get the most out of therapy. Based on her responses to my enquiries, I considered that Carol would respond best to a business-like bond where I emphasized my expertise, but laced with a moderate degree of humour.
9. Finally, I suggested that Carol should read Chapter 1 of *Think Your Way to Happiness* (Dryden & Gordon, 1990) to consolidate her understanding of the REBT theory of emotional disturbance.

THE SECOND SESSION

As you can see from the above description, Carol and I covered a lot of ground in our first session. However, while we outlined and listed her problems, we had not yet started to deal with them directly. As will be shown from the following description, this became the focus of the second session.

1. First, Carol and I discussed her reactions to her reading homework.
2. Second, I asked Carol to select which of her two prioritized target problems she wanted to work on first. She chose the following target problem (which I shall call TP1): I am in trouble at work because I am often late (see pp. 56–58).
3. Then, I asked her to tell me about a typical, specific example of this problem (the knitting example) and proceeded to assess the A and C components of this example (see pp. 76–77; 82).
4. Following on from this I checked to see whether or not Carol had a meta-emotional problem (see pp. 94–96) and on finding that none was present I moved on to the next step.
5. Before helping Carol to identify the irrational beliefs that accounted for the C in this example, I completed my explanation of the ABCDEs of REBT and in particular I reviewed musts and awfulizing and their healthy alternatives and went on to teach Carol about LFT and self-downing and their healthy alternatives (see pp. 84–86).
6. Having filled in the missing gaps in Carol's knowledge about rational and irrational beliefs, I then proceeded to assess her irrational beliefs and stressed the iB-C connection (see pp. 88–89; 101).
7. I then elicited Carol's goals in line with her problem as assessed.
8. Having completed the assessment of TP1, I disputed Carol's iBs to the criterion of understanding the rational solution to her problems (see pp. 106–115).
9. Achieving this enabled Carol to commit herself to her therapeutic goals.
10. Because Carol's target problem was in the realm of discomfort disturbance rather than ego disturbance, I decided to suggest a homework assignment that deepened her understanding of this type of disturbance. Thus I suggested that Carol read step 4 of *Ten Steps to Positive Living* (Dryden, 1994b) which focuses on discomfort disturbance, and she readily agreed to do this.

THE THIRD SESSION

In the third session of brief REBT, I did three things.

1. First, I discussed Carol's reaction to her reading homework.

2. Second, I taught Carol how to use my ABC self-help form, using the steps discussed in Chapter 5 (see pp. 117–124). This took up most of the session, as it usually does.
3. Finally, I asked Carol to complete an ABC form for homework on different examples of the same target problem. She agreed to do this.

THE FOURTH SESSION

In the fourth session, I accomplished four things.

1. First, I checked Carol's ABC self-help form and gave her several suggestions to improve her responses.
2. Second, I taught her that understanding the rational solution is insufficient for change, and I outlined what is involved in integrating the rational solution into her belief system so that her new rational beliefs could make a healthy difference to the way that she thought, felt and acted when faced with the prospect of leaving a significant task unfinished (see Chapter 6).
3. Having introduced the idea of what Carol needed to do to promote integration of the rational solution to her target problem, I initiated the integration process by teaching her how to use the rational portfolio method to weaken her conviction in her irrational belief, 'I must finish an important task once I have started it' and to strengthen her conviction in the rational alternative to this belief (see pp. 142–151). As suggested in Chapter 7, I encouraged her to initiate this technique in the therapy session.
4. I suggested that Carol complete this exercise as a homework assignment. I also suggested that she complete another ABC form on a further example of her target problem. Carol agreed to do these two tasks for homework.

THE FIFTH SESSION

1. I began the fifth session in the normal fashion by checking Carol's homework. Thus, I went over the arguments in her rational portfolio and gave her feedback to improve her skills when completing the ABC self-help form.
2. To further the integration process on her first target problem (TP1), I taught Carol the zig-zag technique (see pp. 151–153) and suggested that she made a start in filling it out.
3. I then considered that we were ready to begin work on Carol's second target problem (TP2): 'I am oversensitive and easily hurt when

criticized'. I asked her to give me a specific example of this problem so that I could assess it.

4. For homework, I suggested that Carol complete the zig-zag technique on TP1 and fill out an ABC self-help form on another example of TP2, which she agreed to do. I suggested that we carry out a review of our work together at the next session which marked the halfway point in the therapy. Carol thought this was a good idea and I suggested that before the next session she should consider what she had achieved and what progress she had yet to make. She agreed to do this.

THE SIXTH SESSION

1. At the beginning of the sixth session I checked Carol's zig-zag homework (TP1) and her ABC self-help form (TP2) and offered her relevant feedback to improve her skills at using these methods.

2. During this session I continued to work on both Carol's prioritized target problems (TP1 and TP2). While the work we did at this point in therapy on TP1 was currently more advanced than the work we did on TP2 (due mainly to the fact that we started with TP1), the rate of progress we made was quicker on TP2. This is quite usual and can be attributed to the fact that when you begin work on your client's second target problem, she has already understood the ABCDEs of REBT and is familiar with a variety of disputing methods. Thus, you are able to accomplish your tasks on TP2 more quickly than you were able to do on TP1 when everything was new to your client. There will be exceptions to this rule: for example when your client's second target problem is much more serious and/or complex than her first problem. Nevertheless, the more your client understands REBT and how to apply it to her problems the less time you will spend on any new problems she may bring up.

Thus, in this session, I taught Carol the rational-irrational two-chair dialogue (see pp. 154–157) to further the integration process on TP1 and disputed her irrational belief ('I need the approval of those close to me') on TP2 and explained how she could do this for herself as a homework assignment (see below).

3. Since we were about half way through our brief therapy contract, I carried out a review of therapy to date. Carol mentioned that she had begun to feel much more in control of whether or not she left tasks unfinished. She also reported that her punctuality at work, while not perfect, had improved. She was glad that we had now started work on the second problem and wondered whether we could have done so

earlier. She was very happy with REBT as a therapeutic approach, but wondered if she could use it for herself. These are typical client concerns at the mid-therapy review. I responded that the thrust of the therapy from now on was to help her to become her own therapist. To this end, I explained that it might be useful if we began to space out our remaining sessions. Carol thought this was a good idea and we agreed that our next three sessions would be scheduled fortnightly.

4. For homework, we agreed that Carol would carry out tape-recorded disputing (see pp. 157–158) on TP1 and both an ABC self-help form and a rational portfolio exercise on TP2.

THE SEVENTH SESSION

1. At the beginning of this session I checked Carol's tape-recorded disputing (TP1), and her ABC self-help form and rational portfolio exercise (TP2). She had experienced a lot of difficulty in focusing on specific irrational beliefs in the tape-recorded exercise, tending to jump from belief to belief. I first brought this to her attention and encouraged her to do a brief reprise of the exercise in the session. While she did this I coached her to keep to the point.
2. This naturally led us to do devil's advocate disputing (see pp. 158–162) on TP1. This had the additional advantage of me showing Carol how to keep focused on disputing one belief at a time.
3. I then taught her the Ellis version of rational-emotive imagery (REI).
4. The final piece of work I did with Carol in this session was a two-chair dialogue on TP2.
5. For homework, Carol agreed to do the following. (i) TP1 – REI and a behavioural/cognitive assignment. For the latter, Carol agreed that she would deliberately start a task knowing that she would not finish it by the time that she had agreed to leave for work. She would leave for work on time and review her rational belief while doing so. From now on I planned to make increased use of behavioural/cognitive assignments. (ii) TP2 – Tape-recorded disputing.

THE EIGHTH SESSION

1. As usual, I began the session by reviewing Carol's homework. She did not find REI useful at all and didn't want to try the Maultsby version (see pp. 164–165) when I described it to her. However, she was pleased that she was able to complete the behavioural/cognitive assignment successfully on TP1. Finally, her tape-recorded disputing on TP2 was

much more focused than it had been on TP1 (see the beginning of the seventh session).

2. After reviewing her homework I conducted devil's advocate disputing with Carol on TP2.

3. Having done a substantial amount of work on Carol's two prioritized target problems I thought that the time was right to start looking for themes among her six problems and identifying core irrational beliefs (see pp. 181–183). This is how I did this.

   (i)   First, I wrote up Carol's two prioritized problems on my white-board. These were:
         • I am in trouble at work because I am often late in the morning.
         • I am oversensitive and easily hurt when criticized.

   (ii) Second, I wrote up the two irrational beliefs that underpinned these problems. As discussed in Chapter 9, I used the general form of these beliefs which were:
         • 'I must finish an important task once I have started it.'
         • 'I need the approval of those close to me.'

   (iii) Third, I wrote up on the board Carol's remaining problems which were:
         • I find it difficult responding to men whom I find attractive.
         • I get used by my friends.
         • I am overweight.
         • I am always in debt.

   (iv) Fourth, I asked Carol if she could see any link between her two prioritized target problems and her remaining problems. In particular, I asked her to focus on the irrational beliefs that underpinned her two target problems and to think whether or not they were responsible for the existence of any of the remaining problems on her list.

         After some exploration Carol identified the following core irrational beliefs:
         • 'I need the approval of those significant to me.' Carol thought that her problems about being criticized and responding to men were explained by this belief.
         • 'I need to get what I want when I want it.' Carol thought that her problems about turning up to work on time, being in debt and being overweight were explained by this belief.
         • 'I must not get what I don't deserve.' Carol thought that her problems about being used by her friends and feeling bad when criticized were explained by this belief.

4. I encouraged Carol to take the lead in assessing a third target problem (TP3): 'I find it difficult responding to men whom I find attractive', using the information derived from the core irrational belief exercise.

5. I reminded Carol that only three sessions remained and explored her feelings about this.
6. Carol agreed to carry out the following homework assignments: TP1 – an emotive 'court discomfort' exercise where Carol would deliberately seek out the discomfort of leaving a very important task unfinished. TP2 – a behavioural/cognitive assertion exercise where she would deliberately put herself in a situation where she would be criticized by a significant person (her father) and practise showing herself that she doesn't need the approval of this person. In addition, she would actively disagree with any unjustified criticism she received. TP3 – an ABC self-help form and the rational portfolio exercise.

THE NINTH SESSION

1. In the ninth session, I reviewed Carol's homework on target problems TP1, TP2 and TP3. While she had completed the last two pieces of homework, Carol admitted that she did not do the behavioural/cognitive assertion exercise on TP2. This was the first time that Carol had not done a homework assignment. We explored the possible reasons for this and discovered that at the end of the previous session Carol thought that the task was too difficult for her, but was scared to say so because she feared that I might disapprove of her. Here we have an example of what psychodynamic therapists would call transference, but what REBT therapists refer to as clients bringing their irrational beliefs to therapy. I handled this issue by using the ABCDE framework in the following manner.

First, I asked her to imagine that she had told me that it was too difficult for her and that I had disapproved of her. You will note that this strategy is the common one of encouraging your client to assume temporarily that A is true. Second, I asked her what her C would be, to which she replied 'hurt'. Then I encouraged her to identify the irrational beliefs that underpinned her hurt feelings and referred her to the work that we had done in the previous session on her core irrational beliefs. Carol recognized that two irrational beliefs underpinned her feelings of hurt. These were:
● 'Windy must approve of me and if he, my therapist, does not think well of me then this proves that I am no good.'
● 'I have been working so hard in therapy that I don't deserve to receive Windy's disapproval the first time I don't do a homework assignment and I must not get what I don't deserve.'

I then asked her to dispute these irrational beliefs in the session using any of the methods she had learned so far in therapy. She chose to dispute them one at a time using the rational-irrational two-chair dialogue method. In the latter phase of this technique I spontaneously 'joined the action' by adopting the position of devil's advocate and attacked her rational beliefs quite strongly. Carol made a spirited defence of her rational beliefs and said at the end of the session that the work we had done on this issue was very valuable. At this point I decided to pay more attention to her core irrational beliefs.

2. I also had time to introduce Carol to the idea of generalizing her therapeutic learning and to reiterate the importance of becoming her own therapist (see pp. 191–194). To this end, I suggested that she set her own homework assignments, which she agreed to do. I did, however, suggest that she should listen to the tape of the session and give me feedback at the next session on what she did not like about my interventions, while disputing the belief that she needed my approval.

3. Finally, we agreed that we would extend the time between sessions and arranged to meet in a month's time.

THE TENTH SESSION

1. First, I reviewed Carol's homework assignments. I paid particular attention to doing so because she had agreed to set her own assignments without any input from me as the first step in becoming her own therapist. She had done the following:

   (i)   She deliberately met her father knowing that it was likely that he would criticize her (TP2). He did so, and during his criticism she told herself vigorously that she didn't need his approval although she wanted it and that he didn't have to be fair to her although it would have been nice if he was. In addition, she disagreed with his unjustified criticisms. This was the homework that she had agreed to do at the end of session 8, but did not do (see my notes on session 9).

   (ii) She recorded a rational-irrational disputing exercise on tape on TP3.

   (iii) She had done an ABC self-help form and a rational portfolio exercise on her problem of being used by her friends (TP4).

2. Then Carol and I spent most of the session on relapse prevention (see pp. 194–195). First, I introduced her to the concept and then we applied it to each of the four problems that we have discussed. Thus she identified the following vulnerability factors:

TP1: Being in the middle of something important AND very enjoyable.

TP2: Being criticized by her father after doing poorly at a work task.

TP3: Seeing a man whom she found extraordinarily attractive.

TP4: Her best friend asking her to do something unfair.

We then did brief devil's advocate disputing on all of them.

3. For homework, I suggested that Carol sought out as many of the above scenarios as she could and practised disputing her irrational beliefs in a forceful manner.

4. Finally, I checked out Carol's feelings about the next session being our last. She replied that she felt sad about it, but was looking forward to coping on her own. We arranged to meet in a month's time.

THE ELEVENTH AND FINAL SESSION

1. As always, I began the final session by reviewing Carol's homework assignments. She had managed to confront her vulnerability factors on TP1 and TP3.

   - On TP1, she had started watching a very enjoyable video and stopped it at the most exciting part.
   - On TP3, she had started a conversation with a man whom she found very attractive, at the end of which he asked her out for a date which she accepted. This ensured that she would continue to work on this issue.
   - Her father had the flu and thus she couldn't do any relapse prevention work on TP2 since the previous session, although she planned to when her father recovered.
   - Working on her vulnerability factor for TP4 was more difficult since it involved another person acting out of character. If Carol had found REI effective I would have suggested this technique to her since she could then see in her mind's eye her best friend using her. Since she did not find this technique useful, she decided to work on it using tape-recorded disputing, having assumed that her best friend had just asked her to do something unfair.

2. In the final session, it is important to review your client's progress over the course of therapy (see pp. 197–198). Carol claimed that she had achieved the following from brief REBT.

   (i)   She was now routinely turning up to work on time and found it much easier to leave tasks unfinished. She considered that while she no longer strongly believed that she had to finish things that she had started, she could see herself drifting back to that belief if she wasn't careful. So she had resolved to keep working at it.

(ii) She felt less tense when in the company of her father and significant others whom she had found critical in the past. She considered that she had made good strides in integrating a non-demanding, healthy desire for approval into her belief system. She was more assertive with her father, in particular, and found that as she did so, his criticisms seemed more petty than she previously thought.

(iii) The progress Carol had made towards adopting a healthy desire for approval also helped her to be more relaxed in the company of attractive men. She realized that she had equated attractiveness with worth and once she really saw that this was not true, she stopped putting such men on a pedestal.

(iv) While Carol claimed to have made some progress on disputing her need for fair and deserving treatment from others, she realized that she had a good deal of work to do before she integrated the relevant rational solution into her belief system.

(v) Carol claimed to have made some gains on her overeating and debt problems. She was making good progress in monitoring her urges to eat and spend and showing herself that she didn't have to have what she wanted at that moment. Consequently, she was beginning to differentiate between healthy and unhealthy episodes of eating and spending. However, she again noted that she had a lot of work to do on integrating this solution into her belief system.

3. I then encouraged Carol to continue to use the REBT self-help skills that she had acquired during therapy and spent some time discussing with her how she could do this, especially on the problems where her progress was less pronounced. In particular, I urged her to commit time every day to maintaining and enhancing her gains and gave her a pamphlet written by Albert Ellis (1984) on this very topic. We then arranged a follow-up appointment in five months time. In Chapter 9, I argued that the follow-up session should take place at a time which exceeded the duration of the therapy. My 11 sessions with Carol were spaced out over a 20-week period and therefore the follow-up session should be arranged no earlier than five months. Finally, Carol thanked me for my help and we duly said our goodbyes.

THE FOLLOW-UP SESSION

The follow-up session that I had with Carol was conducted over the telephone. Three months after the end of therapy, Carol had obtained promotion in her job which necessitated a move to Scotland, making a face-to-face meeting impractical.

Carol reported that she had maintained all the gains that she had made at the end of therapy and had extended those gains in several areas. First, her timekeeping at work was almost perfect and she no longer had any trouble leaving tasks unfinished.

Second, while she did not like criticism, she was able to hear it without feeling hurt or putting herself down and was able to disagree with criticism with which she did not concur in a non-defensive manner.

Third, she claimed that she was no longer intimidated by attractive men and had been dating a handsome Scotsman whom she had 'picked up' at a party.

While Carol said that she was far more in control over spending than she had ever been in her life and was no longer in debt, she still snacked between meals. We did a little bit of work on this and I urged her to use rational self-statements about not needing what she wanted more forcefully than she had been doing.

Finally, she had not yet encountered an episode where someone she was close to had taken advantage of her. One of her friends had remarked that she seemed far less of a 'doormat' than she used to be.

I offered Carol another follow-up appointment in six months time, but she declined this, saying that it was time to cut the remaining ties. I wished her well and we said goodbye for the last time.

I hope this account of my work with Carol has helped you to understand the process of brief REBT. If you wish to find out about where you can train in REBT, please consult Appendix 3.

REFERENCES

Barker, C., Pistrang, N. & Elliott, R. (1994). *Research Methods in Clinical and Counselling Psychology*. Chichester: Wiley.

Beck, A.T. (1976). *Cognitive Therapy and the Emotional Disorders*. New York: International Universities Press.

Bernard, M.E. & Wolfe, J.J. (Eds). (1993) *The RET Resource Book for Practitioners*. New York: Institute for Rational-Emotive Therapy.

Bordin, E.S. (1979). The generalizability of the psychoanalytic concept of the working alliance. *Psychotherapy: Theory, Research and Practice*, **16**, 252-260.

Budman, S.H. (Ed.) (1981). *Forms of Brief Treatment*. New York: Guilford.

Budman, S.H. & Gurman, A.S. (1988). *Theory and Practice of Brief Therapy*. New York: Guilford.

Burns, D.D. & Nolen-Hoeksema, S. (1991). Copying styles, homework assignments and the effectiveness of cognitive-behavioral therapy. *Journal of Consulting and Clinical Psychology*, **59**, 305-311.

Davanloo, H. (Ed.) (1978). *Basic Principles and Techniques in Short-Term Dynamic Psychology*. New York: SP Medical and Scientific Books.

DiGiuseppe, R. (1991). Comprehensive cognitive disputing in RET. In M.E. Bernard (Ed.), *Using Rational-Emotive Therapy Effectively*. New York: Plenum.

Dryden, W. (1986). Vivid methods in rational-emotive therapy. In A. Ellis and R. Grieger (Eds), *Handbook of Rational-Emotive Therapy*, Vol. 2. New York: Springer.

Dryden, W. (1990). *Rational-Emotive Counselling in Action*. London: Sage.

Dryden, W. (1991). *Reason and Therapeutic Change*. London: Whurr Publishers.

Dryden, W. (1993). *Reflections on Counselling*. London: Whurr Publishers.

Dryden, W. (1994a). *Invitation to Rational-Emotive Psychology*. London: Whurr Publishers.

Dryden, W. (1994b). *Ten Steps to Positive Living*. London: Sheldon.

Dryden, W. (1995). *Preparing for Client Change in Rational Emotive Behaviour Therapy*. London: Whurr Publishers.

Dryden, W. & Feltham, C. (Eds) (1992). *Psychotherapy and its Discontents*. Buckingham: Open University Press.

Dryden, W. & Gordon, J. (1990). *Think Your Way to Happiness*. London: Sheldon.

Ellis, A. (1963). Toward a more precise definition of 'emotional' and 'intellectual' insight. *Psychological Reports*, **13**, 125-126.

Ellis, A. (1977). Fun as psychotherapy. *Rational Living*, **12** (1), 2-6.

Ellis, A. (1979). The issue of force and energy in behavioral change. *Journal of Contemporary Psychotherapy*, **10** (2), 83-97.

Ellis, A. (1980). The value of efficiency in psychotherapy. *Psychotherapy*, **17**, 414-419.

Ellis, A. (1984). *How to Maintain and Enhance your Rational-Emotive Therapy Gains*. New York: Institute for Rational-Emotive Therapy

Ellis, A. (1985). *Overcoming Resistance: Rational-Emotive Therapy with Difficult Clients*. New York: Springer.

Ellis, A. (1989). Ineffective consumerism in the cognitive-behavioural therapies and in general psychology. In W. Dryden and P. Trower (Eds), *Cognitive Psychotherapy: Stasis and Change*. London: Cassell.

Ellis, A. (1994). *Reason and Emotion in Psychotherapy*. Second edition. New York: Birch Lane Press.

Ellis, A. & Dryden, W. (1987). *The Practice of Rational-Emotive Therapy*. New York: Springer.

Garvin, C.D. & Seabury, B.A. (1984). *Interpersonal Practice in Social Work: Processes and Procedures*. Englewood Cliffs, NJ: Prentice-Hall.

Horvath, A.O. & Greenberg, L.S. (Eds) (1994). *The Working Alliance: Theory, Research and Practice*. New York: Wiley.

Howe, D. (1993). *On Being a Client: Understanding the Process of Counselling and Psychotherapy*. London: Sage.

Kelly, G. (1955). *The Psychology of Personal Constructs*. New York: Norton.

Lazarus, A. (1981). *The Practice of Multimodal Therapy*. New York: McGraw-Hill.

Malan, D.H. (1980). Criteria for selection. In H. Davanloo (Ed.), *Short-Term Dynamic Psychotherapy*. New York: Jason Aronson.

Marlatt, G.A. & Gordon, J.R. (Eds) (1989). *Relapse Prevention: Maintenance Strategies in the Treatment of Addictive Behaviors*. New York: Guilford.

Maultsby, M.C., Jr (1984). *Rational Behavior Therapy*. Englewood Cliffs, NJ: Prentice-Hall.

Maultsby, M.C., Jr & Ellis, A. (1974). *Technique for Using Rational-Emotive Imagery*. New York: Institute for Rational-Emotive Therapy.

McLeod, J. (1994). *Doing Counselling Research*. London: Sage.

McMullin, R.E. (1986). *Handbook of Cognitive Therapy Techniques*. New York: Norton.

Moore, R.H. (1988). Inference as 'A' in RET. In W. Dryden and P. Trower (Eds), *Developments in Rational-Emotive Therapy*. Milton Keynes: Open University Press.

Persaud, R. (1993). The 'career' of counselling: Careering out of control? *Journal of Mental Health*, **2**, 283-285.

Rogers, C.R (1957). The necessary and sufficient conditions of therapeutic personality change. *Journal of Consulting Psychology*, **21**, 95-103.

Wells, R.A. & Gianetti, V.J. (Eds) (1990). *Handbook of the Brief Psychotherapies*. New York: Plenum.

Wessler, R.A. & Wessler, R.L. (1980). *The Principles and Practice of Rational-Emotive Therapy*. San Francisco: Jossey-Bass.

Appendix 1

LETTER AND INTRODUCTION TO REBT: A CLIENT'S GUIDE

Dear

As promised, I am sending you an introduction to the therapy that I practise. You may benefit from attending my brief therapy clinic in which I offer people 11 sessions of therapy. At the first session, we will discuss your problems and decide whether or not brief therapy is for you. If it is, it is important that you understand the approach that I practise, to see if you think it may be helpful to you. I have prepared the attached booklet with this in mind. If brief therapy is not for you, we can discuss suitable alternatives when we meet. I look forward to seeing you on

Yours sincerely

INTRODUCTION TO RATIONAL EMOTIVE BEHAVIOUR THERAPY*

A Guide for Clients

Purpose of this Booklet

Most of us have ideas about what counselling and psychotherapy are about. But when we actually start to take part in it, there can be surprises in store. Research suggests that people get more out of therapy if they come prepared with a better idea of what is going to happen and what will be expected of them. That is why I have prepared this booklet for you.

Please read this carefully before your first appointment. Some of it may appear to be common sense, while parts may be quite hard going at first. So please read it through more than once so that you can get the most out of it. Some people find that the booklet itself helps them start to tackle their problems even before their first appointment. I hope that will apply to you.

You and your Current Difficulties

You have chosen, possibly on the advice of another person such as your GP, to come to me for help. I expect that this means you are at present aware of feeling 'down', 'stressed', or that things are somehow not going right for you. This is a very common experience. Many of us go through times when we think we are not 'coping' as well as we have done in the past. For whatever reason, when people begin to feel they are not coping, this awareness in itself can make them feel worse.

You may have some idea about why you feel the way you do: it might be problems getting along with a new boss at work, a heavier load of work to do, or difficulties in a relationship outside work. Or it might be lots of different things piling up over a period of time. Or perhaps you can't really work out what has happened to make things get worse for you.

What this tells me is that while there are some things that are much the same for most of the people I see – such as the feeling that they are not coping as well as they have in the past – each person also has their own unique circumstances that bring them to see me. This combination of typical and unique experiences is important in how your therapy will proceed. You will find more about this in the next section.

---

*I acknowledge Dr Michael Barkham's help in the construction of this guide.

For now, the important message I'd like to give you is that coming for therapy is a big step in coping with your problems. Rather than saying to yourself 'I'm not coping because I need to seek help', you could try saying 'Seeking help is my first big step towards coping with my present problems'. As you read on, you will come to see how looking at both yourself and the world you live in in a slightly different way can help to build up a more realistic picture, leading you to feel better and thereby more able to cope with current difficulties.

What is Rational Emotive Behaviour Therapy?

The therapy you will receive is called Rational Emotive Behaviour Therapy (or REBT). It may be useful for you to know more about what it is and how it works so that you can get the most from our meetings. Rational Emotive Behaviour Therapy focuses on two areas: first, the things you *do*, and second, the way you *think* about things. The 'doing' part is concerned with teaching you new skills in the way you do things, while the 'thinking' part is about looking at new ways of thinking about yourself and your world.

As we all know, problems occur every day; we cannot stop them all happening. What is important for you, however, is to be able to try out new ways of doing things or thinking about things so as to be able to solve these problems as they occur. In fact, I often say to people that it's a bit like being a scientist; going out and solving a problem by experimenting with different things until the problem is solved. Even if an experiment doesn't work, then we've learnt something which will help us to look at other possibilities.

To give you a fuller picture of Rational Emotive Behaviour Therapy, I have explained a number of points in the next section which may help you to get more from our meetings.

What Makes Up Rational Emotive Behaviour Therapy?

Rational Emotive Behaviour Therapy is made up of a number of different parts which, when described briefly, may give you a more complete picture of the therapy. This is not meant to be an exhaustive list and it may be that not all the features will be included in your therapy.

Rational Emotive Behaviour Therapy is problem focused and practical. This means that early in the therapy, I will ask you to identify a problem which you want to work on. Once you and I agree on the area you are going to look at, we will then work out, together, practical ways of tackling the problem. This usually means doing something about the problem.

Rational Emotive Behaviour Therapy encourages you to experiment with new ways of tackling problems, and thereby gives you new 'coping' skills. Research has shown us that the difficulties many people experience arise from their using old and ineffective ways of doing things. Often, even when we know things are not going well, it is difficult to change old habits. It is a bit like 'being stuck' and not being able to move forward. What is important for you to know is that things *can* change, and perhaps just as important, that things can change because of *your* efforts.

An important part of REBT is carrying out tasks *between* therapy sessions. REBT is very much about you practising tackling new ways of solving your problems. Because there is far more time between sessions than during sessions, it makes sense to use the time outside sessions to practise and build on ideas discussed during the sessions. Then, progress and difficulties can be discussed at your next meeting with me.

The above points have been to do with the more practical side of tackling your problems (i.e. doing things). Another point about REBT is that it is concerned with how you *think* about yourself and the world. At first, this may sound a strange thing to talk about. For example, you may feel low or down because of things which have happened. Research shows that very often the way we are *feeling* about things (for example, 'down' or depressed), happens becaue of the way we are *thinking* about things. It might be helpful to give a very simple example.

Suppose a friend of yours criticizes you. You may very well feel depressed and say to yourself: 'I'm worthless because he/she criticized me'. You *feel* depressed because of the way you *think* about your friend's criticism. However, you could try thinking about it in another way. For example, you could say to yourself: 'I don't like being criticized, but I'm not worthless'. If you were to think about it in this way, you would probably find yourself feeling sad about the criticism but not depressed, and this feeling would encourage you to find out more about your friend's reasons for criticizing you. However, if you feel depressed, you are likely to withdraw from your friend. This is a very simple example but it shows how distressing feelings can be addressed by thinking about things in a different way.

How Does REBT Tackle Particular Problems?

The above section has presented the two main parts of REBT. What I believe to be particularly important is for you to have some understanding of how these will affect your current difficulties. The more you are able to see how these parts apply to your particular problems, the more you are likely to gain from therapy. It's a bit like looking after a car. Generally, the more we understand about how a car works, the more likely we are to be able to solve a problem with it or possibly take some action before a problem gets too big.

Initially, Rational Emotive Behaviour Therapy focuses on a single problem you are experiencing. This may not necessarily be the 'worst' or most pressing problem. It is more likely to be a problem which, given the time you and I have together, you have the best chance of achieving success with. Often we feel that 'nothing has gone right' and we begin to lose confidence in ourselves. We all need to know that we can change things and the best way of getting this feeling back is to decide to tackle tasks which have a good chance of bringing success.

As you can see, REBT focuses very much on getting back the feeling that you *can* change and improve parts of your life. For example, imagine you have just passed an important exam after studying very hard. If you think to yourself 'That was just luck', you will probably not feel particularly good about your achievement. Suppose instead you say 'I worked hard for that and passed because of my hard work'. The first statement leads you to think that it doesn't matter what you do; it's all luck and there's nothing you can do about it. If you think this, the chances are that you won't feel like you've passed at all, and then you'll start to feel just the same as if you'd failed. On the other hand, if you are able to recognize all the effort you put into it, then you will begin to feel confident.

Have you ever noticed how, if one thing goes right for us, we can often feel much better about tackling different tasks? You will probably find that things you learn from doing one task can often be used in other tasks as well. For example, finding that you can organize your work better during the day may also lead to your finding that you are better able to organize your life in other ways as well. Similarly, if you begin to think about a task in a slightly different way, you may find yourself not worrying so much about other situations because you are thinking about things generally in a more realistic way.

What Will I, As your Therapist, Do During our Meetings?

People have very different ideas about what therapists 'do' during their meetings with clients. For example, you might think the therapist sits back and 'reads your mind', or you might think it is the therapist's job to 'tell you *what* to do'. Well, I believe that giving you an idea of what I will do during the sessions will help you to get more from them by being better prepared for what will happen. In general, I play an active part in the session. One way of looking at the session is to say that it's a bit like developing a 'working partnership' between the two of us. This 'partnership' is very important. For example, we will find it necessary to identify and choose tasks for you to carry out between sessions to help you begin to deal with your problem. The important thing to bear in mind here though is that *we* will be doing this *together*.

During the course of your sessions, you may notice that I have a particular way of talking about or tackling problems. It is probably helpful to tell you about two particular ways in which I will talk with you about your problems. The first way is that I will suggest trying a different method of tackling a particular situation. This is a bit like an 'experiment' – trying something out to see what happens. It may work, which would be fine, or, if it doesn't, it will tell both of us something which will help you devise another way of tackling the problem. It is important to be patient. Learning new skills does not happen overnight.

Just as important as gaining new information and skills is challenging the way you think about things. You will remember earlier in this booklet I pointed out that how you feel often depends on what you are thinking. Let's look at another example. Imagine that you become very anxious about possibly being a few minutes late for a meeting because of the thought that it would be terrible to be late. As this 'thought' leads you to be anxious, then it clearly is not a very helpful way of looking at the situation. In this situation, I might ask you some questions, for example, 'Why would being late be terrible?' You might say that 'People would think I didn't take things seriously if I were late'. I might then ask you whether this, if it were true, would be either (a) unfortunate or (b) the end of the world.

Questioning the way in which you think about things is very important for two reasons. First, it can lead to important changes in the way you think, and therefore feel, about things. And second, with practice, it is something you can do yourself; you don't need someone else, like a therapist, to point it out. It is a bit like learning to think about things, and yourself, in a new way.

Obviously, there is more that I do during the sessions. However, these two areas probably give you a clearer idea of what to expect from me. Of course, this leads to the next question – what do you do during the sessions?

What Do You Do During our Meetings?

Obviously, you will be wondering what you do. Well, the first thing is clearly to present your problem, or problems, to me in a way which makes sense to you. It's a bit like telling your story of the things which have contributed to your feeling the way you do. However, this does not mean presenting a long and detailed account. It may be that you can highlight the particular things which are of most immediate concern to you. I may well pick up on certain points and want to follow them up in more detail. This is all part of me being 'active' with the aim of the two of us working together to solve a particular problem.

Having identified a problem together and agreed on what you want to do about it, you and I will probably question your self-defeating attitudes and beliefs and help you to develop more constructive attitudes. This involves looking for evidence to see whether it supports how you have been thinking about yourself. Indeed, I will probably say to you that you have to become a bit of a scientist. This may sound strange at first. All it means is that you should try and begin to be more 'objective', observe and collect evidence on some issue so that you and I can 'look at the evidence' the following week. So, as you can see, not only is the therapist quite active, but so are you!

Also we will be discussing how you could practise your new, constructive attitude in your everyday life. This will help you to strengthen the new attitude and weaken the older, more self-defeating belief.

Are There Any Problems Which Might Occur?

Clearly, taking part in therapy is not all plain sailing; there are often some difficulties. I believe that pointing to some of the potential problems before therapy begins might well help to minimize some of these difficulties.

It can be tempting to think that just attending therapy, for however many sessions, is enough to bring about some improvement. However, when you think about it, therapy takes only one hour in a week. This leaves more than another 100 waking hours during a week! This will give you some idea about how important it is to put the time *outside* therapy to the best possible use. This will give you lots of time to try out and practise tasks you have discussed with me. In turn, this will provide lots of material for you and I to work on at your next meeting. If, on the other hand, the suggestions made are not carried out because of a shortage of time or not prioritizing them sufficiently, then this makes progress more difficult and less rewarding for yourself. It is sometimes easy to think that things will change quickly. While that is quite understandable, my experience is that improvement can often be slow. At times, it can also be a bit like taking two steps forward and one step back. For example, things might improve over a few weeks but then you may experience a 'bad' week. It is all too tempting to think 'Oh, back to square one', forgetting about the improvement that you have experienced over the past couple of weeks. It is always important to remember and keep hold of the progress that you have made. One way of achieving this is to take notes either during or after the session and then refer back to them as a resource. In addition, an important part of making things better for yourself is *practice*. It's often said that 'Practice makes perfect'. Well, I don't think that's absolutely true. A better way of saying it would be 'practice makes things better'.

Will Therapy Help You?

After reading this far, one question you may still have is 'Will things get better?' From my own experience, that of other psychologists, and from research that has been carried out the answer is that most people do improve. As people get better, they often describe themselves as 'being more like they used to be'. However, the speed at which people improve differs a lot. On the one hand, you might find yourself improving relatively quickly, or on the other hand you might find it takes longer. If this proves to be the case, it is important to be patient. Always try and see the small improvements as these will be the building blocks for the change which comes later.

A final question you might ask yourself is 'Are 11 sessions enough?' Again, research has shown that a majority of people experience considerable improvement during the period over which the 11 sessions occur. It is important to remember that the period of time between sessions will enable you to build on the suggestions made during therapy sessions. The more you put into practice what you have learned in therapy, the more progress you will make.

Finally, I hope this booklet has been helpful. Please feel free to raise with me any questions about what you've read when we meet.

Appendix 2

COST-BENEFIT ANALYSIS

COST-BENEFIT ANALYSIS

Advantages/benefits of problem
SHORT TERM

For yourself   For other people

1:........................... 1:...........................

2:........................... 2:...........................

3:........................... 3:...........................

4:........................... 4:...........................

5:........................... 5:...........................

6:........................... 6:...........................

LONG TERM

For yourself   For other people

1:........................... 1:...........................

2:........................... 2:...........................

3:........................... 3:...........................

4:........................... 4:...........................

5:........................... 5:...........................

6:........................... 6:...........................

Disadvantages/costs of problem
SHORT TERM

For yourself   For other people

1:........................... 1:...........................

2:........................... 2:...........................

3:........................... 3:...........................

4:........................... 4:...........................

5:........................... 5:...........................

6:........................... 6:...........................

LONG TERM

For yourself   For other people

1:........................... 1:...........................

2:........................... 2:...........................

3:........................... 3:...........................

4:........................... 4:...........................

5:........................... 5:...........................

6:........................... 6:...........................

COST-BENEFIT ANALYSIS

Advantages/benefits of goal

SHORT TERM

For yourself   For other people

1:................................1:...............................

2:................................2:...............................

3:................................3:...............................

4:................................4:...............................

5:................................5:...............................

6:................................6:...............................

LONG TERM

For yourself   For other people

1:................................1:...............................

2:................................2:...............................

3:................................3:...............................

4:................................4:...............................

5:................................5:...............................

6:................................6:...............................

Disadvantages/costs of goal

SHORT TERM

For yourself   For other people

1:................................1:...............................

2:................................2:...............................

3:................................3:...............................

4:................................4:...............................

5:................................5:...............................

6:................................6:...............................

LONG TERM

For yourself   For other people

1:................................1:...............................

2:................................2:...............................

3:................................3:...............................

4:................................4:...............................

5:................................5:...............................

6:................................6:...............................

Appendix 3

TRAINING IN RATIONAL EMOTIVE BEHAVIOUR THERAPY

TRAINING IN RATIONAL EMOTIVE BEHAVIOUR THERAPY

If you wish details of training courses in REBT contact:

1. Centre for Rational Emotive Behaviour Therapy
   156 Westcombe Hill
   Blackheath
   LONDON SE3 7DH

   Tel: 0181 293 4114

2. Professor Windy Dryden
   Department of Psychology
   Goldsmiths College
   New Cross
   LONDON SE14 6NW

   Tel: 0171 919 7872

(I run a two-year MSc course in Rational Emotive Behaviour Therapy, the first held in Europe)

INDEX

Index compiled by Caroline Sheard